Five Fingers:
Elegance in Espionage
A History of the 1959-1960 Television Series

By Diane Kachmar

BearManor Media

Albany, Georgia

Five Fingers: Elegance in Espionage
A History of the 1959-1960 Television Series
Copyright © 2015 Diane Kachmar. All Rights Reserved.

No part of this book may be reproduced in any form or by any means, electronic, mechanical, digital, photocopying or recording, except for the inclusion in a review, without permission in writing from the publisher.

Front cover: Luciana Paluzzi and David Hedison starring in the 20th Century Fox Television Series *Five Fingers*. Copyright 20th Century Fox Studios.

All other photos copyright 20th Century Fox Studios unless otherwise noted.

Published in the USA by
BearManor Media
P.O. Box 71426
Albany, GA 31708
www.BearManorMedia.com

Softcover Edition
ISBN-10: 1593938888
ISBN-13: 978-1-59393-888-8

Printed in the United States of America

Table of Contents

Acknowledgments and Introduction — ix
Foreword by David Hedison — xiii

Chapter 1: Operation Cicero in World War II, the Movies and Television — 1
Chapter 2: Creation and History of the *Five Fingers* Series — 13
Chapter 3: Publicity, Reviews, and Interviews 1959-1960 — 41
Chapter 4: Starring David Hedison as Victor Sebastian — 73
Chapter 5: Introducing Luciana Paluzzi as Simone Genet — 97
Chapter 6: Paul Burke as Robertson — 109
Chapter 7: Episodes 1-3: "Station Break," "Dossier," and "Moment of Truth" — 113
Chapter 8: Episodes 4-6: "Unknown Town," "Men with Triangle Heads," and "The Assassin" — 137
Chapter 9: Episodes 7-9: "The Man Who Got Away," "The Emerald Curtain," and "Temple of the Swinging Doll" — 163
Chapter 10: Episodes 10-12: "Final Dream," "Thin Ice," and "Operation Ramrod" — 185
Chapter 11: Episodes 13-14: "The Judas Goat" and "The Search for Edvard Stoyan" — 211
Chapter 12: Unaired Episodes 15-16: "A Shot in the Dark," "Counterfeit," and unproduced/missing episodes — 229
Chapter 13: Recurring Characters: Wembley: Alan Napier; Prince Dimitri Blanc: Michael Romanoff — 235
Chapter 14: The Guest Stars: Episodes 1-8 — 247
Chapter 15: The Guest Stars: Episodes 9-16 — 283
Chapter 16: The Crew — 317
Chapter 17: "The Proper Spy: Victor Sebastian's place in the nascent spy genre: pre James Bond (1962)" by Wes Britton — 351
Chapter 18: "The Real Operation Cicero" by David Goudsward — 359

Index — 373

Dedication

This book is dedicated to my husband, John Kachmar, who always helps me write all my books. I could not do this without him.

Acknowledgments

THERE ARE SO MANY PEOPLE TO THANK FOR HELPING ME WRITE THIS book. First, I have to thank David Goudsward for finding all those "rocks" out there that had to be overturned, no matter what came crawling out from underneath. When it comes to rocks or research, you can't have a better collaborator than David. He found guest stars, and wonderfully bizarre information about said guest stars, when I could not. And he found out more about Operation Cicero than the CIA, um, make that the OSS, ever did!

Mark Phillips also gets a big thank you for all his research in a database I had no access to. I want to thank Wes Britton for his brilliant essay on the spy genre. This book would not be the history that it is without all the help I received from these talented men.

I wish to thank Luciana Paluzzi and Brett Halsey for giving me good interviews about their respective experiences filming this TV series. I especially want to thank David Hedison. He really got behind this book and did almost everything I asked him to, and several things that I didn't. David wrote a lovely foreword and loaned me his four bound scripts and all the pictures from the *Five Fingers* series he had saved all these years. He was a huge help and I could not have done this book without him.

I would also like to thank the UCLA Film and Television Library for allowing me to visit and view two episodes that I would not have seen otherwise. I want to thank all the fans who have told me their memories of this series. My husband John saw *Five Fingers* when it ran the summer of 1962 on ABC; other fans saw it in syndication in 1967 and beyond. There is something about this series that lasts. I hope what has been written in these pages will show you that.

Introduction

THIS SERIES HAS GARNERED MUCH INTEREST OVER THE MANY YEARS since it was filmed. Most of us, who were too young to watch the show when it first aired in 1959, have heard of it through word of mouth, i.e. "Did you know that David Hedison had another series before *Voyage to the Bottom of the Sea?*" or "Did you know he was a spy for the CIA long before he did his first Bond film, *Live and Let Die?*"

Luckily for the interested fans of David Hedison, Luciana Paluzzi, and Paul Burke this canceled series did have a post life. It can still be seen today. Eleven episodes were transferred from 16mm film to VHS tape and then to DVD, shared from collector to collector via the grey market. Some episodes have even made their way onto the You Tube online video platform.

Fox Studio never released the series to home video, but they did syndicate it widely on 16mm film through the early 1980s. The four remaining series episodes in the Fox Studio Archives are now housed at the Film and Television Library, located on the University of California Los Angeles (UCLA) Campus.

I was given VHS copies of some of the episodes in the late 1980s that had been transferred from 16mm prints. That was my introduction to the series. I found this show fun and entertaining. I am happy to share it now with all of you.

Several new shows that premiered in 1959 didn't make it. Perhaps if *Five Fingers* hadn't been counter programmed against the number one TV show of 1959, *Gunsmoke*, it might have lasted. Maybe, as David Hedison has often said, "If NBC had more of a financial stake in the series, they would have kept it on longer." But NBC didn't.

Five Fingers, as a series, had a phenomenal shelf life considering there were only sixteen filmed episodes of this series to syndicate. Come with me and explore this rich history and see why this TV series still draws the interest of fans fifty-six years after it was made.

Diane Kachmar
4/12/2015

Foreword
by David Hedison

When I was a young man in the early 1940s and found a few free hours to take in a movie at the theater in Providence, Rhode Island, I imagined myself being up there on the big screen. My idols were James Cagney, Claude Rains, and Cary Grant. I wanted to be suave, sophisticated, like they were.

After ten years as a journeyman actor, learning my craft in New York City doing theater and early live television, I ended up in Hollywood in 1957. I was put under contract to Twentieth Century Fox, where I made movies and did more television. Fox Studios thought I could be their version of Cary Grant, so they dusted off a film property they had the rights to. This was how television was done in 1959. Fox re-tailored the 1952 film *5 Fingers* to be one of their earliest primetime television series. By the time Richard Berg was done rewriting *5 Fingers* into a series pilot, it bore no resemblance to the parent film whatsoever. We filmed our pilot. NBC liked it and bought the series.

Speaking of tailoring, they gave me the requisite tux that defines suave and sophisticated. They set the show in Europe, the French Riviera, no less, although we never left the Fox lot, and they gave me a lovely countess all my own. Excuse me, this was France. Simone was a Marquis,* albeit one who wanted to model and sing.

Little did Simone know what she was in for the day she so innocently dropped her binoculars down into my lap at that racetrack outside Paris, so we'd meet. She wanted an agent (the talent kind) and she got me. I was another kind of agent, fighting Communists for the CIA. The series never quite came out and said that, but that was what I did.

Action, adventure, intrigue, love. The series wanted to attract the sophisticated late evening viewer, the one who actually *knew* where Cannes was. My series had two very cultured and urbane producers who wanted to do interesting and witty television. These producers lasted one year longer at Fox Television than my series did.

In 1959, everyone was watching Westerns on television. So NBC slotted us against the number one and number three western series on the air, *Gunsmoke* and *Have Gun, Will Travel*. We lasted fourteen episodes before NBC decided that programming wasn't very smart, not if they wanted viewers. Fox Studio did not have great success with most of their early television series, until I signed to do yet another TV series for them that started in 1964. However, that story will have to be told in *another* book!

Five Fingers was made when all the studios were still figuring out what worked on television. The premise was a good one. This same idea took off in 1965 when it was re-made as the *Mission: Impossible* television series. That show became a huge hit in almost the same time slot on Saturday night. What had changed in the intervening years was that spies had now become as popular in 1965 as Westerns were in 1959.

We made sixteen episodes of *Five Fingers* that summer and fall of 1959, documenting a Fox back lot that no longer exists: The Permanent Gardens, The Waterways, Sligon Castle, Adano Square, and Bernadette Street. All gone. They record sound effects on Stage Two now. Stage Seven no longer exists!

I had fun working on those grand old movie sets and what we filmed there still stands up today. Victor and Simone were a great couple with glorious chemistry. I like to think it worked out for them. Fifty-six years later, they have retired to a fine villa in the South of France, where their grandchildren on summer school break come to visit them.

David Hedison
8/30/2014

*Author's note: Simone was given the title of Marquis on the series. David and everyone else called her this all through the series, even though it is not a correct title. Simone should have been a marchioness.

"The Emerald Curtain." David Hedison.
Copyright 20th Century Fox Studio.

Chapter 1

Operation Cicero in World War II, the Movies, and Television

Author's note: The Five Fingers series was supposedly based on a World War II incident involving the British Embassy in Turkey, in which the valet of the British Ambassador sold Top Secret documents to the Germans. The German intelligence officer involved, L. C. (Ludwig Carl) Moyzisch, wrote a book called Operation Cicero *about this incident in 1950.*

Fox Studios optioned this book for a 1952 movie, which they re-titled 5 Fingers. *The 1952 film starring James Mason is an account of the embassy incident with the usual Hollywood liberties, but when this Fox movie property was adapted to be a television series in 1959 by Richard Berg, nearly everything about it changed.*

As part of the history of the making of Five Fingers *the television series,* here is some background on the incident, and the subsequent book and movie that were the source of the writing credit in the TV series saying that the series was "based on Operation Cicero by L. C. Moyzisch."

In 1944, both the Germans and the British wanted to persuade neutral Turkey to be an ally in the Second World War. These countries were ultimately unsuccessful. However, for a short period, a greedy Turkish valet, who once worked for First Secretary Jenke in the German consulate, managed to get hired by the staff of the British ambassador. This gave the Germans an opportunity to know what the British plans were for Turkey to join the war on their side. This valet, code named Cicero by the German Ambassador Van Papen, became the highest paid spy in history. While his information was good and could have easily influenced the outcome of the war in Turkey, the information Cicero stole was never used effectively by either Hitler or the German High Command.

Elyesa Bazna, the valet, should not have been hired. The opportunities Bazna took were handed to him by the British Ambassador, a very old school gentleman named Sir Hughe Knatchbull-Hugessen. Sir Hughe routinely brought top secret papers home to work on. He kept them in a locked dispatch box in his bedroom. Bazna had been recommended to Sir Hughe by another gentleman on his staff. A recommendation was never questioned in those days.

This valet learned Knatchbull-Hugessen's daily routine, which he never varied. Bazna knew when he could access the security box. He would go in, use the keys, take the papers out, and photograph them. Bazna was always careful to return the papers to the box in the same order, so no one would suspect. This went on for four months.

The Turkish government finally told the British they had a leak in their Embassy, based on what the German Ambassador had been telling them. The investigators from England found the British Ambassador extremely resistant to adopting more stringent security safeguards. Sir

Hughe saw nothing wrong in what he was doing, nor any need to change his routine.

Heightened security was implemented at the embassy. It was more difficult for Bazna to continue his clandestine photographing, but not impossible. He stole the key to the new safe, made a wax impression of it, and the Germans supplied a copy key that actually worked. They gave him a better camera when he asked for one. The newly installed safe alarm did not deter him. Bazna quickly learned which fuse needed to be unscrewed inside the embassy fuse box to disarm it.

Bazna photographed the secret documents for money, prestige, and his own class elevation. He had three mistresses and tried hard to become a man of means and wealth, but ended up in one failed venture after another. Bazna was paid by the Germans in counterfeit British pounds, which were later traced back to him for restitution.

Moyzisch, for his part, to avoid going to the Eastern front, did what he was told when Bazna's photos were given to him. Moyzisch was the SD intelligence officer at the embassy. He worked for Schellenberg. He was not a diplomat, as he claimed in his book. He was not to tell Ambassador Von Papen the contents of the photographed documents, but he did.

Von Papen was hated by Ribbentrop, the Foreign Minister, because Von Papen wasn't a rabid Nazi. Ribbentrop's sister was married to the German First Secretary Jenke, the former employer of Bazna. Jenke was the first person Bazna approached with his photographs for sale. It was fortunate that Jenke decided to send Bazna to Moyzisch to handle, or the deal never would have worked out.

SD had the counterfeit funds to pay for the information and their security was much tighter, allowing Bazna's identity to remain concealed for weeks longer. Moyzisch, through his superior Schellenberg, paid their spy and was given genuine documents in return. However, the Germans never believed in *any* of the documents they received from Cicero. He *had* to be a British plant sent to mislead them. No mere valet could have pulled this feat off by himself.

The Germans did not realize how much Bazna wanted to be a respected man of wealth and means, even if he had to steal to do so. He became a valet to learn the secrets of his employers and then use them to make money for himself.

The Americans became involved in this affair through the OSS. They had their own reasons to find out which servant in the British Embassy was leaking top secret documents. Two downed German pilots, in actuality American OSS agents, managed to recruit Cornelia Kapp. Kapp was the daughter of a friend of Von Papen's. They managed to get her assigned as Moyzisch's substitute secretary when the women who worked for him injured her hand. Kapp's job, for the OSS, was to find out Bazna's identity. All Cornelia wanted was a ticket back to America, having been deported as a German national in 1941. She wanted to return to her former lover in Ohio. He, very conveniently for the Americans, turned out to be a current agent at OSS.

Her ex-lover was not one of the two flyers, but he helped set her up with them. The Americans did learn the identity of Cicero, but didn't bother to inform the British. This omission was attributed to the bitter rivalry that had developed between the British MI6 agency and the American OSS during the war.

These flyers helped Kapp escape. They brought her to America, where she ended up in a North Dakota internment camp after it was determined she was mentally ill. A Van Papen relative in the Abwehr intelligence agency also defected at the same time Kapp missed her scheduled train and disappeared from German employment. That left Ambassador Von Papen saddled with suspicion about *his* loyalty. He was recalled to Berlin.

American involvement in this affair was finally acknowledged in 1960. Whether or not a TV series based on Moyzisch's book airing that year had anything to do with this information coming to light then could not be determined.

[Author's note: See Chapter 18 essay for more detailed information on the real Operation Cicero.]

Everyone involved embellished their roles in "the Cicero Affair" and all the principal players published autobiographies. Moyzisch's had the largest printing, but there are also memoirs available by Bazna, Von Papen, Schellenberg and Knatchbull-Hugessen.

Sir Hughe, naturally, did not address the affair in his own record of his public service, maintaining silence until his death in 1971. He retired in 1947. He was allowed to do so. The British maintained an equal silence about the incident. For thirty years. No comment was their only answer.

In Bazna's *I was Cicero*, mostly written by Hans Nogly and first published in 1962, Bazna claimed he was an Albanian and that his father was killed by a British man in a hunting accident. Bazna used many aliases: Diello, Ilya, Pierre, whatever suited the persona he was trying to project at the time. He was a performer. Bazna tried to sing professionally more than once, but that never worked out for him, either.

Bazna had three mistresses, none of whom were a Polish countess, and he had eight children by them. He never moved to Rio, but stayed in Ankara, Turkey, failing at every post-war venture he was involved in. He spent his counterfeit pounds so lavishly that he is credited with exposing the Germans' counterfeit operation.

His fake pounds were made in a prison camp by Jewish prisoners to destabilize the British Currency. These bogus pound notes kept circulating for many months after the war and eventually forced the British to change some of their currency.

The prison camp operation was broken up. The pound notes were to be destroyed before they were seized by advancing Allied forces. That plan quickly went awry in a series of multiple misfortunes that befell the German convoy charged with this task. Most of the fake pound notes were recovered. They were brought up from a river bottom, but still salvaged.

Darryl Zanuck purchased the film rights soon after the details of "the Cicero Affair" became public in 1950 with the publication of Moyzisch's book. Zanuck gave Michael Wilson the task of creating a screenplay and persuaded Joseph Mankiewicz to direct. Mankiewicz was coming off the huge success of *All about Eve* (1950) and had four Oscars to his credit. However, like many artists, he had experienced difficulties with Zanuck and was willing to make this movie his last project, so his contract would lapse.

On May 12, 1951, Mankiewicz read Wilson's screenplay and was very enthusiastic about it, knowing he could add more ingenuity, humor, sex, and excitement to the story, if Zanuck would let him helm the film.

Movie still from *5 Fingers*. Valet Ulysses Diello (James Mason) shows what he has to sell to Col. Von Richter of German Intelligence (Herbert Berghof). Copyright 20th Century Fox Studios.

Zanuck agreed, but Mankiewicz could take no writing credit, no matter how much dialogue he added to the film. He also had to agree to keep Otto Lang on as the producer. James Mason was cast as the valet and Danielle Darrieux was given the role of the (fictional) expatriate Polish countess who is his accomplice/partner. The film was very well done in a semi-documentary style, which best served the seriousness of the subject, and specially filmed scenes in Turkey added an exotic touch.

This was a witty, well-crafted drawing room film that was very entertaining and filled with mocking humor. The known ironies of this incident were all included and new ones (the betrayal of the valet by the countess) were added, as well as other fictional characters and twists. Mankiewicz's trademark of reworking dialogue as the film was being shot added yet another layer of sophistication to the film.

Despite what the film claimed in the voiceover narration, it did not deal truthfully with the real events of the story. Bazna was nowhere near as suave and glamorous as Mason played the role, nothing about the real valet (called Ulysses Diello in the movie) could match that actor's worldly charm, knowledge, easy English diction, and urbane manner.

Moyzisch was portrayed as a comic bumbler, not the competent intelligence officer he was. The weak Michael Rennie character (Travers), who was sent from London to uncover the leak, came into the story to help the Embassy Security man find the leak. This pair suspect Diello, but never could catch him, leading to a totally fictional and sensational escape by the valet at the end of the film. In truth, Bazna had already left embassy employment of his own accord, several months before the British staff was recalled and their Turkish Embassy was closed down.

Equally fictitious is the assertion that Diello actually stole plans for the D-Day invasion. Disaster was only averted in the film when German Intelligence tore up the stolen documents, convinced they were a clever British plant to misdirect them. Great drama, but nowhere near what happened. Sir Hughe would never have been given D-Day documents to read in Turkey, much less the actual invasion plans.

Filming went well. Mankiewicz worked well with Lang. But afterward Mankiewicz became quite angry over the cuts Zanuck made to his final edit after he had left the studio. Zanuck came up with the title 5 *Fingers*, thinking a number would tie it to semi-documentary Fox movie predecessors like *13 Rue Madeline*. He had some studio art made up that showed a clutching hand (symbolizing greed and theft) with each of the digits labeled with a "sin" such as Lust, Greed, Passion, Desire, and Sin, starting with the thumb as Lust.

Mason was pleased with the film, calling it one of the best sensible spy films made up to that time. The movie was intended to be popular entertainment. It succeeded brilliantly at that, winning Oscar nominations for Wilson and Mankiewicz and even an Edgar. It was the last good film Mankiewicz would do. None of his later projects had such brilliant manipulation of the facts to improve the drama of the story.

Bazna didn't make any money off the movie, either. He did meet with Mankiewicz during the seven weeks the director was in Turkey filming the final chase scene with doubles. Bazna contributed nothing to the story that Mankiewicz wanted to use, therefore he received no fee.

Mankiewicz later used their meeting, along with the secret photos he had taken of Bazna during it, for publicity in 1952 when the film came out. One of the Bazna photos appeared in an April 7 *Life* Magazine spread. In another ironic twist, the film cost $1.5 million to produce and never made that money back, for all its later acclaim.

I found very few reviews for *5 Fingers:* The Movie.

Pauline Kael hated it. She found Mason to be "cold and no one she wanted to care about." From her book *5001 Nights at the Movies*.

Philip Scheuer (*Los Angeles Times*) loved it, calling the film "cleverer and more urbane than Mankiewicz's previous two Oscar winning films." He also called it the "year's slickest spy yarn" in his end of the year (1952) wrap-up.

Other Fox versions of the *Operation Cicero* story were made, since Fox now owned the rights to it. They include a *Lux Radio Theater* program starring James Mason that aired on October 13, 1952. Production #798. This same program was rerun on *Hollywood Radio Theater* on February 1, 1955.

The next version was part of an anthology TV series called *20th Century Fox Hour* that aired from 1955 to 1957. These episodes were one hour versions of movies Fox owned, filmed with already paid contract players to fill air time. "Operation Cicero" was made in the second season. The original air date was December 26, 1956. It was episode seven of the season and number twenty-five of thirty-seven episodes made.

It was directed by Hubert Cornfield and starred Leon Askin as Siebert, Romney Brent as Sir Frederic, Eduard Franz as Von Richter, Peter Lorre as Moyzisch, Ricardo Montalban as Degalo aka Cicero, Gavin Muir as MacFadden, and Alan Napier as Travers. Robert Sterling was the host of this sixty minute version, filmed in black-and-white.

The *20th Century Fox Hour* series was revived on the Fox Movie Channel in 2002. Here is an online review of the 1956 "Operation Cicero" episode posted during that time.

"This long-lost series has been remastered and restored, and is currently being shown on the Fox Movie Channel under the new title *Hour of Stars*. It is a fascinating curio made up of one-hour condensations of 20th Century Fox's biggest hit films, with entirely different casts.

Author's note: Unproduced scripts were featured on this series as well.

The scripts, photography, and camera angles on these hour-long shows are virtually identical to those in the films they are based on. Although this is part of what makes this series so fascinating, and although it raises the level of writing and photography far above that in the average TV series, this is unfortunately where the resemblance ends, at least judging from the episode I caught last night. The episode was entitled "Operation Cicero," and was adapted from the hit 1952 spy film *5 Fingers*. It had one advantage over the original in that the main supporting role of Moyzisch, Cicero's contact man, was played by

Peter Lorre. But the episode was compromised by the fatal miscasting of Ricardo Montalban (of all people) in the role of Degalo, the traitorous valet, played so memorably in the film by James Mason. Montalban may be a great Khan in *Star Trek*, but he is the last person one would ever imagine playing a dryly cynical spy who is willing to betray the Allied cause in World War II for money and his own amusement. He brings almost none of the nuances that Mason brought to his portrayal. The other actors in this episode are not miscast, but strictly unmemorable in comparison to those in *5 Fingers*. The only other actor who can stand comparison with his movie counterpart is Alan Napier, who plays Travers, the British intelligence agent played in *5 Fingers* by Michael Rennie.

There will be more episodes in this series, and they will certainly be of interest as early TV artifacts, but if you expect the same experience that you had in seeing the original films they are based on, you might be disappointed. The impression this series gives is similar to that of watching a touring company of a Broadway show when you have already seen the original Broadway production."

Casting Montalban as a Hispanic version of the valet in the 1956 remake almost makes sense from a story point of view, since the valet plans to run away with Countess Anna to Argentina. This series runs irregularly on the Fox Movie Channel, but I was unable to record this specific episode to do my own review. It's now 2015. I'm still waiting for it to air again.

20th Century Fox Hour was a quick money maker for the studio at a time they needed cash badly. Buddy Adler was no Darryl Zanuck and his unexpected death in 1960 didn't help the financial situation at the studio. In the spring of 1959, when Martin Manulis was developing new television series, the next version of *Operation Cicero* became the pilot for *Five Fingers: the Series*.

5 Fingers movie poster. Hand artwork as described in this chapter.
Copyright 20th Century Fox Studios.

Chapter 2

Creation and History of the Five Fingers Series

David Hedison credits creation of this series to Richard Berg. Berg invented the characters of Victor Sebastian, Simone Genet, "Robbie" Robertson, Wembley and "Prince Dimitri" Blanc. He came up with Victor's cover as a talent agent and his double agent role. The series evolved over the sixteen episodes that were filmed. A full year of series television in 1959 would have been thirty-nine episodes. NBC committed to buy twenty-six episodes. They canceled the show after sixteen were filmed.

Only fourteen episodes actually aired in that initial NBC run, but the show immediately went into syndication and was well distributed overseas between 1961 and 1965. The additional two filmed episodes were shown in most of those syndicated runs. The first national syndicated run in the United States was in the summer of 1962 when the series was shown, mostly late at night, on ABC affiliates across the country.

Simone was supposed to be a spy in the original pilot script, but producer Herbert Swope changed his mind and made her a model instead. That was "a wrong move by Swope," David Hedison told me. That incarnation of her lasted for about four episodes. Simone was a "club singer" for a while and was brought in as a spy-in-training around episode ten. Sadly, we will never know where the show would have gone with her character if the series had lasted an entire season of thirty-nine episodes.

There was plenty of publicity for the new series beyond the 1959 Fall Preview issue of *TV Guide* where *Five Fingers* was featured in a color spread called "The Eyes That Never Close." 1959 apparently was not a particularly good year to be a spy or a private eye. Of the six new shows introduced in that preview spread, four of them had been canceled by the end of the 1959-1960 season. Several syndicated spy shows did not fare any better. The Western TV series was king in 1959.

NBC described their new series in various publicity releases: "*Five Fingers* . . . code name for America's top counter-intelligence agent, master of espionage and split-second action. In the shadowy world of international intrigue, he stalks and is stalked by his countries' enemies in chilling undercover battles of a grim Cold War. A full hour thriller starring David Hedison [and] introducing the lovely Luciana Paluzzi.

[In] an hour-long series dealing with international intrigue, David Hedison stars as a counter intelligence agent and Luciana Paluzzi will be introduced as a regular. *Five Fingers* is based on the spy story *Operation Cicero*. It's the story of an American agent assigned to break up a Soviet espionage ring by joining its rank and file. It was written by L. C. Moyzisch. To conceal his true identity, [the agent] goes by the name Five Fingers."

"NBC's new full hour series of international intrigue will...premiere Saturday, October 3, from 9:30 to 10:30 p.m. with "Station Break," a drama of adventure and espionage on the French Riviera. The filmed series stars David Hedison as U. S. counter-intelligence agent Victor Sebastian and introduces Luciana Paluzzi as fashion model Simone Genet. Featured in the premiere episode are Eva Gabor, restaurateur Mike Romanoff and singer Greta Keller. Victor Sebastian is known to most people as a theatrical agent who books musical performers for plush cafes and casinos in European capitals. To a select few, he is known as a valuable agent for Russia. Actually, he is a counter-intelligence agent [for the United States.]"

In April 1959, the NBC television network bought a one hour continental spy drama from Fox Studios for the upcoming 1959 season. Considered effective counter programming to the plethora of westerns currently running on the television air waves, it was a continuation of the spy and detective series beginning to be produced, such as *Peter Gunn, I Led Three Lives,* and *77 Sunset Strip.*

The series was supposedly based on the book *Operation Cicero* by L. C. Moyzisch, which had been optioned by 20th Century Fox for the 1952 film *5 Fingers,* starring James Mason. In the movie, Mason portrayed an Albanian employed as the British Ambassador's valet at their embassy in Ankara, Turkey, during World War II. Ulysses Diello (an alias) turned spy. He copied top secret papers the British Ambassador brought home to study by taking photographs of them. The valet then sold his photos to the Germans for money. He wanted to raise himself from what he considered a poor station in life. This is the story detailed in the *Operation Cicero* book.

For the 1959 TV series, the story was moved to the present day and nearly all the original story details were changed. The series lead became an American named Victor Sebastian. Victor was recruited by American Intelligence to fight the growing Communist threat. As a cover, Sebastian became a world-famous bon vivant and theatrical agent, a fellow who knew everyone who was anyone.

While Victor Sebastian was employed by the Americans, he spent most of his television missions convincing the Russians/Communists he was still a loyal Party member. In the second episode, we are told Sebastian is a long-time mole planted into the Communist ranks.

Fox tapped a rising young contract player named Al Hedison to play this double agent. As an American of Armenian descent, he had the right "continental" look. Victor was born in Sedalia, Missouri, from the fleeting glimpse of his file we are given in the pilot, but his speech suggests an Ivy League education, probably Harvard.

Victor Sebastian's cover as a theatrical agent, along with assistance by American Intelligence, allowed him to travel with impunity all over Europe, with his various entertainment acts in tow. He continually foiled Communist plots, no matter what those nefarious plans were.

Wembley and Sebastian, in which Victor was the junior partner, had talent offices in Paris, New York, and London. For the duration of the series, Victor worked out of the Paris office. Wembley was cast, but only made two appearances in the series. Victor's main touring act during the series was his brand-new club singer, known as a chanteuse, named Simone Genet.

Genet was a French aristocrat, the show (wrongly) declared her a Marquis and model, who decided one day in 1959 that she wanted to do club singing as a lark. She had "arranged" to meet Victor at the famous French race track [Longchamp] by dropping her binoculars down into his lap. He was smitten with her almost immediately. Sebastian was very happy to see Simone again when she traveled to his other home in Cannes to ask him to sign her as a client.

They became lovers almost immediately after she was signed, even though they were almost never allowed any time together to consummate their relationship. Sebastian was always being called away to deal with yet another Communist plot. Given the restrictions on what could be shown on television in 1959, this was inevitable.

Victor wasn't above using Genet or her singing to cover his spying activities nor was he shy about using her jet set friends to further his counter-espionage goals while he was (supposedly) searching for new talent to sign in-between her singing gigs. It was high society and continental glitz, with mysterious clandestine meetings in salons and palaces around the world.

Sebastian was constantly juggling his cover, his clients, his love life, and his double mission to fail at whatever the Communists asked him to do. He also had to insure his cover remained intact and most of the time that caused the demise of the Communist agent who was opposing him.

Vic rarely worked alone, however. His American Intelligence contact was an agent named Robertson, who would pass messages by leaving a single glove behind for Sebastian where it could be easily found. Victor also had agents embedded among his clients to aid him with his missions and provide support, equipment, and intelligence. His clients were multi-talented and not only in the arts. This idea would be resurrected and redone for the hit 1965 TV series *Mission: Impossible*.

Sebastian's partner in his theatrical agency, an older Englishman named Wembley, is hardly involved. He doesn't keep track of where Victor goes or what he does, as long as Sebastian checks in from time to time and keeps sending in new client contracts. He doesn't question anyone Sebastian signs, even acts that end up blatantly assisting Victor on his missions. He is genuinely fond of his younger partner. He teases Sebastian in one of the episodes he is in about always chasing after that girl; their newest client.

Wembley is so totally blasé, it's obvious that he was recruited by American Intelligence long ago to be the London office front and turn a blind eye to whatever Victor and his acts are doing out on the road. Simone's seamless integration by Robertson into the spy end of the business in later episodes only reinforces this. It was a long standing operation by 1959. In the second episode, the script states that Victor's cover as "Code Name: Five Fingers" was almost blown eight years earlier (1951) in Berlin.

Al Hedison, as a Fox contract player, had made three successful motion pictures for the studio since April of 1957 and had received enough fan mail for the studio to give him a try-out as a television lead. The series pilot "Station Break" was shot and sent around to the various television networks. NBC loved the concept and bought it. The pilot episode has him credited as Al Hedison.

David Hedison. Copyright 20th Century Fox Studios.

The NBC network *then* decided they didn't like that name. Al wasn't glamorous enough. They suggested several other names, but finally were finally persuaded to go with Al's middle name, David. So Al Hedison became David Hedison professionally, in a move that really wasn't necessary and would cause no end of name confusion for the actor for years afterward.

David was not happy with this development and took his case to the press, as was chronicled (off the wire) in *The Charleston Gazette* (West Virginia) July 4, 1959, in an article written by Harold Heffernan. "The hottest name change row in recent years raged between NBC and Al Hedison. Following his unique starring role in *The Fly* film, Hedison piled up such a heavy load of fan mail that he was boosted to starring role status in the new spy adventure *Five Fingers*. But the executives at NBC took a very dim view of the name Al Hedison. They felt that it did not suit the actor who was playing such a dignified and sophisticated international spy and that this would affect how he would be received by viewers. They ordered Hedison to change his entire name. Hedison refused. A stubborn stalemate lasted for three weeks. It ended up as a compromise as Hedison agreed to change his first name in favor of David. But he insisted that the name Hedison stay as it is! David's parting shot to NBC: 'It seems to me a fellow named Jolson did all right with the name Al.' Years later, David would mention, 'it never seem to hinder Al Pacino, either.'"

Five Fingers aired on Saturday nights at 9:30 p.m. with the newly christened David Hedison. Al Hedison was quite well known for his second Fox film, *The Fly*, filmed in 1958, thus Fox's new TV lead would invariably get asked that first year if he was related to the movie actor.

Eventually his current fans became used to seeing him billed as David instead and the actor later went on to have great television success under his changed professional name. Several more generations of fans would come along who only knew him as David and the name change ceased to be an issue for them, even though it remained an inevitable (and perennially asked) interview question for Hedison.

A line item dated April 27, 1959, stated "the new series was a sure starter for . . . NBC-TV next fall in the spot now held by the [canceled] western, *Cimarron City*." NBC formally announced the show had been purchased for the fall season on June 9, 1959, with a second announcement appearing June 12.

Martin Manulis, the new head of Television for 20th Century Fox, green-lighted the series and Herbert Swope, Jr. was put in charge of production. There were two other Manulis shows in production at this time: *The Many Loves of Dobie Gillis* based on an earlier Debbie Reynolds film and *Adventures in Paradise*, based on a treatment written by James Michener, of *South Pacific* fame.

Manulis and Swope put together an experienced crew and filming began on *Five Fingers* in June of 1959. Their first task was to extend the thirty-two minute pilot to fit the new one hour time slot. The episodes did not air on NBC in the order they were made. The series was originally slated to debut on September 12. The first episode actually aired on October 3, 1959, with this opening:

> "To the entertainment world on two continents, I am Victor Sebastian, theatrical agent. These are my offices, but the business I'm about to transact can never appear on the company books; not if I'm to survive. As it so happens, I'm another kind of agent: counterespionage.
>
> My employer: The United States Government, although sometimes I pose as its enemy. My code name: Five Fingers."

This voiceover by David Hedison runs at the beginning of each *Five Fingers* show; the Morse code you hear almost spells out *Five Fingers*. The sequence is missing the N.

The cast and crew completed sixteen episodes before the crew took the traditional Thanksgiving/Christmas break. Everyone was told to

CREATION AND HISTORY OF THE *FIVE FINGERS* SERIES

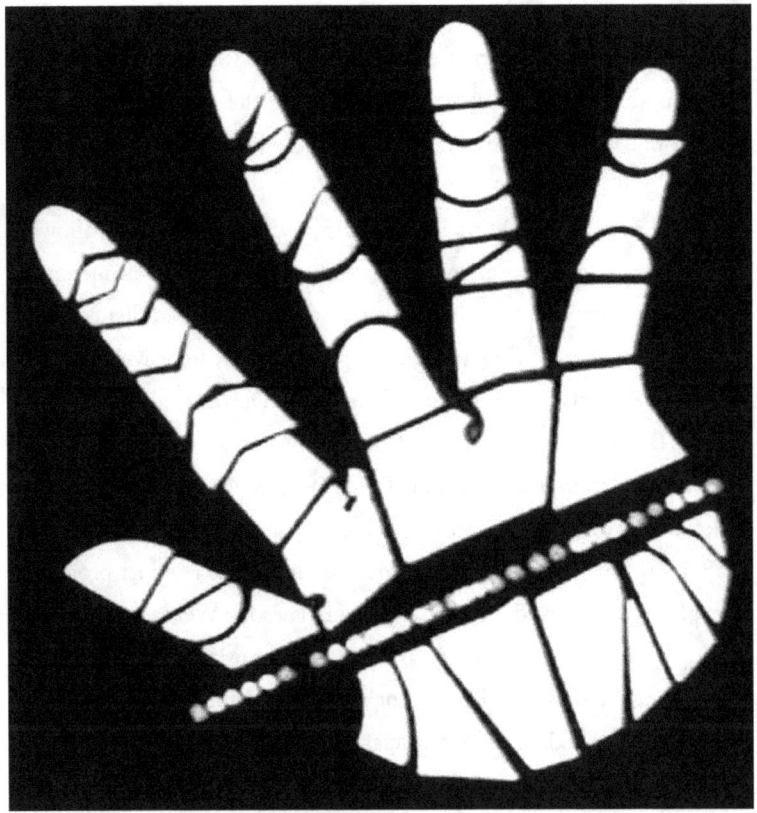

Five Fingers logo. Copyright 20th Century Fox Studios.

report back in January to resume work. Several notices that the show was renewed came out in late November.

In *The Press Telegram* (California) November 28, 1959, Terry Vernon writes: "*Five Fingers* has recently been renewed by NBC for an additional thirteen weeks."

Dover Daily Reports (Ohio) also reports on November 28, 1959, "NBC has just announced it will renew *Five Fingers*. The network has exercised its option to order an additional thirteen episodes for the hour-long spy drama starring David Hedison and Luciana Paluzzi."

TV Guide in their December 9 issue, along with a profile of newcomer Paluzzi, mentioned that the show, despite low ratings, had been picked up for "the rest of the season." NBC's commitment to filming another thirteen episodes was announced on November 28. That would bring the total episodes filmed to twenty-nine, fulfilling the contract NBC made to buy twenty-six episodes when they purchased their share of the series back in April.

The *Lima News* (Ohio) December 5, 1959, stated: "The following newcomers, who are receiving stellar notices and billing on upcoming NBC shows this fall, promise to gain wide favor with audiences. They are Pernell Roberts, Michael Landon, Jeanne Bal, Jody McCrea, Bob Matthias, Robert Crawford Jr., Allen Case, David Hedison, Luciana Paluzzi, Betty Lou Keim and Burt Reynolds."

In *The Gazette Mail* January 17, 1960, Jay Fredericks wrote, "The national poll of all television critics and columnists are now in for the 1959-1960 TV season and those with the top votes as most promising stars of TV are in. Edd Byrnes (men) and Tuesday Weld (women) were the top vote-getters. Runners up as most promising new actors were Nick Adams and Bobby Darin. For actresses, runners up were Connie Stevens and the Italian actress, Luciana Paluzzi (of *Five Fingers*)."

The San Antonio Express (Texas) writes from the wire on January 10, 1960, "David Hedison is considered one of TVs most prized guys and even though his *Five Fingers* departs from the schedule this month, Hedison will be popping up on movie screens again soon. He's already done three films for Fox and he has plenty of fans who want to see a lot more of him."

The Gazette Mail (West Virginia) January 17, 1960, writes: "David Hedison, of the fading *Five Fingers* series, has been keeping steady company with Maria Cooper, Gary's daughter."

No one ever documented why the NBC executives changed their mind about extending the *Five Fingers* series and put on a public affairs news program instead. It did not survive the Saturday night "time slot of death," either. Anyone staying home that night, the least watched night of the week, was apparently watching *Gunsmoke*.

By spring, this time slot had been returned to the local stations. The last *Five Fingers* episode aired January 9, 1960. Art Carney hosted a special for a week until the news program was ready to broadcast.

The decision had fallout. Fan dismay over the cancellation began showing up almost immediately. *The Oakland Tribune* (California) December 31, 1959, "TV Mailbag" published this. A reader said: "I feel as so many other viewers do that *Five Fingers* is a fine show and I hate to see it go off the air." P.G., Oakland. "Answer: Many of our readers have reported that they would rather lose their own hand than *Five Fingers*. But sadly, NBC still plans to cancel the show next month."

This item ran in *The Oakland Tribune,* January 1960, where Columnist Bill Fiset answered your TV questions: "Question: The romantic scenes between David Hedison and Luciana Paluzzi on *Five Fingers* seem very believable. Are David and Luciana really in love? Answer: No. They only kiss like that on camera because that is the way they earn a living."

The Press Telegram (California) published this on January 21, 1960. Earl Leaf writes: "NBC has really goofed by announcing the cancellation of *Five Fingers*. Its stars, David Hedison and Luciana Paluzzi have been getting close to 1,000 fan letters a week. There are not too many other TV stars who can make such a statement. Relenting a little, NBC now says it will give the series another try as a summer replacement and see what happens."

In March of 1960 David Hedison talked to UPI News' Vernon Scott about the show's demise. Scott wrote: "In the shambles following a collapsed TV show almost everyone cries the blues, blaming the sponsor and then going off to look for new work. It's almost a tradition. Hurrahs, however, were raised when that international spy series *Five Fingers* took the final count last month.

Luciana Paluzzi ran off to get married to actor Brett Halsey [January 25] and she has not set [foot] on the Fox studio set since the show finished filming. David Hedison, the handsome hero of the defunct thriller, was just as happy and says he can now settle down to being a movie star, which is what he had in mind all along. He has now stepped from the *Five Fingers* wreckage to star in the new feature, *The Lost World*.

The only shadow on the horizon of his career is that his old TV show may actually be reinstated to the NBC fall schedule. 'NBC has realized that it made a mistake in canceling the show. This summer they are going to rerun the thirteen episodes. If the reaction is good, the network will attempt to put the show back into production. But if they do, they plan to cut the series down to a half hour. Also, Luciana would not be in the series. They might just as well change the show's title and forget about me, too. The series would not be the same without her.'

The actor does not want to see *Five Fingers* return but he is very grateful to it for rocketing his career to the big-time. 'Before the show, my name was Al Hedison and I had made three movies. I was just another newcomer to the business. No one paid much attention to me. *Five Fingers* made a star out of me. People now recognize me on the streets and my fan mail has been terrific.' He says the show had a busy schedule. 'I worked twelve hours a day and during the series I lost twenty-two pounds. I've now gained it back and feel much better.'

NBC never did bring the "revamped" *Five Fingers* series back that summer or in the fall of 1960. The network or Fox Studios sold it off into syndication almost immediately. No additional episodes were ever filmed and the series was never resurrected. Luciana and David quickly moved on and into different film projects.

In the *Pittsburgh Post-Gazette* July 29, 1960, there is an article by Win Fanning entitled: "*Five Fingers* demise is explained by star David Hedison." Fanning wrote: "Visiting here in Pittsburgh on behalf of his new *Lost World* movie, David Hedison, star of the ill-fated *Five Fingers*, had some thoughts on why his series was canceled while the marginally-rated other new NBC entry, *Riverboat*, was renewed. 'I think our show's cancellation simply came down to a case of economics,' he says. 'NBC owns all of *Riverboat* but had only a 40 percent financial interest in the sixteen episodes of *Five Fingers*. Fox had the other 60 percent.'

There were plans earlier this year to bring *Five Fingers* back for summer reruns, along with two new episodes that were filmed, but not telecast. 'My hopes for that were high,' says the actor, 'especially since our original ratings showed a marked uptrend in audience numbers toward the end of our run.' But those summer reruns didn't happen and David admitted that he is now, 'Completely fed up with television.' He is under consideration for major film roles such as in *Sanctuary* (based on William Faulkner's novel), *Return to Peyton Place* and *The Chapman Report*. With a movie schedule like that, who needs television?"

David's next interview that mentions the series was in December 1960 when he was promoting his appearance in the "Lesson in Fear" episode of the Fox TV series *Hong Kong*. The article states that *Five Fingers* was killed before its time. "'It was just a year ago that I returned from a Christmas vacation to report for the Seventeenth show. I was told I didn't need to come in, because the series was canceled. Luciana was all broken up about it, [but] I didn't really care. The show had done me a lot of good, working with people like Viveca Lindfors and Monty Woolley and Eva Gabor was great experience.'

Hedison agreed that *Five Fingers* should have been given a better chance to attract an audience. As proof of its potential, Hedison observed, 'it is one of the top shows in Australia [syndicated market] and my fan mail from Down Under is immense.'

What killed it? 'NBC owned only a part of it and so wasn't [as] interested [in keeping it] as [they would have one of] their wholly owned shows. We had weak sponsors, a lot of little ones so the story was interrupted every ten minutes. When we didn't get a [high] rating at first, they panicked. How could we get a rating? We were up against *Have Gun, Will Travel* and *Gunsmoke!* NBC must have recognized [the time slot] was impossible, because we were replaced with a public affairs program.'

Hedison [has] since done a feature [for] 20th Century Fox, *The Lost World*. He is set for another [movie], *Marines, Let's Go,* to start in Japan next month [January 1961]. So [he] came out the series unscathed, armed with some good acting experience and a new name."

David would work under his contract for Fox for one more year, until they let everyone go in 1962. When he did get work again, *Five Fingers* always seemed to come up. When Hedison was cast in *Voyage to the Bottom of the Sea*, Erskine Johnson wrote over the wire and it was picked up by *The Joplin Globe* (Missouri) in April 1963. "David Hedison's television series *Five Fingers* was disintegrated like *The Fly* a couple of years ago. It was a good series, but NBC made the mistake it could outdraw *Gunsmoke* in the ratings!"

David's final word on the series came in December of 1973 in a syndicated column by Joan Crosby in the *TV Scout* newspaper magazine. "David Hedison, who starred with Richard Basehart on the *Voyage* series, dropped out of sight when that series left the air. He materialized in Europe, got married, did some films, appeared opposite Lee Remick in a BBC production of *Summer and Smoke* and did a James Bond film. He also became the father of two daughters along the way. Now Hedison and his family are back in Los Angeles to stay.

'I'll go abroad for a role, but not to live,' he says. 'It is now practical to live here.' He recalls that after *Voyage*, there wasn't much going on in town. 'My wife was seven months pregnant and since she was British, I could work in England. We took our first daughter over there and our second was born in London.' He has been doing TV work this season, including *Cannon* and *The New Perry Mason*. He would like to do another TV series. 'But not one with monsters and submarines,' he says. 'Any actor who says that he wouldn't do a TV series... well, I don't know who would say that except for Paul Newman and Robert Redford. And one day they will probably do one too.'

His first series was *Five Fingers*, which ran from 1959-1960. It had a short, but well remembered run. 'It was a television series ahead of its time,' he says. 'I would like to do that show again, and with the same actress, Luciana Paluzzi. One problem with the series was that they put us up against *Gunsmoke*.' If it's possible, he may also play Felix Leiter again in the next James Bond film, if Hedison doesn't have a schedule conflict when it films next spring."

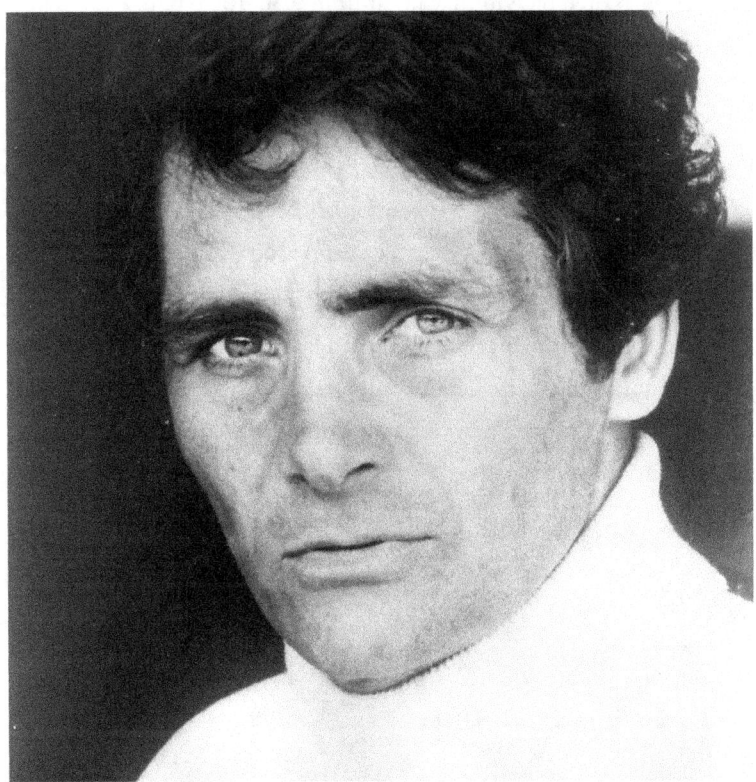

1973 TV Scout Sketch Picture. Photo copyright David Hedison.
1973 Head shot from his then agent.

Five Fingers had very high production values and Fox did do a lot of press to promote this series. Unfortunately, given the six week (or more) lag time between the release of the material by the studio and the actual publication of the magazines, most of the best publicity for the show came out as the show was going off the air and long after it was canceled. These myriad publicity articles and reviews are chronicled in the next chapter.

Five Fingers: Elegance in Espionage

The Broadcast History of the *Five Fingers* series is as follows:

The initial series run was on NBC: October 3, 1959-January 9, 1960. The episodes aired on Saturday night from 9:30-10:30 p.m.

There was a theatrical release in the UK: January 1961 to January 1962. Referred to as the *Operation Cicero* series, each "film" ran forty-eight minutes.

Nine episodes were reviewed in the British Film Institute's *Monthly Film Bulletin*: "Dossier," "Moment of Truth," "Emerald Curtain," "Temple of the Swinging Doll," "Final Dream," "Thin Ice," "The Judas Goat," "Shot in the Dark," and "Counterfeit." Quad Posters and front of the house B&W photo lobby cards were produced to publicize the series, like the one below.

"The Judas Goat": Unmasked man [unnamed extra] running into the street after he was mugged by the villain for his "carnival" mask. Copyright 20th Century Fox Studios.

TV Times Star Gallery: David Hedison, star of NINE'S [sic] new series, Five Fingers. Copyright 20th Century Fox Studios.

The series was syndicated to Australia in 1961. The premiere of the series is touted in *Melbourne TV Times* dated August 18-24, 1961. *Five Fingers* aired on Friday nights at 9:30 p.m. on Channel 9 in Melbourne. The episode listed for Friday August 19, 1961, is "Dossier." It is also stated the series was replacing *77 Sunset Strip* on the schedule.

There were two articles from *The Sydney Morning Herald* announcing the series Down Under. On July 10, 1960, *The Herald* said: "The international sleuth is the current fashion in TV, taking over from the small-time private eyes. One example is the exciting new *Five Fingers*, which will start here next Friday, replacing *77 Sunset Strip*. David Hedison is the star, with a twenty-one year old named Luciana Paluzzi, an Italian actress, as his co-star. Hedison, who once worked as a paint brush salesman and a bellhop at New York's Waldorf Astoria before turning to acting, will play Victor Sebastian, a counter-espionage agent working for the U.S. government under the cover of being a theatrical agent. Friday's opening episode is set in the south of France, with Eva Gabor as [the] guest star."

The Sydney Morning Herald ran a review by Valda Marshall on July 24, 1960. "Channel 7 looks like it has come up with a winner with *Five Fingers*. David Hedison is cut from familiar spy material and the opening shot had him in the arms of the beautiful Luciana Paluzzi. Then David strolled away casually to catch a plane to Cannes. As a 'love them and leave them' investigator, he joins the good company of other TV heroes such as Michael Rennie of *The Third Man* and David Janssen's *Richard Diamond*. Where *Five Fingers* really looks to score big, however, is in its story department."

Five Fingers finally ran as a summer replacement series in 1962 on ABC. I found listings for WABC in New York City that have the show airing 11:35 p.m. to 12:35 a.m. in the Historical *New York Times* Database.

There was also a very brief Los Angeles syndicated run later that year. The series aired from 9:30-10:30 p.m. on Channel 7 KABC from December 2, 1962, to January 19, 1963. These listings were found in the Historical *Los Angeles Times* Database.

Five Fingers was honored at a Television film festival in Cairo, Egypt, in 1963. David Hedison was given an engraved tea service: a tray, pot and cups that he promptly gave to his mother, Rose. She kept that tea service until she sold her house in 1994.

The show was distributed by Fuji Television in Japan in 1965 and in France in May of 1965. It was also distributed in Spain as *Cinco Dedos* and in Finland as *Viisi Sormea*.

The show was syndicated to South America at this time. It ran in Buenos Aires. It was mentioned in a South American TV guide offered for sale on EBay. The show also aired in Chile.

Copyright 20th Century Fox Studios.

Another American run, which aired episodes in both English and Spanish, was on the air from February through August 1967 on UHF Channel 47 WJNU. This station served the tri-state area of New York, New Jersey, and Connecticut. The series aired on WJNU at 10:30 p.m. for the first two months (February 2-March 30) and then at 7:00 p.m. for the duration of the run (April 6-August 17). There may have been other, later syndicated runs on WJNU, but this was the only one I could document.

There may have been other syndicated runs of this series in America, but they ran on broadcast and cable stations that I did not personally get at that time. I have been unable to verify from anyone who did see them when and where these runs aired.

Syndicated *TV Guide* listing. Cincinnati edition with picture. June 9, 1962. Copyright *TV Guide*. Photo copyright 20th Century Fox Studios.

Creation and History of the *Five Fingers* Series

The *Five Fingers* series was filmed at Fox's Beverly Hills Studio. In the summer of 1959 the studio was huge, stretching on for blocks and blocks. There were two gates: one on Sunset Boulevard and the main one on Pico Boulevard, which came to be known as the "*Hello, Dolly* Gate" after the 1969 film was filmed on the lot.

From Rodeo Drive, turn southwest on Santa Monica Boulevard and follow it until you reach Avenue of the Stars. Turn right. Proceed on Avenue of the Stars until you reach W. Pico Boulevard. Turn right. The Beverly Hills Studio will be on your left. Turn left onto Motor Avenue to enter the studio. Do not take the 405 Freeway as stated by the Studio web site.

Fox opened their studios there in 1928, on land that once was the personal ranch of western movie star Tom Mix. Seven years later, Fox merged with Twentieth Century Pictures, which had been founded in 1933 by Darryl Zanuck, after he left Warner Brothers. The combined studios became 20th Century Fox in 1935.

The studio did well under Zanuck. He was as tyrannical as Goldwyn or Warner, but he respected the talent he had and was collaborative in a way that was good for production of high quality material. Fox didn't have a particular niche, like MGM, which was known for making musicals, or Warner Brothers, who made gangster films. Due to Zanuck's personal tastes, however, the studio did become known as a producer of "adventure" films.

Fox had a huge back lot. It was built up over many years on the old ranch site. You could find almost anything from a South Seas lagoon to an old western town to downtown New York City. The lot was 230 acres and stretched from Pico Boulevard to Santa Monica Boulevard. Within the studio high fences were Plantation House (used for southern films), Old New York Street, which had a trolley and an elevated train tracks, New New York Street, Suburban Street (for neighborhood shots), New England Street, Midwestern Street, Tombstone and Omaha Streets (two western sets), The Train Station, Adano Square (an Italian square),

Bernadette Village, Old French Street, Algerian Street and The Keys of the Kingdom Church, Sligon Castle, plus Chicago Lake, Sersen Lake and The Waterways (South Seas Lagoon). The Dutch Moat was a small tank with a sky backing. Sersen Lake was a larger rectangular tank with a huge backdrop and the adjacent Chicago Lake (made for the film *In Old Chicago*) was the largest body of water. Underwater scenes were scheduled for The Green Tank; it had portholes built into it for the cameras to shoot through. It was located on Stage Sixteen, until the tank part of this stage was torn down in 1967.

To give you an idea of the scope of these old sets, today off Santa Monica Boulevard, adjacent to Beverly Hills High School, there is a cluster of office buildings where *The Waterways* used to be. This was the sleepy lagoon and Tahitian village, with the sixty-five foot replica of the Schooner *Tiki* anchored in concrete and asphalt in four feet of water, which stood for the first two seasons of *Adventures in Paradise*. Everything on the sold section of the back lot (176 acres) was demolished in August of 1961.

Fox caught a real break in the early 1950s when they patented Cinemascope, a wide screen process that made movie going an event again. They used the process to film a biblical epic called *The Robe* which made a ton of money, spawning both imitators of the process (Vistavision for one) and a whole host of other biblical films for the rest of the decade. These cinemascope event movies became known as "road shows" and would usually play in theaters for over a year.

These event films helped stave off television until mid-1950. As the movie studios lost more and more money on expensive road show flops and lost their audience for B and mid-range movies, those considered not worthy of road show treatment, the studios began to seriously produce series programming for television.

Television had been around since 1948, but the shows aired were mostly done live; first in New York and then in Los Angeles. They were mainly anthology shows with rotating casts doing stage plays live or some kind of talent contests or variety and burlesque skit shows. The studios adapted every medium out there to the "new" one, trying to figure out what worked and what received the highest ratings.

Warner Brothers was the first studio to seriously film prime time dramatic series for television in 1955. These TV series still had rotating casts, the principal difference being these episodes were filmed and they starred mostly unknown or newly signed contract actors.

Fox produced their first series, *My Friend Flicka*, in 1956 at the Sunset and Western studio. They came out with *20th Century Fox Hour* in 1957, which aired one hour staged versions of their old movies. TCF Television kept that part of the studio busy and profitable at a time profits were hard to come by. Movie audiences were dwindling for the aforementioned B-movies which had always fed the immense bottom line of studio overhead, talent contracts, and development costs of (ultimately) unused properties.

Also in 1956, to raise capital, Fox leased the rights to fifty-two of their old (pre-1948) films that they were convinced they would never re-release again. They made money doing this, but in the long run, this only drove more viewers out of the theaters and home to their televisions. In six years movie attendance dropped from 90 million in 1950 to slightly above 60 million.

In 1959, three series were green-lighted from Fox pilots and twelve pilots were ordered. *Hong Kong*, *Bus Stop*, and *Follow the Sun* became series in 1960; *White Hunter* and *Brock Callahan* did not.

The Fox studio commissioned a master-plan development from Welton Becket Associates in an attempt to raise more revenue. This plan was unveiled at a major press event on the Western back lot in 1957. Welton Becket was an architect who designed many of the most famous buildings in Hollywood and Los Angeles. The first studio land sale was made in 1958. One hundred seventy-six acres went to Webb and Knapp of New York City to develop Century City. They paid Fox $40 million. Webb and Knapp was a real estate development firm, founded in 1922 by Robert C. Knapp and W. Seward Webb, along with Eliot Cross, a noted architect, who, with his brother John Walter Cross, formed the architectural partnership of Cross and Cross. William Zeckendorf joined this firm in 1938 and acquired it in 1949.

William Zeckendorf, Sr. was known as "the real estate mogul's real estate mogul." He was years ahead of his time. He assembled the parcel for the United Nations in 1947, built the Roosevelt Field shopping center on Long Island, the Century City complex in Los Angeles, and did several urban renewal projects in Philadelphia and Washington, D.C. Then he went broke.

Fox sold the remaining back lot (fifty-four acres) for $43 million to Zeckendorf and Alcoa (partners) in 1961 and then leased it back so they could continue film production there. Acreage of the current Fox Studio is fifty plus acres. The Fox back lot was 230 acres. There are sixteen sound stages on the studio lot off Pico Boulevard, currently numbered through twenty-two in 2015. Stages Seven, Twelve and Thirteen no longer exist. Stage One and Stage Two have been re-purposed. Stage One is now the scoring stage and Stage Two is used for ADR/Foley work (sound effects). Stage Sixteen is still on the map, but has been renovated.

There was also a Westwood Studio, a Sunset and Western Studio (TV show production), and The Fox Ranch, in the West Valley. Brett Halsey remembers filming at *The Train Station*, which was used in three *Five Fingers* episodes; in particular, "Final Dream." Halsey does not specifically remember using *Algerian Street*, which appears in the episode "The Assassin" in addition to Halsey's "Thin Ice" episode.

Dobie Gillis filmed at Sunset and Western Studio, according to Brett Halsey. *Adventures in Paradise* filmed on *The Waterways* and other locations on the back lot in Beverly Hills. The Studio Head during *Five Fingers* production was E. Maurice "Buddy" Adler, who died unexpectedly in 1960 of lung cancer at age fifty-one. Hedison mentioned he talked to Adler frequently during his earlier (pre-series) days at the studio.

Darryl Zanuck returned as Fox studio head in 1963. Spyros

Skouras, the studio head who took over after Adler's death, had basically mismanaged the place into the ground by then, squandering assets and personnel. Skouras sold off everything he could.

Under Skouras, Fox suffered a string of expensive movie flops, culminating in the box-office disaster *Cleopatra*. The new owners had already conceived Century City as "a city within a city." They started building it in August 1961, demolishing the Fox back lot for the land beneath it.

In 1963, the first new building, Century City Gateway West, was completed, followed the next year by Minoru Yamasaki's Century Plaza Hotel. Minoru Yamasaki was a United States architect best known for his design of the twin towers of the World Trade Center. Yamasaki was a prominent architect of the 20th century and his firm, Yamasaki & Associates, continues to do business today.

Century City is a commercial and residential district on the West Side of Los Angeles. The West Side consists of Bel-Air, Beverly Crest, Beverlywood, Century City, Brentwood, Cheviot Hills, Pacific Palisades, Palms, and Rancho Park. Beverly Hills and the neighboring city of West Hollywood are entirely surrounded by the city of Los Angeles, on the northeast.

The major thoroughfares in this area are Santa Monica and Olympic Boulevards. Olympic Boulevard is a major artery. It stretches from 4th Street on the western end of Santa Monica to East Los Angeles, farther than Wilshire Boulevard. Pico Boulevard runs from the Pacific Ocean at Appian Way in Santa Monica to Central Avenue in Downtown Los Angeles. Wilshire Boulevard is one of the principal east-west roads in Los Angeles. It was named after Henry Gaylord Wilshire, an Ohio native who made and lost fortunes in real estate, farming, and gold mining.

Century City was to be served by the Beverly Hills Freeway. This never-built highway would have linked the Los Angeles districts of Westwood, Los Angeles, California and Echo Park along the route of Santa Monica Boulevard to the north, providing a rapid transit corridor.

Most people assume Century City's main street, Avenue of the Stars, refers to movie stars. The project was considered a city of the future, so they named the streets Galaxy, Constellation, and Avenue of the Stars. Century City has many law firms and executives, mostly with ties to the film, television, and music industries. Buildings in Westwood appear to blend with Century City, although they stand over three-quarters of a mile apart. Century City's gleaming high-rises are in stark contrast to the small apartment buildings and single-family detached homes in the neighborhoods surrounding it. They were some of the first skyscrapers built in Los Angeles after earthquake-related height restrictions were lifted in the early 1960s.

Some of the most recognizable buildings in Century City are: Fox Plaza, 20th Century Fox headquarters. It was "Nakatomi Plaza" in the first *Die Hard* movie. The MGM Tower is 491 feet tall. It was constructed from 2001 to 2003, has thirty-five floors and was headquarters of the historic Hollywood studio Metro-Goldwyn-Mayer, which is now owned by Sony. The Hyatt Regency Century Plaza Hotel is a landmark nineteen-story luxury hotel. Its sweeping crescent design fronts the spectacular fountains on Avenue of the Stars adjacent to the twin Century Plaza Towers and the Creative Artists Agency building. Century Plaza Towers I and II are two forty-four story, 571 feet tall towers located at 2029 and 2049 Century Park East. The Hyatt Regency Hotel was blown up in 1993 thriller *Point of No Return*. And the whole neighborhood was destroyed in *Fight Club*. The twin Century Plaza Towers were featured on TV in both *Remington Steele* and *Moonlighting*, and the fountains on Avenue of the Stars are in multiple films and TV shows. Around the corner at 1888 Century Park East was the headquarters of Orion Pictures. They were sold to MGM and are now also owned by Sony.

The ABC television network had its corporate headquarters in the ABC Entertainment Center across the street from the Century Plaza Hotel, where many U.S. Presidents stayed when they were in town. The Shubert Theatre was there. Both these buildings were demolished in

2004. Steven Spielberg once opened a restaurant in the Century City Shopping Center called Dive! Patterned after a submarine. It was a sub shop. Across Pico Boulevard from the 20th Century Fox Studios is the famous Hillcrest Country Club. Fox Studio actors who were members would go and eat lunch there when they did not want to eat on the lot in the Fox commissary.

Our history of the *Five Fingers* series continues in the next chapter as we chronicle the publicity and reviews that were published about the series that summer and fall of 1959.

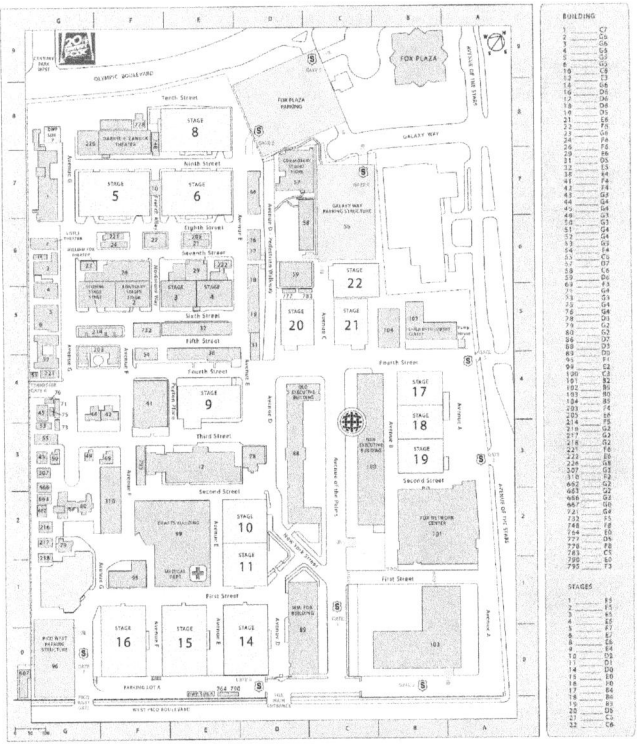

Copyright 20th Century Fox Studios.

Chapter 3

Publicity, Reviews, and Interviews 1959–60

On June 19, 1959, Harvey Pack wrote one of the first interview/publicity pieces for the *Five Fingers* series in the *Troy Record* (New York). How much of this piece is Fox Studio publicity department boilerplate is unknown. They packaged these anecdotes and put them out for anyone to print in the myriad newspapers and magazines of the day.

"David Hedison knows well about pounding the pavement for work. He used to sell Fuller brushes in order to make the money necessary to pursue an acting career in New York. His jeweler father would shout, 'What have I done to deserve this?!'

David went door to door selling brushes to save up $1,000 for an acting career. Now, he feels his father has accepted him as an actor and he is quite proud that David was selected to star in NBC's new *Five Fingers* series. This series is considered one of the network's brightest new dramatic properties for 1959-60, based on the popular James Mason film.

After he starred in *The Fly* and *Son of Robin Hood*, David was turned over by Fox to producer Martin Manulis and he's now bidding David for TV stardom. David is now fortifying himself for the grueling TV series by eating his favorite food, yogurt diluted with water plus chopped up garlic and cucumbers. Some counter-spy! The enemy will smell him coming.

David begged me to include that although he was known as 'Al' in *The Fly*, he has now changed his name to David. As we finished our coffees, comedian Pat Carroll walked into the restaurant and posed a big question to David, 'Hi Ara, how have you been?' When Pat left, I asked David who Ara was. 'Pat has known me for a long time,' he said. 'My [Armenian family] name is Ara.'"

The New York Times reviewed the upcoming series on July 9, 1959. John Shanley writes: "In the new *Five Fingers*, David Hedison is the handsome but rather bland hero. Despite its hollow storyline of international counter-espionage, this series might draw a large audience. The photography is very attractive and so is Hedison's co-star, Luciana Paluzzi."

The *Joplin Globe* (Missouri) ran the following on August 25, 1959. "Al Hedison will become David Hedison this fall for his new *Five Fingers* series. It is a decision based on what some unknown genius calls, 'more dignity.' But has name will still be Al when Fox releases its made-in-the-U.K. film *Son of Robin Hood*. The film was made in the same studio where British star Richard Greene shoots his *Robin Hood* TV series. One day while on this lot, Hedison, with feather in his green cap, passed Greene, who also wore a feather in his green cap. Hedison yelled out a friendly, 'Hi Dad!' 'All I got from Greene was this very cold stare,' says Hedison. 'I don't think he was very happy about our film! And neither was I!'"

In *The Pittsburgh Gazette* on August 10, 1959, Win Fanning previewed the show by saying, "The success of the sexy by-play between men and women on shows like *Peter Gunn* and *77 Sunset Strip* has now led to other shows following the same formula. The most promising is pretty Luciana Paluzzi and her co-star David Hedison in the new *Five Fingers*. It will be showing up opposite *Gunsmoke*. Cowboys, move over! This gal is coming for you!"

The Troy Record on August 10, 1959, runs a commentary by Steven H. Scheuer. "For the upcoming television season there is a mass of westerns and mysteries, such as a private-eye based in Honolulu, but these are nothing to get excited about. They will be the same old junk with new faces but written by the same old tired writers who move their plots from show to show. But not all is black and white this fall. Former *Playhouse 90* producer Martin Manulis, a very shrewd fellow, is hiring not only new talent for his three new TV series this year but many of the writers from his prestigious *Playhouse 90*. One of these shows is *Five Fingers*, about international intrigue. The premise may have a familiar ring as it is based on a James Mason movie. But one difference is that the hero, played by David Hedison, will be an American agent sneaking into a Soviet spy ring.

Producer Herbert Swope, Jr., has cast the fairly unknown movie actor Hedison as the lead and has handsome Italian actress, Luciana Paluzzi, as his feminine co-star. She is liable to really warm up a movie set. Swope is also pouring good money into this show's writing staff and has already hired talented people such as Dick Berg and director Bob Stevens. This is indeed the tip-off that will distinguish *Five Fingers* by the talent involved and indicates a genuine attempt to make *Five Fingers* better than the usual weekly television series.

Swope himself has impressive credentials, having directed John O'Hara's *Appointment to Samarra* and produced the acclaimed anthology *Lights Out*. He has also spent time working for Pat Weaver when Weaver was head of NBC. Swope is still carrying around the excitement he had when he worked for Weaver in which he produced a host of exciting and different projects. Now Swope hopes to put that same life into *Five Fingers*. 'Really, this is not going to be some pulp series,' he says. 'We have the freedom and opportunity to try something different here. Things have changed in Hollywood. We are not limited to using people who are only under contract to 20th Century-Fox. We can talk to, or use, anyone we want for this show. That's a big step and our writing crew for *Five Fingers* is pretty impressive.' Mr. Swope's comments are encouraging and the very fact he is involved certainly means something!"

Howard Pearson writes about "Video Laughs on the set of TVs *Five Fingers*" in *The Deseret News* (California) on September 7, 1959. "Luciana Paluzzi, David Hedison's co-star in *Five Fingers*, was about to do a scene where she finishes making a phone call and then was to walk across the room. When the scene was over, the director said, 'That was fine, only you didn't mosey along as I told you to. And why, may I ask, were you so carefully studying the room as you walked across it?' Luciana was puzzled. 'Mosey?' she asked. 'What is this mosey? I thought you said I should be NOSY as I walked across the room, so that's what I was doing!"

The *Star News* (California) September 11, 1959, has a comment by syndicated columnist Mike Connolly. "The new 20th Century Fox series *Five Fingers* looks like it is set for a long run on NBC. At least, its future looks good to co-star Luciana Paluzzi because she is bringing her mamma Maria all the way over from Italy to live in Hollywood for the next year!"

The *Blytheville Courier News* (Arkansas) September 17, 1959, has a wire byline by Erskine Johnson. "The biggest target this year will be on *Gunsmoke* and *Have Gun, Will Travel*. They are currently riding high on CBS Saturdays and when NBC tried to knock them off with a western last year, it didn't work. But this year could be different. The competition is *Five Fingers*, an hour of international intrigue and sophisticated settings. NBC has slotted this ambitious program against the CBS cowpoke heroes. The *Five Fingers* producers can afford to go all out for quality with a higher than usual TV budget. One network run would not even begin to pay back its production costs but eventual reruns on TV would. One angle to recoup the costs of an expensive show like *Five Fingers* is to release episodes abroad as motion pictures [with] two episodes combined to make a feature. And since this series already has a European background, the actors don't even have to leave Stage Six at Fox."

In the September 1959 *TV Star Parade*, David is listed for *Five Fingers* in "Your Pocket Guide to TV's Top New Stars."

On October 3, 1959, *TV Scout* was of the opinion that "The premiere of *Five Fingers* is the best bet on TV tonight. In this era of the Western, it is such a pleasure to report on a new adventure series without a horse in sight! *Five Fingers* is a new spy story, pure and simple. It is enlivened by the presence of a beautiful girl, Luciana Paluzzi, as the hero's best friend. She is a genuinely rare find for television. But the hero, played by David Hedison, is another slick haired guy and he is the biggest drawback to the show. He is a theatrical agent who is a spy on the side and tonight he must break up spy ring on the French Riviera. Although Eva Gabor and Mike Romanoff guest star, it is international cafe singer Greta Keller as a blind chanteuse, who nearly steals this show from everyone else. Keller is a Viennese-born singer and she is well-known throughout the world. This pilot film for *Five Fingers* did have the disadvantage of being two episodes in one. It was originally made as a half-hour pilot but enlarged into an hour show after a request from NBC. New characters and scenes were added at the last minute so it is somewhat choppy as result. Still, if its stars were more worldly and mature, this could really be one crack of a TV series!"

In the *Arkansas Hope Star* October 8, 1959, Cynthia Lowry of *The Associated Press* wire service wrote: "*Five Fingers* is a new interesting espionage series but the only way I can tell that I'm not watching an old B movie is by the slim lapels on the suit of its hero, David Hedison."

FIVE FINGERS: ELEGANCE IN ESPIONAGE

Reviews of the expanded series pilot "Station Break" were mostly favorable. Bill Fiset wrote in the *Oakland Tribune* (California) on October 14, 1959, "*Five Fingers* is a new series with quality. It is NBC's answer to ABC's slick hit, *77 Sunset Strip*. *Five Fingers*, however, is a much better package. This is the most original suspense show on television and is a definite bright spot for Saturday nights. *Five Fingers*, you might say, deserves a hand. Martin Manulis is producer and the show has an unmistakable touch of class. The hero (David Hedison) and heroine (Luciana Paluzzi) are attractive and pleasant to watch.

It also has its own gimmicks. There are long, long intimate kisses between the two, which became fashionable on *Peter Gunn*. There's tricky camera work, such as where the camera pans back and forth over a woman's figure in a bathing suit at Cannes without ever once showing her face. But then, hey, what's a face? It has name-dropping (Hedison's front is that of a theatrical agent) and intriguing guest stars such as Eva Gabor and Mike Romanoff. It also has good music. Greta Keller played a blind singer in the opening episode and her rendition of 'La Vie En Rose' was fabulous! Sadly, her character gets stabbed to death with scissors near the finish. David Opatoshu was a totally bald villain who looked and talked like Yul Brynner. This alone kept lady viewers on the edge of their seats. The show has a lot of beautiful women wearing a lot of beautiful clothes and the entire series exudes glamour. Women viewers see the clothes, and men viewers see the women models.

The premiere show also had a lot of exterior location filming in the French Riviera. Such pains are usually reserved only for feature films. Indeed, *Five Fingers* suggests a feature film quality and much credit in the premiere must go to director Andrew McCullough. The producers have also taken the time and trouble to bring an Italian actress to Hollywood for this show and Miss Paluzzi has now grown into stardom. All in all, *Five Fingers* is such a glittery and easy to watch show that its spy plots, the kind about dastardly microfilm messages scribbled on matchbook folders, etc., seem superfluous. It is running opposite *Gunsmoke* and *Have*

Gun, Will Travel so the pretty girls and music should be enough. But really, there was one unforgivable thing that happened in the first episode. The hero, the international intelligence agent, wore his handkerchief with a square fold in his breast pocket and that is definitely out this season. [Wardrobe] should know better than that!"

Ron Burton wrote in the *Lima News* (Ohio) on October 26, 1959, "The new *Five Fingers* is a top new TV spy thriller. 'I'm a theatrical agent as far as this girl is concerned.' The 'girl' is Luciana Paluzzi. Luciana is a beautiful Italian import. It is Hedison's task to lie to her to avoid letting her know he really is a US spy operating in [the] various countries. 'Each week, a private eye [remains] a private eye. Not me. I play the same role each week, [but] this variety [of roles is] better.' *Five Fingers* is a series of many things: roles, names and languages. 'One of the roles I play [here] is liar to a pretty girl. I like [that] I don't play the same role all the time, although I do preserve an identity as Victor Sebastian, theatrical agent. I'm supposed to be [that], most of the time. I'm something of a private eye. I'm a counteragent. And a liar.'

David is also known by several names on the Fox set. Victor, which is his name on the show, Al, which was his early name, David, his current name and the name of Dave, which irritates him. He does not like the name Dave. 'My real name is Albert David Hedison, Jr. My last name was [always] Hedison, but my grandparents [were Heditsians until they changed it when they became American citizens in 1917.]"

"All it took was a name change to go from Fly to Spy. That's what happened to David Hedison, who plays the lead in *Five Fingers*, a new spy series being seen Saturday evenings at 9:30 p.m. on NBC-TV. He is listed as David Hedison, but he's the same person as the Al Hedison who starred in the highly successful film *The Fly* [a year] ago. He's a natural athlete, likes water skiing, tennis, ice hockey, snow sports, horseback riding and most recently bull fighting. This last is more than a hobby. David makes no bones about the fact that he would like to do a re-make of *Blood and Sand* and has been studying [with] a former professional matador [Patrick Cunningham], so he will be able to play the role in style.

David has another ambition as an actor, a more usual one, he wants to play *Hamlet*. Eventually, he'd like to direct. David is single and playing the field romantically; says he's not even going to think about getting married for a while. In the meantime, he gets around with a wide assortment of screen lovelies. He has plenty of room for a wife and a batch of kids in his rented old Spanish stucco house. [Now] he's starring in a weekly TV series, like the other unattached guys in the same boat, he's finding he has little time for dating. And it's tough to locate a wife when you haven't even time to take a girl to the movies," according to the 1960 annual issue of *TV's Top Stars*."

In an article called "When a Bachelor Entertains" in the November 1959 issue of *Movie Life*, David is a guest at Bob Horton's [*Wagon Train*] house party. He demonstrates his newly learned bull fighting skills with a borrowed tablecloth and Horton's totally uncooperative black poodle.

Hedison is still unhappy with his network mandated name change when he is interviewed in Japan while making his fifth film, *Marines, Let's Go*, for Fox. In *Pacific Stars and Stripes* (Japan) March 10, 1961, Al Ricketts writes: 'David Hedison would not hurt a fly. Mosquitoes? Yes, possibly. And perhaps all other kinds of other creepy crawly insects. But not flies, because his career got such a big boost from *The Fly* film. 'That movie was a good break for me,' he says. 'It was a sympathetic role and I received a lot of fan mail because of it. But I don't want to play any more insects!' The likeable actor was also the victim of an old Hollywood malady, a name change right in the middle of his career. When he was about to star in the NBC series *Five Fingers*, the powers that be decided he had to change his first name Al to David. The producers felt it was a necessity. 'I still don't know why they insisted on that,' says Hedison. 'But who knows? Next week, I'll probably be Frank Hedison!'"

The name change was attributed to an "unknown [network] genius" who feels Hedison's name needed "more dignity," according to an August

25, 1959, article in the *Joplin Globe*. In the 1960 *Movie Screen Yearbook*, they reiterate, "... for TV, David was more dignified." And then they tell the readers to be sure to write to him at NBC on Hollywood and Vine.

The *Steubenville Herald Star* (Ohio) December 9, 1959, review by Jonathan Crosby is not kind: "On *Five Fingers*, a new spy drama, a very pretty girl standing out in the moors looks up and screams. There is a mysterious face peering at her from a window. Then you get a commercial. That pretty much sums up how things go in this series, which is NBC's Saturday night espionage thriller. It contains all of the good and bad aspects of motion pictures from the last fifty years. The camerawork is excellent and all of the girls are beautifully gowned while all of the boys are husky and handsome. The setting of the series is absolutely superb. Well, so much for the good things about *Five Fingers*.

The bad may be summed up by saying that the stories are simply incredible but to say that does not really express it. *Peter Pan*, for instance was incredible, too, but writer James Barrie really believed in it when he wrote it and the actors who played in it took it seriously. But I get the idea that the writers on *Five Fingers* make up this malarkey that they themselves don't take seriously and that the actors are just doing it for the money. Even the directors are just engaging in a piano exercise.

The show's trouble is that it falls between two levels; it is not arrant derring-do for the kids and certainly is not serious drama for the adults. It just does not come up with anything near the imagination of Alfred Hitchcock's thrillers. What you are left with every week is an exercise in technical competence, which Hollywood excels in. This is yet another one of 20th Century Fox's contributions to television and *Five Fingers* takes a stand right next to Fox's *Adventures in Paradise*. If they keep up their TV work on this level, Fox may yet put Warner Brothers aside as proving a hallmark of mediocrity on television."

Two months after the series ended, in March of 1960, David Hedison was hard at work on his fourth Fox film, *The Lost World*, but the press kept right on talking about the now canceled *Five Fingers* series.

An extensive sixteen page interview, illustrated with set photos from the filming of *Five Fingers* episode "The Emerald Curtain," that was obviously meant to push the series was published in the March 1960 issue of *Stardom* magazine, which lasted only few months longer than this series.

Rona Barrett wrote: "David Hedison and I have been friends for several years. I hadn't seen him in quite a while until we met at the 20th [Century Fox] commissary the other day. His black curly hair clung close to his head and his suntan made his brown eyes darker and more dancing. It was noon time and neither one of us had breakfast. David ordered a cold salad plate while I had some eggs and toast.

I had already selected the angle for our story, *The Lonely Life of Al Hedison*, when Al (all his old friends still call him that) said, 'Please. Rona, let's not do that. Can't we do something else? Something different, something really honest and truthful?'

For one hour, Albert David Hedison and I sat discussing different aspects of his life. David's life has been a determined one. His two feet were always planted on terra firma. He was going to be an actor, no matter what.

'I am not neurotic or sick, nor am I lost,' he blurted out. 'Every time I pick up a magazine the pages are filled with stories like *The Day so and so almost died! Or My Mother hated me! Or I was a Juvenile Delinquent!* None of these things ever happened to me! I guess I will never be "good copy" for the fans.' David shook his head in disbelief and continued eating.

It was there and then I decided if this was the way David's life was, why not tell it that way? *What makes David run? All the things he hates!*

David Hedison hated going to the jewelry design school his father sent him to. He also hated college. Time was precious. An education [can be valuable], but David wanted to act. Life was too short to spend time doing things he didn't want to. But his mother and father knew best. *There was no such thing as an acting career. That was nonsense!*

David's father had a successful jewelry [enameling] business. He was their only child and, being a son, his father wanted to hand the business down to him. David said, 'I want to be an actor!' They laughed. They thought their son was as normal as blueberry pie. Every child goes through a period wanting to become a movie star. Only with David, it was different. *He was going to be one!* There was no way he was going back to jewelry design school for another summer. His father thought if he went [there] long enough he would begin to like the work and give up this acting nonsense.

So David enlisted in the Navy at seventeen. After his tour, he went to college and finally got his chance to do summer stock in 1949. He had finished his junior year at Brown University and that summer he went away to Wellesley, Massachusetts. For the first time, he was introduced to the world of acting. The more he became involved with the theater, the harder it was to in think about going back to school. He hated school. He wanted to act. He loved the theater. It was the very soul of his existence. David never finished college. He quit to earn money as a Fuller Brush salesman so he could to go to New York, pay for his tuition and study acting.

In New York he learned to hate sitting in coffee shops and listening to other actors talking about this and that and doing nothing about it. 'I had to be prepared,' David said, 'I wanted to learn. I want to know everything I can possibly know. As actor can be anyone he wants to be. I wanted to be everyone! There was no time for nonsensical talking. Talking was a waste of time and I hated time to be wasted. It was too precious. There was too much to be done.'

He had saved enough money [to pay for his classes] at the Neighborhood Playhouse. He was the first one in class and the last to leave. He got a night job at the Waldorf Astoria. He snuffed candles, he polished silverware, and he did anything else that needed doing. During the day, he'd walk the cold, grey, rainy streets of New York looking for acting work. Work wasn't easy to find. 'Some days I didn't even have a dime for a frankfurter or the bus. I'd tramp the city from the east side to the west side from uptown to downtown. I guess that's why I hated rain. Every time it rained, it would cost a buck to get my suit cleaned. I couldn't afford to miss an interview. I never knew from one day to the next if this interview might be the one. I needed a job so badly at that time. You can only keep going so long and if nothing happens you begin to wonder, maybe it will never happen. So many times I felt my confidence being knocked out from under me. But I kept going. I knew that without confidence I had nothing. Confidence was half the battle won.'

David paused to order more coffee. 'You know what else I hate? I hate elevators! I'll walk up six flights before I'll take [one]. It's much quicker walking. I can't stand waiting around for an elevator to come. I have to get where I'm going now, not five minutes from now. I also hate waiting for people. I'm always on time. I hate wasting a minute and I get irritated when people make me wait. In those extra few minutes I could have been doing something constructive.'

'I [was studying] with Uta Hagen. Several months later my luck began to change. I was in the play called *A Month in the Country*. I won a Theatre award for that which led to me being spotted by Fox. I was flown to California and put under contract to do movies.' Life in California [was different] than life in New York. The slow pace made David uneasy. Life was too relaxed. He hadn't learned to relax yet. Just because he had a contract, didn't mean he could stop. *You want to be a good actor? Then work for it.* So David pushed. He continued studying. He worked hard. He was looking for the right part and in his looking he met all kinds of different people.

'Luciana, who co-stars with me, has really got 'it' and I predict great things for her in the months to come. In this series I play a theatrical agent who is a counterspy. The scripts have been exciting and I've enjoyed each role immensely. But I must admit, even if it sounds a bit calculating, that I'm doing this series in hopes that one day I can play the roles I want to play. It's become a known fact that through the medium of TV, one can gain immediate recognition. Like any actor, I'd give anything to play a role that had everything from A-Z in it. But until I can reach that stage, I'll keep working, keep studying, and keep learning.'

'Don't you ever stop running?' I queried, 'Isn't there ever time for relaxing?'

'Well, if you can call it relaxing, It took me quite a while to realize that you have to stop somewhere along the way, even if it's to evaluate what's going on. I did that one morning not too long ago. It was [right] before I got this series. I was discouraged. Then it hit me. Perhaps I needed a rest to think over my plan of operation. So, I took off and headed for Catalina. Now I go there all the time to relax. I skin dive and swim and fish and try to take my mind off everything I've done the previous days.'

While he appears to be sitting idly on a small cabin cruiser, David Hedison's brain is turning like the hands of a clock. He's thinking about tomorrow and all the things he will do once he hits the mainland.

Now the interview is over, I couldn't help but say to myself: 'Who would want to change such a guy?' For all the things [David] hates, there are hundreds more he loves: like Christmas in New England, his house in the hills, motion pictures, Simone Signoret, the sea, bullfights, the color red, James Thurber, horses, Erroll Garner, girls. What I admired most was what David represented: The determined people who under adverse circumstance never gave way to the weakness of the moment. That's why they succeed."

Author's note: Barrett's complete Five Fingers set interview with David Hedison is sixteen pages.

David related the following story that happened during the filming of the series in the January 1960 issue of *Movie Stars TV Close-ups*. "It was a bright, sunny day when David Hedison headed south on Highway 101 toward Laguna Beach and the Mexican border. All he was thinking of as he chatted gaily with the girl next to him and the couple in the backseat were the bullfights they were going to attend in Tijuana that afternoon.

Although the traffic was fairly heavy in both directions, David felt safe in sticking close to the legal speed limit, which was fifty-five miles an hour. He was safe, too, [until] the hood of his car suddenly unlatched and sprung up against the windshield, blocking his view as he was just about to go into a long curve.

The girl next to him let out a scream. The couple in the back seat turned deathly quiet. David himself [said,] 'Oh, God, let us get to a safe stop.'

Gripping the steering wheel with both hands, he tried to peer out the side of the car but couldn't see much. He could hear the screeching [of] brakes and tires as other cars swerved to avoid hitting him. Twice, less than a couple of inches separated him from on-coming cars. One came so close that David hastily pulled his arm away from the window.

In spite of the heavy traffic and his inability to see ahead, David managed to bring his car to a safe halt. Only he doesn't think he should take the credit. He firmly believes a power far greater was responsible."

On June 19, 1960, *The Odessa American* (Texas) ran a profile by Hedda Hopper. "If you think David Hedison has come up fast in Hollywood, he will soon put you straight that he is no overnight star. He had just completed his fifth film when we spoke and had recently finished a TV series, *Five Fingers*. He is even better known in Europe because *The Fly* was such a sensation there and so was *Son of Robin Hood*. '*The Fly* cost $450,000 to make and it made $5,000,000,' he told me. 'It's the kind of film you dream of doing!'

Hedison is always faultlessly groomed and dressed with conservative good taste. He is a fluent talker and his ease, poise, and excellent manners are impressive. He lives up to what he considers are a movie star's responsibilities. He drives a Mercedes, entertains in his Beverly Hills home, which once belonged to Jean Harlow. 'I love it because of the huge rooms and high ceilings. There is a lot of space in which to roam.'

When we spoke of actresses today, it included his former co-star of *Five Fingers*, the Italian Luciana Paluzzi. 'She is one actress who came through like a blockbuster,' he said. 'Her merriment, her beauty and her capability as an actress register instantly.' He noted that foreign actresses such as Miss Paluzzi have it all over the American actresses in one respect. 'They have a willingness to work hard. Most have come from poor families, where they had to do more than their share work while in childhood. Our actresses in America have been handed everything on a silver platter and they expect stardom to come to them in the same way.'

Hopper Article picture June 1960. Head shot.
Copyright 20th Century Fox Studios.

But he pointed to some American actresses who have potential. 'Dolores Michaels should have a future. She has a definite quality. She's kooky off-set but very professional and capable at work. Sandra Dee is the best ingénue in the business. Elana Eden is a complete actress in every sense. Judi Meredith is beautiful and can make good if she will continue working. I no longer consider Hope Lange as a beginner but she and Joanne Woodward are the best young talents in the business and they have made it.'

And actors? 'Paul Newman is the best all-around younger actor.' Hedison thinks Doug McClure, Rod Taylor, Cliff Robertson, Brett Halsey and Gardner McKay are also sure to make the big time, as well as Tom Tryon and Stuart Whitman.

David is often seen nowadays dating such girls as Venetia Stevenson, Susan Oliver, Lea Di Lea (a sculptress), Joi Lansing [*Love that Bob*] and Vicki Trickett."

By the end of 1960, David is being described in the fan magazine annuals as a major movie "bachelor" heartthrob. "Girls usually sum up their feelings about David Hedison in one full-throated word: WOW! And we can't say we blame them. David is sensationally handsome, sensationally attentive and is quite the hand at keeping the conversational ball rolling. All of which makes him fun to be with. As for falling in love, that could be fun, too, if and when Mr. Hedison would just let go and give his freedom the heave-ho. That's hard to do when girls of every description – all beautiful – keep him busy." Interestingly, this "movie" article in *Movie Screen Yearbook no.7 1961* is illustrated with a photo of David from the 1959 *TV Guide* premiere photo shoot of *Five Fingers*. The series had been off the air for nearly a year.

David was in competition to be named "The King of TV" in 1960. There was a fill-in-the-blank ballot to mail in and vote for your favorite "sigh guy." He was also named one of TV's "Most Exciting Dreamboats" in the 1960 *TV Star Annual*. "Don't be afraid to be a dreamer," David said. "All great accomplishments begin with a dream. I had a college professor who told me to 'stop dreaming' and learn a real trade. I find great joy in learning something I never knew before," he said in the *Movie Mirror Yearbook, Number 10* (1966).

"I like being a bachelor. I really enjoy calling my life my own, not having the responsibility involved with marriage and having the freedom to do whatever I want whenever I want. It's great. It's probably the last time, outside childhood, [of] complete freedom any man enjoys in his lifetime. When a man can see as many women as he wants, enjoy their company and [then] move on. The last days he can revel in the glories of being unattached, plucking the fruits, as it were. I imagine I'll get married one day. It's in the cards for everyone. But [I want] to make these days of inhibited luxury last as long as possible," he said in *PhotoTVLand* in August of 1967.

David was often snapped with Maria Cooper during the time of the series, going to weddings and parties with her, but according to *Movie Stars TV Close-ups* December 1959, "They enjoy each other's company, but it's nothing serious. David is busy with his *Five Fingers* series; Maria sees many others, Gardner McKay among them."

As for our other *Five Fingers* star, here is some of the publicity that was written about Luciana Paluzzi for the series. Most of the writers were quite taken with this "new" star and Luciana received a lot of notice.

Erskine Johnson writes in *The Redlands Daily Fact* (California) April 11, 1959, "Dial G for Glamour. Just arrived from Rome is Luciana Paluzzi, with wonderful black eyes bigger than giant-grade ripe olives. She will certainly make history as the first foreign glamour girl to star in an American TV series. This Italian charmer will be on small screens this fall as a sexy gowned, mink-dragging spy in *Five Fingers*. And I bet all of the dear old Dads across America will not fall asleep on their couch while Luciana is in the living room. She certainly cuts quite a figure in her blue jeans but she assured me that these clothes were not a sign that she was pulling some kind of act or going Hollywood. 'Blue jeans in Rome are considered smart,' she said, flashing me a big smile that has mowed down Victor Mature and Victor McLaglen in their upcoming movies with her, *Tank Force* and *Sea Fury*.

She has already made sixteen European films and when *Five Fingers* producer Herbert Swope Jr. saw one of them on TV, he had her do a screen test and that was it, she was on her way to Hollywood! As a kid growing up in Italy, she was a fan of Hollywood movies and now that she is here, she has found several surprises. One big surprise was when she recently met Johnny Weissmuller at her first Hollywood party. He had played Tarzan on the screen when Luciana fell in love with him the age of eight. But in finally meeting him in person, her eyes popped wider than usual. 'I recognized him but I didn't recognize his soft, low voice. In Italy, his films were dubbed and they gave him such a big deep Italian voice that you could hear him outside of the theaters.' Meanwhile, she has turned out to be the most exciting thing to happen at 20th Century Fox since oil was once discovered on its back lot. There is serious talk of her playing a dual role on *Five Fingers*, as twin sisters on opposite sides of the law. That may very well happen because once you take just one look at Luciana, you immediately want to take two!"

In *The Blytheville Courier News* August 17, 1959, Erskine Johnson writes more about her. She couldn't ask for a more dedicated publicist. "Sex, weekly changes of scenery, an Italian glamour girl and a handsome Cary Grant type leading man; these ingredients will all go up against the CBS powerhouses *Gunsmoke* and *Have Gun, Will Travel* this fall. It promises to be this season's most interesting ratings duel for audiences. NBC is really determined to win Saturday's audience this year and take viewers away from those strong westerns. It failed to do this last year with a western of its own called *Cimarron City*. They are trying again this year with *Five Fingers,* a one hour spy show with David Hedison and Luciana Paluzzi. She has black eyes, curves like an Italian coast line and a record of sixteen Italian movies to her credit before she was brought over to Hollywood. This show indicates that there could finally be audience trouble brewing for *Gunsmoke*. If *Five Fingers* works, you can bet the rival networks will be throwing sex into all the other top-rated TV westerns."

On September 9, Erskine Johnson strikes twice. In the *Blytheville Courier News* he says, "While Italian eyeful Luciana Paluzzi will dazzle all of the dear old Dads who watch NBCs new *Five Fingers* series Saturdays, the ladies of the house will discover her co-star, David Hedison. David will play a sort of TV version of Cary Grant in this spy thriller." In *The Redlands Daily Fact* Johnson states, "The title Italian Grace Kelly tag fits Luciana [Paluzzi]. She has red hair, striking eyes (bigger than the headlights on most foreign sports cars) and something seldom found in Hollywood imports of glamour girls from Italy, a well-scrubbed look. The Italian Grace Kelly [moniker] fits her as well as her tight blue jeans that she likes to wear off stage during *Five Fingers*, her new TV series. She has appeared in fifteen European films but is unknown on American screens.

The producers of *Five Fingers* hope she will establish herself as one of the first foreign stars by the very nature of the medium of television itself. Producer Herbert Swope Jr. is giving her 'the works,' with [a] fabulous wardrobe and photography by Oscar winner Joe MacDonald. And the sets for *Five Fingers* are as lush and as plush as you will find in any major feature motion picture! In this series there is romance and a variety of sundry beauties, the most sundry being Luciana. Co-starring with her is handsome David Hedison as a sort of electronic Cary Grant, a counter-espionage spy, roaming the glamorous spots of Europe. When I first met Luciana, this sexy pixie had just arrived from Rome and came to the studio in US made blue jeans. 'Blue jeans in Rome are now considered smart,' she said. 'They fit tighter, you see.'

Luciana Paluzzi said about *Five Fingers*: "What kind of girl am I? In this episode, he's [Victor] in Mexico. And I turn up in Mexico. Next time, he's in Venice. And I'm in Venice! But we are not married! What do I do? Live in sin? We see each other every time in the series but he is always like a young lohver. [sic] He is still looking!"

She made her debut at age fifteen in *Three Coins in the Fountain*. She considers *Sea Fury* her best part to date. Now at twenty-one, her career is moving upward. "I never had such a big luck [sic], but maybe it's good; keep improving. All my life, I dream to be a naval engineer when I grow up. You know naval engineer? To build boats? Not little boats, big big boats. I love boats all my life, but you know a fonny [sic] thing. I can't swim."

In *The Paris News* September 10, 1959, Lydia Lane writes: "Luciana Paluzzi of this fall's *Five Fingers* is a name that we will all soon know in America. This wonderful and charming Italian girl greeted me in perfect English when her publicist introduced us at my hotel. We then walked to Via Veneto and had lunch at Gigi Fazzi. She ordered for us: a melon, prosciutto, lasagna, chicken mixed with green salad, with espresso coffee. We asked her how she keeps so thin. "Every morning I do fifteen minutes of exercises. I hate it but it keeps my figure in line. I need all the willpower I have to keep that going. And before I flew to Hollywood for my *Five Fingers* screen test, I tried dieting only on tomatoes and eggs. I did NOT enjoy it!"

Vernon Scott for *UPI* wrote in the *Buffalo Evening News* on October 3, 1959, "Movietown's newest Italian import, a lollapalooza named Luciana Paluzzi, is the first European beauty brought to Hollywood expressly for the TV series. Her black, snapping eyes, titian [red] hair and eye-woggling [sic] curves will be seen opposite videos two biggest westerns, *Gunsmoke* and *Have Gun, Will Travel*. Her new hour-long show, *Five Fingers*, will be pitted against the oaters at 9:30 this evening.

Luciana, she's not the kind of girl you'd call Lucy, originally was to play a one shot role of [a] slinky European spy in the series, but 20th Century Fox producers took one look at the pilot film and changed plans. They increased the series to an hour in length and gave her co-star billing along with David Hedison, who portrays a U.S. counterintelligence agent.

'I play David's girlfriend, in the European tradition,' she explained.

'It's not exactly said what our relationship is, but I travel all over the world with him.'

Only six months in these palm tree climes, Luciana has already nailed herself a fiancé. He's actor Brett Halsey. 'We plan to be married January 25.'

Why that particular date?

'Because Brett's divorce doesn't become final until the 24th. If we have enough time after that we will go to Rome to visit my parents. But we are going to make our home here in Hollywood.'

Luciana, who is not yet twenty-one, was a movie star in England, France, Germany, and Italy before coming to Tinsel Town for her TV series. She's anxious to return to movie making.

'The show is sold for twenty-six weeks,' she smiled. 'If it is a big hit, they will make another thirteen, but I hope not.'

Luciana is genuinely dedicated to upholding the tradition of other Italian lovelies as Gina Lollobrigida and Sophia Loren, whom she admires greatly.

'In Italy, we concentrate on being girls and wives,' she said. 'This is a career in itself. We leave the competition to the men and they like it better this way.'

'I haven't been in America very long now, but it is long enough to watch and learn. It is also long enough to make me wonder if many American women really want a man cluttering up their lives, the way they so much pretend. They work so hard to make themselves attractive, physically; they spend so many hours and so much money on it. But they ignore the most important point of all, I think. They will not be dominated. They will not let a man believe he is the center of their universe.'

[This] young Italian actress, new to American audiences, [is appearing] opposite David Hedison in NBC TV's hour-long counterspy series *Five Fingers*, filmed on the 20th Century lot.

'Maybe American women [are] too clever, no? In Europe, we think a man is to be waited on, catered to, even obeyed. In America, girls are too smart, too independent... why should I wait on him? I am no servant! Then they wonder why they cannot get a man or cannot hold the man they have. It is sad.

'Sometimes when I have worked long hours ... and Brett and I are having a late dinner at my house, he will say... you forgot the sugar... and I will look straight at him and say, 'I have worked long hours today, and I am tired. Go get it yourself.' But just a little of that, [only] enough to keep him from taking [me] for granted.'

With the informality that prevails on television sets, it was inevitable that Luciana be nicknamed, [particularly] with a last name like Paluzzi... Hours after shooting started, [she] became 'Lala' to everyone in the crew. Now everyone knows what a lalapalooza [is], but Luciana was not conversant with American slang. She passed it off as American whimsy, until someone asked her if she minded. When it was explained to her what it meant ... 'something superior, extremely striking,' she grinned and declared. 'This I like! Now I smile when they call me, Lala.'

And there is much to smile about. It was a dream part for any young actress. Her leading man is David Hedison, as amiable as he is handsome. Since she plays a high fashion model, her gowns are being designed by Fox's award winning Charles LeMaire. The story line is international. [One] segment was set in Istanbul, another in Mexico City and subsequent weeks will see them all over the globe. 'How nice if we could go on location and really visit all those places,' Luciana sighs. But she is becoming rooted in Southern California. Even though Hollywood gave her a 'warmer' welcome than she wanted when she arrived.

Her home, high in the hills off Laurel Canyon was one of those threatened by the fire that destroyed forty three homes in that area last July. 'It was the Friday before we started shooting. I was at the studio, finishing up some costume fittings. They knew I live off the canyon and they did not tell me! They know I can do nothing. Police are not letting anyone up there [and] they will lose me for the day, if I go! Finally, the last costume is fitted and they tell me what has been on the radio.

'I race out of the building, tear across town in my Jaguar. There is a little back road I know. Everyone is yelling at me as I pass, "You can't go up there!" Finally, I arrive at the point where the police stop me. I am in tears. I point out where my house is, how it is still a long way from the fire, how I must get there and get some things out. They let me through. The fire stopped about two blocks from my house! I was so lucky.

'I want my mother to come from Rome for a long visit and I want the maid I had for so long in Europe; she would love it here and be such a help to me.'

Luciana can hardly be described as the domestic type. 'I like best to have a girl in the kitchen with me, so when I make dirty a dish, she takes and washes it. Sewing I do not like, much, but I can do it. Cooking, I love. Now that work has started on the series, I may never cook again. I have not the time. In the months between the pilot film and the series, I have much time and I cook up all kinds of things for my friends, lasagna, spaghetti, polenta.

'So what happens? The producer says, "Luciana, you are getting fat! You must take off ten pounds!" But I do not do it right away.' Luciana waited until only a few days before shooting. 'I just starve those few days.'

What cooking Luciana does these days is almost always for Brett. Two weeks after she landed in Hollywood, she met Brett Halsey. Two weeks later they were engaged. How have her parents felt about this? 'They write they are much surprised. They think it may be a little fast, even for an Italian.'"

The *Dover Daily Record* (Ohio) ran this on October 10, 1959. "His co-star on *Five Fingers* is Luciana Paluzzi, who is nicknamed la-la Paluzzi. She is from Italy but she has adjusted well to California. 'I am delightfully surprised by Hollywood,' she says. 'I was sure, as I left from Rome to fly here, that I wouldn't like it. I thought it would be a busy place, full of businessmen and all business. But I have found it very friendly and very pretty. I want to live here eight months out of the year.' Her English is very good considering that the young actress learned our language in the last three years, mostly self-taught by reading books and especially by watching American movies. 'Fortunately I have a good ear for languages.' She is the only child of an Italian Army Colonel. She grew up in Milan during the war. When she was sixteen, a friend of her father's asked her to appear in a small part in an Italian movie. Soon after, she moved to Rome and began her film career. Now she lives on the hillside of a canyon near Hollywood where she cooks Italian goodies and invites her pals to dinners!"

Luciana Paluzzi. Copyright Luciana Paluzzi.

The Reno Evening Gazette (Nevada) November 27, 1959, claims that "Luciana Paluzzi, the Italian beauty who co-stars in *Five Fingers*, says she is so involved in her career that she has no time to get married."

Luciana is profiled in *TV Guide* on December 9, 1959. "The young Italian girl with the stream-lined chassis, the large, limpid brown eyes and the name that looks like a cross between pal and pizza was doing a little on camera schmoozling [sic] with a well-set-up leading man named David Hedison. The name of the girl was Luciana Paluzzi. The show is NBC's *Five Fingers*. And the scene [was] clearly designed to celebrate in celluloid some of La Paluzzi's more spectacular equipment. [It] was being played poolside, which of course necessitated a bathing suit with a bodice that wouldn't give up.

As Hedison leaned over and kissed La Paluzzi you would have sworn there was a faint sizzling sound. Even the fronds on the palms near the pool seemed to wilt.

'Cut and print,' yelled the director. With the jubilant air of a man who has just made a gold strike. 'That's the kind I like to see!'

Hedison, an excellent young American actor who got his start in a popular movie success a year or so ago called *The Fly*, looked [satisfied.]

'Now we talk, yes,' she said, turning to [this] reporter [as her co-star left the set.] It turned out that La Paluzzi hasn't been in this country very long. In fact, considering that she's been in movies or, as they say in Europe, 'films' five and a half years, she hasn't been in this world very long. The daughter of a retired Army officer, she's twenty-one years old, just barely. She got one of her first jobs, a bit in *Three Coins in the Fountain* in her home town of Rome in 1954, and has since been dazzling audiences. She dazzles in three languages.

Herbert Bayard Swope, Jr., producer of *Five Fingers*, which, in case you don't know, is an international spy piece, never left home to discover Luciana. It seems that earlier this year that ever vigilant gentlemen happen to be looking at a screen test (made two and a half years ago by the J. Arthur Rank organization in London) of another actor, Stephen Boyd (also subsequently signed by 20th Century Fox), with Luciana Paluzzi.

La Paluzzi sizzled. Swope flipped and immediately made arrangements to rescue the lady from European films (she has made about sixteen of them) and land her in American television. La Paluzzi couldn't be more delighted.

'I love, how you say it, the bessball. I am a Dodgers fan. I adore all the runs and the stealing of besses. I love America. It is like a beeg Italia.'

Luciana learned English (she is fluent in French and currently studying German) in the natural course of events. Having landed in an American picture (*Three Coins*) she began to study English and found she had a natural aptitude for it. Later she went to France, made a picture with Maurice Chevalier, and another with Bridget Bardot. Was there any friction working with the temperamental Bardot?

'Do not be ridiculize,' she says. 'I love her very much. She does not imitate. She's natural, fresh and young and when she's on the screen she fills it.'

Still later Luciana went to England and made several pictures, one called *Tank Force*, with Victor Mature, and another called *Sea Fury*, with the late Victor McLaglen. Then Hollywood.

To show how much she approved of America, Luciana promptly bought herself a Thunderbird, in lieu of a Ferrari, and announced her engagement. The lucky young man is Brett Halsey, also under contract to 20th Century Fox. She telephones him half a dozen times a day from the set, and sometimes he drops in on her.

Luciana doesn't agree that she sizzles. She only agrees that she can be 'saxy' when the 'screept' calls for it. She denies that American women are very different from European women except that, 'Italian womans [sic] are more housewives. American womans are clever at business and are very full of sax appeal even at five o'clock coming home from the office.'

As for TV and her career: 'I never worked so hard and I watched the thing with Sammy running and *The Bob Hope Show* and *Playhouse 90*. I

Tank Force: Luciana Paluzzi with Victor Mature.
Copyright Columbia Pictures.

have only one regrets. I like the blue jeans. Then they forbeed me! They said I deedn't want to look like the Actors Studio.'

Luciana is 'allowed' to go visit Brett Halsey on the set of his Mexican movie right before series filming begins because he is 'lonely.'

The fan magazine writers noticed the chemistry between the two stars. 'Just as we were being served coffee [at the 20th Century Fox commissary] David Hedison and Luciana Paluzzi came in and took the next table. Gardner McKay [the popular star of the Fox series *Adventures in Paradise*] jumped up to greet the brown-eyed Italian beauty. When [she and Gardner] put their heads together and whispered laughingly, Hedison playfully pushed McKay aside and made like a jealous suitor...'

'What's between those two?' I asked a studio exec.

'Some say there is and some say here isn't,' he replied. 'But I know this: she's a popular girl around here. And working with her in *Five Fingers* Hedison seems mighty happy...'

We turned to wave as Hedison and Miss Paluzzi got up and headed back to their sound stage. Her red hair bobbed as she laughed at something David was telling her.

David told me there was nothing between him and Luciana. David saw himself as her big brother (he was eleven years older) and that 'it was his job to see that no one put the move on his good friend Brett Halsey's fiancée. That is what a friend did.'

Once the show was over, Luciana found herself in demand. *The Gazette Mail* (West Virginia) January 17, 1960, writes, "20th Century Fox head man Buddy Adler has put out immediate word for his people to find a big fat motion picture for Luciana Paluzzi, the popular co-star of NBCs *Five Fingers*."

The *UPI* wire seconds that thought on April 19, 1960. Fred Danzig writes, "I would like to see more of new TV actress Luciana Paluzzi. It was really nice to see this former *Five Fingers* star appear on *Adventures in Paradise* last week. If she wants to do more episodes of that series that is okay with me!!"

The Waterloo Daily Courier (Iowa) on January 25, 1960, announces that "*The Heroine of TVs Five Fingers weds.*" Byline Las Vegas: "Several members of Hollywood's younger set attended the wedding of Italian actress Luciana Paluzzi and actor Brett Halsey. The guest list for the Sunday ceremony included Gardner McKay, Edd Byrnes, David Hedison (Paluzzi's co-star in *Five Fingers*), Jean Seberg, Greta Chi and Don

Adventures in Paradise Gardner McKay and Luciana Paluzzi.
Copyright 20th Century Fox Studios.

Kennedy. It was the first marriage for the twenty-two year-old Paluzzi. Halsey had just received his divorce papers from wife Renata Hoy, Miss Germany of 1954. The wedding ceremony was performed in the Hotel Sahara by U. S. District judge David Zenoff."

Not everyone made it to the first wedding. *The Progress Index* (California) January 31, 1960, writes, "Luciana Paluzzi (*Five Fingers* co-star and an all-eye-full) and actor Brett Halsey will become Mr. and Mrs. *February 24.*"

Their marriage was not destined to last even a year. In *The San Antonio Light* (Texas) September 5, 1960, Lee Mortimer writes, "Is it possibly true? Brett Halsey and Luciana Paluzzi in a reconciliation?"

Even Louella Parsons is tracking the troubled couple, given this second item in *The San Antonio Light* (Texas) November 21, 1960. "Come next June, Brett Halsey and Luciana Paluzzi will have a date with the stork. Let's hope this will bring about a reconciliation for the couple."

In *The Evening Standard* (Pennsylvania) December 29, 1960, Leonard Lyons gives us the next update. "In the movie *Return to Peyton Place*, Luciana Paluzzi (of TVs *Five Fingers*) plays an expectant mother. In reality, she really is expecting a baby. In the film she plays Brett Halsey's wife and in real life, the couples' divorce suit is now on the calendar."

And it goes from bad to worse. *Racine Journal Times* (Wisconsin) December 15, 1961. "TV actor Brett Halsey and his estranged wife, Luciana Paluzzi (formerly of TVs *Five Fingers*) are exchanging angry accusations against each other in a bitter court hearing that involves their pending divorce. Superior Judge Alton Pfaff ordered the two actors to bring their son, Christian, here from Italy by January 1st, 1962. The Judge directed Halsey to pay his actress wife 200 dollars in monthly support for the six-month old boy and 400 a month in temporary alimony."

The last word on the matter comes in *The Los Angeles* Times June 26, 1966, in an interview by Kevin Thomas. "Luciana Paluzzi was perhaps the first European beauty brought over to America to star in a TV series, *Five Fingers*, when she arrived here in 1959. She created a certain impact

Return to Peyton Place Luciana Paluzzi and Brett Halsey.
Copyright 20th Century Fox Studios.

in that show. She then married actor Brett Halsey, but later both her marriage and career began to flounder. 'I signed a seven year contract because I did not know any better,' says the very pretty and determined actress. 'I became pregnant and let time slip away. So there I was sitting around doing nothing... never again will I ever sign such a contract.'

Her second chance came with a choice part in *Thunderball*. 'James Bond has been so important to me. He has been the touch of gold for everyone involved.' In [the films] *Thunderball, To Trap A Spy* and *The Venetian Affair*, she has come to a bad end, but she is not worried. 'In Italy, we say that it is good luck for you to die in your pictures!' While she attempts to re-establish herself in America, her ex-husband, Brett Halsey, with whom she is now friendly, has been starring in Italian films. Years after her divorce, she is still too scared to consider marriage again. Right now working and taking care of her small son are her major concerns."

That's all the press that was still out there for me to find. It is by no means exhaustive, but I hope these interviews and stories and information were informative and entertaining. Now we will hear from the stars of the *Five Fingers* series. They will tell us what it was like to work on this series; in their own words.

Luciana from *Thunderball*. Copyright Eon Productions.

CHAPTER 4

STARRING DAVID HEDISON AS VICTOR SEBASTIAN

ALBERT DAVID HEDISON, JUNIOR WAS BORN MAY 20, 1927, IN Providence, Rhode Island. He is the only child of Albert and Rose (Boghosian) Hedison. Tavit Heditsian (David's grandfather) had his entire family anglicize their names to Hedison when they became naturalized citizens of the United States in 1917. Tavit became one of many David Hedisons and Tavit's youngest son, Abraham, chose to be re-named Albert David.

When Albert, Jr. was two years old, his father decided to give up his trade as a jeweler and start his own business. The family moved to Medford, Massachusetts, and became the owners of a small store called Al's Spa on Hillside Avenue. They lived at 15 Hamilton Street. David remembers attending Hillside Grammar School, near Tufts College. [Renamed Tufts University in 1954].

It was 1930, in the middle of the Great Depression, so the store did not do well. They closed it and moved to another location in West Roxbury for a time. That location was not a money maker for them, either.

From fifth grade to tenth grade, young Al attended a different school every year. His family moved back to Providence and in with his uncle when he was twelve, while his father started a jewelry enameling business. The enameling business eventually became successful and prosperous enough for his family to move into their own home at 221 Vermont Avenue.

Al attended Roger Williams Junior High, then Norwood Grammar, and finally settled in to stay at Hope High School. He became active in the community theater with the Benefit Street Players, as he had decided at the age of eleven to become an actor.

At sixteen, Hedison spent the summer at the Rhode Island School of Design learning to make jewelry, but that did not dim his acting ambition. In the summer of 1945, as soon as Al graduated from high school, he enlisted in the Navy. However, Al was still in basic training in upstate New York when World War II was declared officially over. He spent his year and a half in the Navy stationed in Jacksonville, Florida, typing discharge papers and acting at the local community theater in the evenings.

Seaman Second Class Hedison came home after his tour was completed. His parents wanted him to go to college, not acting school in New York City, so Al acceded to their wish and deferred acting for a time. He enrolled at Brown University and began working toward a degree. Al found that he did well in the classes he liked, but Brown was not where he wanted to be. He became active in the college theater group, the Sock and Buskin Players, but it was not the same as studying his chosen craft in New York City. Al met a girl at Brown that he thought he wanted to marry, but she did not share his enthusiasm for acting as a future career and would not even consider going to New York with him to pursue this dream, so their wedding never happened.

Al left Brown at the end of his third year to earn the money to pay his own tuition at the Neighborhood Playhouse of the Theatre. Two theater apprenticeships and three jobs later, one at the Wellesley Summer Theatre in 1949 and the other at the Newport Theatre in Rhode Island in 1950, he had made enough cash for one year's tuition. Hedison packed a bag and finally went to New York to study to be an actor under Sanford Meisner. At the end of his first year there, Al auditioned for the Barter Theater Award, which was a job for the summer season at their theater in Abingdon, Virginia. Al won the audition; he was #116 of 250 aspirants. He came back to New York when the season ended to continue his training at the Actor's Studio. He graduated from there in 1953. His first job after graduation was four parts in the summer pageant *Thunderland* in North Carolina, where he also worked as a DJ on local radio. 1954 found him at the White Barn Theatre in Pennsylvania, doing fifteen plays in sixteen weeks. Once again, Al returned to New York, where he did some off-Broadway work, several bit parts on live television and studied acting with Uta Hagen for another year.

Hagen was so impressed with him she set up an audition for him with Sir Michael Redgrave for an off-Broadway version of *A Month in the Country* in 1956, for which Al won a *Theatre World* Award. This play brought Hedison to the attention of Charles K. Feldman, the famous agent. Feldman decided he wanted to represent Al and had him travel to California to audition. 20th Century Fox liked what they saw and on April 1, 1957, they signed Al to an exclusive seven year contract.

His first film was made in Hawaii, a World War II destroyer versus German sub tale called *The Enemy Below* which starred Robert Mitchum. It was filmed at Pearl Harbor on board the *USS Whitehurst*. Al was given fourth billing in his debut in an effort to build him up as a new star.

His second film, in which Fox gave Hedison the star billing, was made in April of 1958. *The Fly* was a mid-level science fiction tale that went through the roof. Al knew it was a good story the minute he read it, but no one, including the studio, expected the film to have that kind of box-office sales.

Hedison was promptly loaned out afterwards to do *The Son of Robin Hood* in England. He starred in that one, too, but he wasn't the son of Robin Hood, in fact, there wasn't even a son of Robin Hood *in* the picture. There was a daughter of Robin Hood. So naturally, at the end of the picture, David's lead character became the son-in-law of Robin Hood!

Now that Al was a movie star, Fox decided to give him a try-out as a TV series lead. The property they chose for him was the 1952 spy movie *5 Fingers*. His name was mentioned to the studio's new head of Television, Martin Manulis. Manulis screened *The Fly*, liked what he saw, had a meeting with David and he was cast.

A pilot was shot in April 1959 and NBC bought it, mostly because they liked the chemistry between the two leads, Al and a vivacious newcomer (from several films made in Italy) named Luciana Paluzzi. The two stars clicked as continental jet-setters, bumming around Europe. He was a talent agent, she was a singer, but it was an elaborate cover for his real job as an undercover counterespionage agent defending American interests against Communist plots.

NBC liked everything about the series, except the first name of the male lead. They wouldn't rest until he changed it to his more "glamorous" middle name, David. So Al became David Hedison for this series and all his roles after this one. NBC also decided to anglicize Luciana's last name, (from Paoluzzi) for good measure.

The TV series was well mounted and publicized by both NBC and Fox, but NBC scheduled the show on Saturday night up against the number one and number three shows at the time, the then half hour westerns *Gunsmoke* and *Have Gun, Will Travel*.

European spy intrigue was good counter programming, but there wasn't enough audience left give *Five Fingers* a high enough ratings

Al Hedison 20th Century Fox Player. Copyright 20th Century Fox Studios.

number to stay on the air, so it was canceled, unexpectedly, in December of 1959. The public affairs news show that replaced it didn't get any better ratings. Before the end of the season, NBC gave up programming for that time slot and returned it to their affiliates to fill.

Sixteen episodes of *Five Fingers* were filmed, fourteen aired. The show was then sold overseas as forty-eight minute short films to be shown in theaters. The show aired again very briefly in series format in the United States two years later. It was syndicated in Los Angeles in December 1961 and nationally on ABC during the summer of 1962.

David was a popular subject of the many fan magazines of the day, so Fox lost no time putting him back into their movies. He was cast in *The Lost World* as the male love interest, and then Fox sent him to Japan to film a Korean War movie. Fox had wanted him to follow the success of *The Lost World* with another similar film called *Voyage to the Bottom of the Sea*. David chose to do *Marines, Let's Go* instead, playing a rich blue blood who enlists to prove he can be "one of the guys." He does. A chance to work with director Raoul Walsh had a lot to do with that choice.

David also appeared in two other short-lived Fox television shows that were based on Fox movie properties: *Bus Stop* and *Hong Kong*. These two series did not garner high enough ratings to air more than one season each.

David was supposed to do two films in 1962, but the first one was given to Elvis Presley instead and became a musical. The second one, after going through a couple of title changes, was filmed as *It Happened in Athens* and ended up as the launch for a newly contracted actor, who had been rechristened Trax Colton. With all the studio name changes at this time, David could have done a lot worse than being told he had to use his middle name. Hedison told me he was put on studio suspension for his refusal to do this film. Suspension was commonly done in those days to keep contract actors in line.

David was cast in the Halloween episode for the sixth season of *Perry Mason*. He then found out his contract had been dropped by Fox, as had all the contract players, because of the continuing financial problems at the studio that had started back in 1958. The studio had decided to sell all their land to the developer of Century City. They then leased back whatever acreage it took to keep sixteen of their sound stages from being bulldozed and managed to stay in business.

David signed on with United Artists. His first job was as the Apostle Philip (there were twelve more apostles cast) in the biblical film, *The*

Greatest Story Ever Told. Hedison spent most of 1963 filming this epic in Page, Arizona. The final print was over four hours in length. The film was cut to make it a three hour road show. Most of David's scenes ended up being cut. The nine bachelor actors shared a dormitory and many good times, going en masse to movie premieres and Jamie Farr's wedding, biblical beards and all. David ended up with many new friends, who are still his friends today.

When his servitude in Arizona ended, David was invited to a TV festival in Cairo, Egypt, to honor *Five Fingers*. Also being honored was Roger Moore for *The Saint*. They became friends almost immediately.

Roger invited David to come to London to play a part in a *Saint* episode about an American that Roger knew David would be perfect for. While there, David got a call from Irwin Allen to do his TV series *Voyage to the Bottom of the Sea*. David didn't really want to do a series, but Roger talked him into it. The money was too good to say no.

Richard Basehart had also signed on. David wanted to work with Richard, so he finally agreed to do the series. The pilot was filmed in November of 1963 and ABC bought it. In June of 1964, David became series co-star, Captain Lee B. Crane, of the Submarine *Seaview*. He and Richard worked hard that first year to make a good show. The long hours paid off as the show was renewed for a second season and would now be filmed in color.

David was receiving so much fan mail he had to hire Bridget Price to help him. Price set up a fan club for him. Fox was sending out hundreds of signed photos and picture cards to fill requests sent to their PO Box 900. David didn't quite realize how popular he was until the studio sent him out in the fall of 1965 to plug the second season of the show.

Several of these in-person appearances ended up being hastily rearranged on site in order to manage the unexpected overflow of fans who came out to see him. David tried his best to meet everyone he could, often doing more than one appearance per day and then taking additional time to visit sick kids in hospitals wherever he could. Hedison was a great ambassador for the show. He continued to be sent around the country for the duration of the series.

Voyage came to an end in the spring of 1968, when ABC decided not to pick up their option for a fifth year. The network gave the show's Sunday time slot to a new Irwin Allen series, *Land of the Giants*. Neither David nor Richard had any desire to do a fifth year, so it worked out well for all concerned.

David was in Italy, completing work on his company's independent film, *Kemek*, when the cancellation of *Voyage* was announced. He had already proposed to the girl he had been dating for the past year, Bridget Mori. He had met her in Italy the previous spring while scouting locations for this film. They were married six weeks later in London on June 29, 1968, and spent the summer traveling all over Europe.

Returning to America in the late summer, David began looking for work. He was offered *The Brady Bunch* series by producer Douglas Cramer, but turned it down. He did a *Love, American Style* and was sent to England to do a *Journey to the Unknown*. Bridget was pregnant with their first child when he went on tour with Edd Byrnes in the stage production of *Under the Yum Yum Tree*. The tour ended three weeks before Alexandra was born on July 10, 1969.

Dissatisfied with the roles he was being offered here in America, David packed up his family and moved to England in the fall of 1970. His second daughter, Serena, was born there on January 22, 1971. David stayed and worked in England until 1972, doing plays and TV movies on the BBC and ITV networks.

One of the last jobs he was called for in the UK was a meeting with the producers of the eighth James Bond film, *Live and Let Die*. They wanted him to play Felix Leiter. David initially thought he would work with Sean Connery, but Connery pulled out of the movie and Roger Moore was hired. These two old friends had great fun making this film in New Orleans and New York City.

The Hedisons returned to America in 1972. David began doing

multiple television guest star roles and TV pilots. He played a cruise ship doctor in the pilot for a show about the *Queen Mary* in 1975, that didn't sell. David was asked to play the Captain of *The Love Boat* in 1977, but passed on the role. He was in the pilot for *Benson*, but he didn't like his character and declined to play the part when the series sold to ABC in 1979.

Moonraker 1979 premiere photo.
Copyright Rona Barrett's Gossip magazine.

Very shortly after that, Hedison signed for a national tour as the lead in the Neil Simon play, *Chapter Two*, and was on the road through February of 1980. David had two leading ladies and three different casts. The tour crisscrossed America from San Diego to Maine to Palm Beach, Florida and remains a highlight of Hedison's long theatrical career.

David returned to the screen in 1979 with *North Sea Hijack*, an adventure film starring Roger Moore as Rufus Excalibur ffolkes. Why they thought calling the film *ffolkes* was a better title for distribution in America still has everyone scratching their heads. David and Roger are terrific in this movie, which also starred James Mason and Anthony Perkins.

David would do one more film with Roger in 1984, a murder mystery based on the Sidney Sheldon novel *The Naked Face*. Roger played a psychiatrist; David was an obstetrician and his brother-in-law. Again they worked very well together.

Hedison continued to do both summer stock theater and television guest star roles the entire decade. Some highlights include *The Marriage-Go-Round* play with Jane Powell in the summer of 1981, parts on *Dynasty* in 1983 and a semi-recurring role in *The Colbys of California* for nine episodes in 1985, and the plays *Return Engagements* and *Come into My Parlor* in 1988.

It was during the Florida winter run of *Parlor* that David was asked to reprise his role as Felix Leiter in *Licence to Kill* with Timothy Dalton as James Bond. David filmed in Key West and Mexico in August of 1988. He then went to Poland to film *Undeclared War* and did a play, *Catch Me if You Can*, in London in 1990. His contract for the London play kept him from accepting a role in the cult TV show *Twin Peaks*.

In the summer of 1991, David was given a five year contract to play the corrupt businessman Spencer Harrison on the long-running daytime drama *Another World*. This entailed him moving to New York City. He spent the next four years going home to California once a month to see his family. If he had a Friday off, David would take the train up to

Warwick, Rhode Island, to spend the weekend with his mother, Rose, who was now ninety years old. David credited those frequent visits for delaying Rose's move into an assisted living facility until much later.

Hedison started doing theater again while in New York City and managed quite a run of summer stock appearances at East Coast theaters after he left the soap in 1995 through the summer of 2002. He also did a play, *Rough Crossing* by Tom Stoppard, in Lincoln, Nebraska in 1996.

David also began doing the occasional personal appearance at autograph shows. He started doing more of these in 1998, at shows in New Jersey and Los Angeles until 2003, then all around the country after that. In 1999, an Atlanta con appearance lead to him being cast as a senator targeted for assassination in the Fred Olen Ray film, *Fugitive Mind*.

David also appeared in *Mach 2* and the sequel to *The Omega Code*. In *Megiddo: The Omega Code 2*, David played his character at three different ages: forty, sixty and eighty. His last film to be released was *Spectres* in 2005, in which Hedison played a ghost. David made another film after that, *Reality Trap*, but it was unable to find an American distributor. He played a TV executive involved in a murder plot.

Starting in 2003, as the result of appearing at a Bond event in Long Beach, California, David recorded a series of audio books. His first job was doing the excellent twelve minute introduction to the eight hour series, *How to Live the James Bond Lifestyle*. Then he recorded a part in Edd Byrnes' *Casino Caper* in which he played himself, and another part in Barbara Leigh's *The King, McQueen and the Love Machine*, in which he played the head of Universal Studios, Jim Aubrey. His last speaking role was that of McKnight, on the Robert Culp/Nancy Kwan thriller, *McKnight's Memory*. These audio books were first released as CDs and now can be downloaded as MP3s. He also began working at the Actors Studio West with moderators Mark Rydell and Martin Landau at this time.

In 2004, David was signed to a two-year contract to play Arthur Hendricks, Katherine Chancellor's ex-lover and the biological father of Jill Abbott on *The Young and the Restless*. Once his paternity was revealed, the three of them tried to become a family, but it didn't work out. A retired judge, Arthur was wrongly accused of killing his wife for her insurance. Although the accusation was false, Arthur was heartbroken his family would believe he was a murderer. He called off his engagement to Katherine and left town for good. David was in fifty-one episodes of this daytime drama during his year on the show. His option for a second year was not picked up. The budget of the show was drastically cut by the CBS network and five other actors were also let go.

In 2005, 2006 and 2007, David continued to make personal appearances. He did two plays: *The Scent of Jasmine* in Los Angeles and *Love Letters* in Monmouth, New Jersey. David travels extensively. He celebrated his milestone eightieth birthday in Italy with many old friends. Roger Moore then came to Los Angeles to celebrate his eightieth birthday, also in 2007, and receive a star on the Hollywood Walk of Fame. David gave a lovely speech at the star presentation, which was promptly posted on YouTube. David has two very active social media pages and a store on Facebook.

David spent time in 2008 contributing to the book *The Fly at Fifty*, which is a history of his classic science fiction film. David has contributed to books about other people in the past, but this was the first book to focus solely on one of his films. He was also the major contributor to this *Five Fingers* book. Hedison made appearances in New Jersey and Boston to celebrate the fiftieth Anniversary of *The Fly* in October and November. David remains busy at the Actors Studio West and with the Academy of Motion Picture Arts and Sciences when he is not traveling abroad or making appearances. Hedison visited San Francisco in February 2009 and did a comic book convention in New York City in October. David attended the Memorabilia Autograph show in Birmingham, England, in November 2009.

He visited friends in London in March 2010 and appeared at a monster convention and a comic book convention, respectively, in Burbank and Anaheim in April. He was a judge for the Southern California Chapter of the Special Olympics in June. In September, he was the guest of honor at a screening of *The Fly* at the Hollywood Palms Theater in suburban Chicago, right before he attended the Hollywood Celebrities and Memorabilia show. He spent the Christmas holidays visiting friends and relatives in London and South Africa.

Hedison began 2011 with an appearance at Monster Mania 17 in March as part of a Classic Sci-Fi Reunion which included the two of the three remaining stars from the Irwin Allen series *Time Tunnel*, Lee Meriwether and Robert Colbert, plus Roy Thinnes from *The Invaders*. In August, he was a guest at the LA Comic Book and Science Fiction convention at USC's Shrine Auditorium. As part of the 2011 Halloween celebrations, he was part of the "100 years of Vincent Price" celebration in Nashville and part of a *Fly* reunion with his son, Charles Herbert, at MonsterBash in Butler, Pennsylvania.

David spent the first six months of 2012 being filmed for two projects having to do with the fiftieth anniversary of James Bond. David was also filmed for M*ad Scientists, Monsters and Maniacs: Horror in the Atomic Age*. He attended the Hollywood Show again in April and did a *Fly at Fifty* book signing in June, after celebrating his eighty-fifth birthday in Italy. He did the Memorabilia show in Birmingham, UK, in November 2012 and was the most popular member of the Bond Group there.

In April 2013, he attended a *License to Kill* screening and Q &A at the historic Alex Theatre in Glendale, California. He was interviewed for *The Green Girl* documentary by George Pappy, Jr. This documentary covers the life (and death) of Actress Susan Oliver, who played Vina, the Orion Slave girl, in the original Star Trek episode "The Menagerie." Susan was a fan favorite. David has known her since 1950.

Hedison attended the preview screening of this documentary held in Santa Monica in March 2014. *The Green Girl* was released on DVD to much fanfare at the Star Trek Las Vegas convention on July 30, 2014, and now can be ordered on-line from the website and from Amazon. It can be obtained on-demand through several outlets. This documentary has received two awards, most notably the Jury Prize at the Valley Film Festival, and has screened at other festivals in Los Angeles, including the Los Angeles International Women's Film Festival on March 21, 2015. The documentary film was also nominated for the 2015 Rondo Hatton Classic Horror Awards.

Now eighty-seven, David participated in the last 50th anniversary *Voyage to the Bottom of the Sea* Cast Reunion at the Hollywood show at the Westin LAX in October 2014. The *Classic Chillers of the Silver Screen* DVD that he is featured in is scheduled to be released in 2015. He remains active, doing four web interviews with *Tinseltown Talks* and *Blast from the Past* among others during 2014. David looks forward to whatever fifth act 2015 and beyond will bring him.

Photo from *The Green Girl*. Courtesy of George Pappy.
Copyright George Pappy, Jr.

Starring David Hedison as Victor Sebastian

David Hedison talked to me about starring in the *Five Fingers* TV show:

Who created the character of Victor Sebastian? Was it Richard Berg, who wrote the screenplay for the pilot "Station Break"? The show is not really based on anything in the L. C. Moyzisch book Operation Cicero, *no matter what the series credits say.*

DH: Richard Berg created the characters of Victor Sebastian and Simone Genet. Richard also wrote the screenplay. I checked this morning and was told that *Five Fingers* was originally a half hour pilot screenplay. The network flipped over this pilot. They really liked the Hedison/Paluzzi chemistry, so they decided to make it into a one hour show.

Unfortunately, they scheduled our show opposite *Have Gun, Will Travel* and *Gunsmoke*, the two top rated shows on TV at that time. NBC was totally pleased with everything about the show, *except* they loathed my first name, Al. I was born Albert David Hedison, Junior, and that name had served me perfectly well for 37 years [up to this point].

Since I was under exclusive contract with 20th Century Fox and not on a two picture deal, as I should have been, had I been a little wiser in those days, I really had no say about this. The network had their way and I was rechristened David (much more glamorous). So David I became. I have always regretted that decision.

As soon as *Five Fingers* hit the air I received a lovely, but rather amusing, fan letter from a woman. She wondered if I was related to Al Hedison, the movie actor. She ended the letter with this comment: "Mr. Hedison, although you are better looking, I think Al Hedison is a better actor." This remains my most famous and enjoyable fan letter.

Five Fingers: Elegance in Espionage

Did Martin Manulis (Head of TV production at Fox) have any input into the series?

DH: Manulis did have a great deal of input at the beginning, but then became more involved with another show of his on the lot that was taking off, *Adventures in Paradise* with Gardner McKay. Nick [Dominick] Dunne was the Exec in charge of that show, so basically I ended up working more with Herbert Swope, who was in charge of our show. I was always pushing him for more steamy love scenes between Victor and Simone. We were allowed to kiss at the end of the episodes, such boring innocent kisses, to show we were in love, but that was about it. This could only be expected, I suppose, since it was 1959 television. Ouch!

Swope was doing two others series at the time. How hands-on was he? How helpful was he in helping you find the character of Victor? Did the director of the pilot offer any help?

DH: I had no discussion with anyone about how to play Victor. The two directors probably offered some suggestions, as the pilot did sell. Robert Stevens directed the pilot, then Andrew McCullough was brought in later to extend the thirty-two minute pilot to a one hour episode length.

Did you make up a biography of Victor Sebastian to help you? Were you allowed to offer ideas to make the scripts you were given better?

DH: I did not write up any formal biography, but I obviously had several ideas of my own, otherwise I'd have never been able to play the part. I'm sure I must have suggested some cuts or added new material to the scripts, with, of course, Herbert Swope's okay. Although I don't remember any of the script writers particularly, I do know that all the scripts I was given, even the first drafts, were first-rate.

Starring David Hedison as Victor Sebastian

Victor was a "theatrical" agent, but I never saw him book any plays. Did the word "theatrical" have a different meaning in 1959? Sebastian apparently booked ventriloquists, band leaders, ice skaters, as well as a singer who wanted movie roles . . . twice!

DH: Victor would book anyone with talent. A lot of the series stories were deliberately tailored to showcase whoever was the guest star of the week.

Someone at the studio told Vernon Scott (UPI) *that Luciana was only supposed to be a guest star in the twenty-eight minute pilot. Who made her a series regular?*

DH: I don't know anything about that. Luciana was, from the beginning, signed to be my co-star. We received the same salary, an amazing $750.00 a week. Herb Swope discovered her. It was probably his decision.

When was the additional footage (with Eva Gabor as the countess) for the pilot shot? She is not in the thirty-two minute version of the pilot I have seen.

DH: When NBC decided to do *Five Fingers* as a one hour series, Eva Gabor was added as a guest star and most of the half hour version of the pilot was included in the first episode. It worked. Fox never wasted anything.

Luciana could barely speak English in some of her early interviews for the show. Did this cause any problems with filming?

DH: She actually spoke English quite well, and I certainly had no problems understanding her. I found her Italian accent charming as did many (actually all) of her audience. The studio publicity department probably encouraged this, as a hook for the magazines. Luciana was, and still is, a beautiful human being with a great heart.

In my case, the studio had included in my bio that I stuttered when I was young, which was a total fabrication. There are several articles out there that mention this "handicap" I had to overcome. It was the way studio publicity was done at that time.

Did you find your first series difficult to do? How did you adapt to the increased work load and the faster pace of television?

DH: Yes, it was difficult sometimes. You had to know your lines. Cue cards were never used. I had to study a little harder to keep up with the pace of filming. It was very hard work and long hours that summer and fall.

"Moment of Truth." Copyright 20th Century Fox Studios. Photo courtesy of David Hedison.

Luciana was part of Buddy Adler's "Fox class of 1959" as was Gardner McKay, as well as Five Fingers *guest stars Brett Halsey and Michael David. You were part of the "Fox class of 1957," which included Joanne Woodward and Stuart Whitman. Do you think Buddy Adler's strategy to recruit and groom his own Fox stars worked?*

DH: Fox was in the business of creating stars by giving them top billing on their films to build them up with the movie theater audiences. The studio would then make a bundle of money loaning out "their stars" to other studios for their films.

I was loaned out for *Son of Robin Hood* in 1958, which was filmed in England. Fox received a hefty sum from Argo to do this, and all I was being paid was my contract wage, a princely sum of $500.00 per week. It was standard practice, one that would not change until the strike in the spring of 1960.

Speaking of my billing, I can't tell you how embarrassing it was to see Al Hedison billed over Vincent Price and Herbert Marshall in *The Fly*, but that was the way Adler decreed it be done.

Tell us about Charles Feldman, who he was and what influence he had on your career in Hollywood.

DH: Charles K. Feldman "discovered" me, when I was on the stage in New York City in 1956 doing *A Month in the Country* with Uta Hagen, who was one of my acting teachers. He was with the Famous Artists Agency in Hollywood and represented some of the biggest stars in Hollywood. He was the one who arranged for Marlon Brando and Vivian Leigh to be cast in the classic film *A Streetcar Named Desire*.

Five Fingers: Elegance in Espionage

He wanted to represent me. Feldman brought me out to Hollywood and then sent me out to several studios to audition for a movie contract. I was hoping Warner Brothers would sign me, but Fox made an offer and we signed with them for seven years (the standard work for forty weeks/ off the remaining weeks' contract) with graduated salary increases each year.

I didn't make it to seven years with Fox; the studio went bankrupt in my fifth year (1962). My option was dropped, along with everyone else under contract, and we were all let go to fend for ourselves. I then signed with United Artists and ended up in Page, Arizona, doing a biblical film with George Stevens for nearly all of 1963.

You mentioned the guest stars you remembered working with the most were Eva Gabor in "Station Break," Monte Woolley in "The Men with Triangle Heads" and Viveca Lindfors in "Temple of the Swinging Doll." Why these three?

DH: They were the only three guest stars I remembered at the time the interviewer asked me that.

You were friends with another guest star. Tell us about Edgar Bergen in "Dossier."

DH: Edgar Bergen was one of the nicest actors I've ever worked with. He had invited me to dinner at his home several times. I was particularly fond of his beautiful and gracious wife, Frances, and their very young and totally, unbelievably gorgeous daughter, Candace. A terrific family.

You worked with Peter Lorre in the episode "Thin Ice." I heard he was a handful at that point in his career. Did he actually learn his lines for this episode or did he ad lib?

DH: Peter was very professional and knew his lines. There were no problems and we had a lot of fun. There was one scene in the script when he and I (in character) were eating lunch at a fancy restaurant. He was supposed to order some caviar. Normally the prop department would come in and provide a small bowl of something cheaper that resembled caviar, probably strawberry jam.

Before the take, Peter asked the real waiter for some Beluga caviar. As we played the scene, there he was, nibbling on his caviar. He then offered me some, which I gratefully accepted, after the scene was shot. We were on location, shooting at the Hotel Bel-Air.

When the tale of the caviar episode (and the bill for it) got back to the production department, they went ballistic at the unnecessary expense and never forgave poor Peter for doing this. Not that he gave a damn!

Who cast Luciana's fiancé, Brett Halsey, in the "Thin Ice" episode?

DH: I would say that was the casting department, but I'm sure we were both trying to get him on the show. They were married in Las Vegas about a month after the show was canceled. Herbert Swope was always open to our suggestions for casting. I'm happy it worked out. Brett and I are still great friends.

How much of your own stunt work did you actually do? You have an older, heavier stunt double at times, but not that often.

DH: I did as much as possible, but I let the stunt man handle the more dangerous stunts like falling off a roof! George Robotham was my stunt double, who also happened to be my next door neighbor where I first lived in Beverly Hills. There were days when I would return home exhausted. So George and his wife, Jeanne, would fix me a drink, and we'd barbecue a steak. Very thoughtful people.

What kind of training did you get to do those stunts? You mentioned Patrick Cunningham taught you to bull-fight.

DH: Patrick Cunningham was an American bull-fighter who lived on Catalina Island. At one time, I thought I might have a shot at playing the lead in a remake of *Blood and Sand* opposite Sophia Loren. I'd go over to Catalina on a weekend and spend a lot of time working on cape passes, etc. I thought I was doing well. Henry Ephron, who was producing the picture at Fox, promised that he would give me a screen test. But it was not to be. The picture was shelved. Robert Evans was cast as a bull-fighter in *The Sun Also Rises* for the film that *was* produced. C'est la vie.

When did you start working at the Actors Studio West? You originally joined the Studio in New York in 1953.

DH: I started working at the Actors Studio West around eleven years ago. It has given me a great deal of pleasure working with the new, young, undiscovered talent. Mark Rydell, the Director, and Martin Landau, the great actor, are the moderators of the acting sessions. They are great inspiration to us all.

Herbert Berghof was in the 1952 movie version of 5 Fingers *playing one of Moyzisch's German bosses. You studied under Berghof and became an alumnus of what is now HB Studio.*

DH: I worked mostly with Uta Hagan at the Herbert Berghof Studios. She was Mrs. Herbert Berghof. She got me the theater role (in 1956) that got me noticed and led to my movie career at Fox.

Who was your favorite director on the series and why? Lamont Johnson, Allan Reisner, Montgomery Pittman, Andrew McCullough, Paul Wendkos, Gerald Mayer, David Greene, or Charles Rondeau?

DH: I liked them all. As I remember, Lamont Johnson and Alan Reisner directed more than the others. Johnson did four episodes and Reisner did three. I worked again with Charles Rondeau on *Voyage to the Bottom of the Sea*.

Did you like any particular writer? Did any of them write for you?

DH: The show had really fine writers, but I don't remember ever meeting any one of them. Jerry Devine later directed the *Man-Beast* episode in late season four of my *Voyage to the Bottom of the Sea* series. That episode remains one of my favorites. Not that the script was all that great, but I had a lot of fun doing it.

Do you have any other memories of the series that you want to share with us? Every week you went to a different country (on the Fox back lot). Can you tell us about working at the studio before their back lot was sold off and bulldozed in 1961?

DH: Fox Studios in 1959 was a magnificent studio with acres and acres of land. I was put under contract there in April of 1957. Friends of mine would fly out from New York and visit me on the set. I'd take them over to the studio commissary and buy them lunch. As we ate, I'd point out the various movie stars to them who would be eating at other tables, which would be followed by lots of oohs and ahs. Then I would pour my friends into my red and white Ford Fairlane convertible and off we'd go traveling all around the studio; to the French village where they filmed *The Song of Bernadette*, to the western town where *The Ox-bow Incident* took place, along with so many other famous westerns. Then we would drive through the New York streets in case they got lonesome for home. On and on we would travel until we visited every location on the set. What an educational and thrilling day it was for them. Such lovely memories! I'd love to turn back the clock.

David Hedison
8/21/2014

Wedding photo of Brett and Luciana and David with both guys kissing the bride. Copyright UPI.

CHAPTER 5

INTRODUCING LUCIANA PALUZZI AS SIMONE GENET

LUCIANA PALUZZI WAS BORN JUNE 10, 1937, IN ROME, ITALY. SHE IS AN Italian actress, best known for playing SPECTRE assassin Fiona Volpe in the fourth James Bond film, *Thunderball*. The only child of an Italian Army officer, Luciana really had no desire to be in the movies. She was studying Naval Engineering in Milan and ballet at La Scala at the time her film career took off.

Paluzzi's very first film was an uncredited walk-on part in *Three Coins in the Fountain* (1954). She played Rossano Brazzi's little sister. Luciana went on to appear in many more movies, most of which were made in her native Italy. In her early films, she is billed as Luciana Paoluzzi. She was

Five Fingers: Elegance in Espionage

discovered in 1958 by Herbert Swope, Jr., when she was making *Sea Fury* in England with Stanley Baker.

In 1959-1960, she appeared with David Hedison in the short-lived espionage television series, *Five Fingers*, on NBC. She was also a guest star on the Fox series *Hong Kong* and *Adventures in Paradise*.

In 1964, she played the villainess in another espionage based creation, *The Man from U.N.C.L.E.* She appeared as the seductive T.H.R.U.S.H. agent Angela in the first season episode "The Four Steps Affair" and in the movie version of the show's pilot episode, which was released to cinemas as *To Trap a Spy*. She was also second female lead in the Frankie Avalon and Annette Funicello comedy vehicle *Muscle Beach Party* (1964).

Even though Paluzzi had an extensive resume before and after her brush with Bond, audiences still remember her best as the fiery, red-haired villainess Fiona Volpe that she played in *Thunderball* in 1965. Paluzzi originally auditioned for the part of the lead Bond girl, Dominetta 'Domino' Palazzi.

After she was cast, the producers decided they wanted use this part to "discover" a new actress and launch her career with this role. Eventually the part of Domino was given to a former Miss France, Claudine Auger, who had no acting experience whatsoever. They changed the Domino character from Italian to French to accommodate this.

Paluzzi, with way too much film experience to become an ingénue again, was then recast (more appropriately) as the world weary "bad" Bond girl, which Luciana said was "loads more fun to play than a 'good' Bond girl, any day."

Years later, Paluzzi admitted that being a Bond girl was a double-edged sword. She was amazed at the level of fame, publicity, and recognition she received from *Thunderball*, but as a result of being in such an outlandish film, she felt she was taken less seriously as an actress upon her return to the Italian film industry.

Introducing Luciana Paluzzi as Simone Genet

Luciana Paluzzi and Robert Vaughn in *The Venetian Affair*.
Copyright MGM Studios.

Paluzzi was married to actor Brett Halsey from 1960 to 1961. They met at a party given by Gardner McKay and promptly fell in love. Halsey later guest starred in the "Thin Ice" episode of *Five Fingers* after he completed a film assignment in Mexico. Their one year marriage ended in divorce, after which they appeared together in the film *Return to Peyton Place*. The couple had a son in 1961, Christian, but were already living apart by the time he was born.

Luciana's mother, Maria, had been vehemently opposed to her marriage to Halsey. Brett was not Catholic and divorced. Brett and Luciana loved one another but, apparently, could not make a life together. "Next time I will marry an Italian," Luciana said in 1961, after the bitter divorce. "We just could not get along. We had different views on family life. We had different educations." Luciana took child support for Christian, but no alimony. Christian did not live with nor get to know his father until he was an adult.

Halsey said they lived together before his divorce from Renate Hoy became final. It was 1959 and a couple could not live together unless they married. Luciana rented the house across the street from Brett (in Rosilla Place) and that was her official address, but she lived with Brett.

They married as soon as Brett was free, in a civil ceremony that was held in Las Vegas at the Sands Hotel on January 25, 1960. Brett's whole family was there, as were David Hedison and Gardner McKay. Several photos were published of the Las Vegas wedding at different times. The one that came out in May 1960 named Greta Chi, who was Gardner McKay's then girlfriend, as the maid of honor. The couple found out they weren't legally married because Brett had not signed his divorce decree. So they married again, only to separate again in less than a year.

Halsey was dating Barbara Steele after their separation and Barbara was also in the running for the part of Brett's wife in *Return to Peyton Place*. Luciana got the part, and the estranged couple did not speak to each other for the first three days of filming.

In 1979, Luciana married producer Michael Solomon and retired from the movie business. The couple currently resides in Los Angeles, California, and Mexico. They also have a son, Lee, from Solomon's first marriage.

Luciana's "official" NBC biography states: "Luciana Paluzzi, co-star of "5 [sic] Fingers" on NBC TV Network, Television's first foreign glamour girl to star in a weekly series, is a brown-eyed redhead of twenty-one nicknamed Lala Paluzzi.

The charmer from Rome will co-star with David Hedison in NBC-TV's new television spy series, Saturdays 9:30 to 10:30 p.m. EDT starting Oct. 3. She will portray a sheath-gowned fashion model who flits in and out of danger with Hedison during the full hour episodes.

'I am delightfully surprised with Hollywood, but I sure, back in Rome, that I wouldn't like it. I thought it would be a busy place, full of businessmen, all business. Instead, it's very friendly and pretty. I want to live here for at least eight months of the year.'

Introducing Luciana Paluzzi as Simone Genet

Luciana Paluzzi. Copyright 20th Century Fox.

Luciana's English, which still carries a slight accent, is remarkably good considering she learned it in the past five years, mostly self-taught from watching American movies. She also speaks French as fluently as her native Italian. 'Fortunately, I have a good ear for languages.'

The only child of an Italian Army colonel, Luciana grew up in Milan. When she was sixteen, a friend of her father asked her to play a small part in an Italian movie. She began her film career as Rossano Brazzi's little sister in *Three Coins in the Fountain*.

Since then she has played in sixteen European films, including pictures made in Paris and London. Most recently she played opposite Victor Mature in *Tank Force* and Victor McLaglen in *Sea Fury*.

She lives in a hillside canyon home near Hollywood where she cooks Italian goodies and invites her pals to dinner." NBC Studios, New York, September 4, 1959.

Luciana Paluzzi talked to me about her *Five Fingers* role:

Herb Swope "discovered" you. He saw your screen test for Sea Fury, *which was filmed in England in 1958. Would you talk a bit about your work in Italian cinema before you were brought to America?*

LP: He did, he actually did. And I remember Dominick Dunne worked on our show, and I remember Martin Manulis. Herb was a character. I had to look absolutely stunning. He was very concerned about how I looked. I was out in the jungle and he has me in lipstick with my hair nicely fixed, which I thought was ridiculous, but he was always watching over me, making sure that I looked good. I was the star. It was the fashion in which movies were made in those days. I just loved Herb Swope.

Your first film was Three Coins in the Fountain?

LP: I only had one or two lines. I was going to be a naval engineer. I wanted to build big boats. In Italy, you went to different schools until you are thirteen. One taught classical subjects and the other taught scientific subjects. I was the only girl in my class. The rest were all boys. I met the production manager. We had a casual dinner with my father. There was this small role in the film that was driving him crazy. He didn't know any young actresses. So he looks at me and says, "Luciana, come up tomorrow." He was a friend of my father, so [my father] didn't mind. My father was very strict. He wanted me to be a teacher. Acting was not for young ladies.

I went up and I got the role. I went with my Mom on location. It was a wonderful experience. Now, I have [sic] to go back and tell my father I wanted to be an actress. So I did one role and then another role and, before I knew it, I was in the movies.

You didn't plan to be a movie star. How did that happen? Did your father approve?

LP: He wasn't as upset as I thought he would be. My mother was on my side, which helped. So I kept working, getting more and more parts, and by sixteen I was working in Italy and England and had made about a dozen films. That's how it happened.

What was your first impression of America when you arrived here?

LP: I arrived and it was dark; it had been a very long flight. Planes were slower in those days. In 1959, I remember the [prop] plane had a curtain with four beds in the back, like bunk beds. That's how I arrived; it makes me sound so ancient. I am pro-American from the day I set foot here. Everyone was so nice to me. I loved the United States as soon as I arrived. A great country. So open. You can do anything here.

Five Fingers: Elegance in Espionage

How and where did you first meet your co-star David Hedison?

LP: I met him at Fox. We were having wardrobe fittings and pictures taken for the pilot. We filmed it and then they sent us to New York to promote the show to NBC. They brought me over to do the series. I was given a seven-year contract. That was what they did in those days.

Were you excited when the pilot for Five Fingers *sold? Do you agree with David Hedison that the chemistry between the two of you is what sold the series?*

LP: What sold the series was it was an original idea at the time. But our time slot was terrible. We were different. There was not another series like that on at the time. It was one of the first hour shows. We were up against cowboys. We were an adventure that went all around the world and were very different, but our competition was too great. It was like being on up against *60 Minutes*. There were more cowboys than anything else on then. This was Pre-Bond and a great idea. After the Bond movies came out, series like ours became more popular.

Charles LeMaire dressed you beautifully for this series, but later on you wore Petite Sophisticate by Ann Klein. Did they let you keep any of the clothes and were you contracted to model any of them?

LP: I did not know Anne Klein existed then, but if you say there was a credit for her clothes at the end of the episode "Thin Ice," I have to believe you. I have not seen the show for fifty years. There was no contract with me, but the credit indicates that the clothes were given to the show to promote their line.

I did not keep any. After I worked in those clothes for hours and hours I had no desire to keep any of them. They had makeup stains and were truly "work" clothes. Nothing glamorous about them at all. I did not want them anymore.

Why did they make you French? Weren't there any famous Italian chanteuses they could pattern your character after?

LP: Good question. I have no idea why. There was nobody of Italian descent who was a famous singer that I remember, but there was Edith Piaf and other French singers of note, so they probably thought the audience would relate to that and then gave Simone that background.

Was that you singing? Or did Fox dub you with someone who sang (in French?)

LP: That was my voice. I went into a recording studio, and I recorded the songs. Then when I was on the set, they would play my recorded song very loud and I would try to match my recorded vocal. [Standard Fox practice] No, they did not have Marni Nixon or anyone else who did that at Fox sing for me on the series.

"The Emerald Curtain." Copyright 20th Century Fox Studios.

Five Fingers: Elegance in Espionage

Do you have a favorite episode?

LP: I love them all. I really had a great time doing them.

A favorite guest star?

LP: I had a ball with the marionette Charlie... and the ventriloquist. [Edgar Bergen] Such a nice person.

Did you ever meet anyone famous on the lot that you had always wanted to meet?

LP: I saw Marilyn Monroe on the lot. Wow. I had arrived. She had a certain something. When she would walk into the commissary to have lunch, you always knew when she was in the room.

You seemed to like "teasing" Victor with former flames in this series. Did he really need to worry?

LP: Not at all. But I really don't remember all these boyfriends you speak of. You need to send me DVDs, and I will watch them to see what you are talking about.

[For the record: There was Alfred Ryder as the Count and Cesare Danova as Alain, a former childhood friend in episodes five and ten.]

The Five Fingers series is quite popular with David's female fans, they love how romantic he is with you. Do the fans that come to your table at autograph shows mention the series?

LP: Yes, absolutely, the older fans, in particular, come and remember the show and talk to me about it.

Oh, I have something for your book. Do you remember the book *In Cold Blood*? This is a true thing; the family was watching *Five Fingers* that night they were murdered. Then they were killed. So the last TV that family saw was our show. I was reading the book and I had no clue this was coming. Took me totally by surprise. But let's talk about something less bad. Next question!

Tell us a little about your career post series. Everyone knows you did a Bond film. Was there another film, perhaps somewhat lesser known that was a favorite of yours?

LP: One that I did with Lina Wertmuller. An Italian film. She is one of our best directors. We did the film *This Time Let's Talk about Men*. I loved working on that with her. She was so creative.

There were a lot of young actors and actresses on the lot when you came to Fox in 1959. Who befriended you first and brought you into the group?

LP: Gardner McKay. He was a friend of Brett. We were a very small group; I wasn't hanging around a lot of people. We did not go out much in those days. We were working. It was a different time. We didn't hang out in nightclubs like they do now. I had very early calls for hair and makeup.

We are at the end of our interview.

Thank you for sharing your memories of Simone Genet with me.

LP: I am celebrating my 30th wedding anniversary this year [2009] with Michael Solomon. I have been out the movie business for thirty years. When I married my husband, I quit. I don't know why people still write to me and want to talk to me. It amazes me.

Luciana Paluzzi
April 2009

Luciana Paluzzi at *The Hollywood Show* in January 2013. Copyright David Elkouby.

Chapter 6

Paul Burke as Robertson

Paul Burke (1926-2009) was born in New Orleans. He was the son of Marty Burke, a champion boxer who lost bouts to future world champion Gene Tunney in 1921 and 1924. Marty was also a sparring partner for Jack Dempsey for many years. After retiring from the ring, Marty Burke ran a bar in the French Quarter that was considered so rough that New Orleans police would show up only in groups.

Seeing the sad characters pass through the club gave Paul a sense of purpose. "I stayed up late watching the barflies, the brawlers," he told *TV Guide* in 1962. "I listened to the stories of wasted lives; I watched the effect of wasted lives. It gave me a strong feeling of urgency about my own life. Acting is exciting. It's the excitement of re-creating a human experience. Acting is more exciting than living; more electric, more immediate than living. That's because life is full of random elements. In acting, you select, you choose the elements. This selection allows you to get to the essence of the character, the essence of an experience."

He studied acting at the Pasadena Playhouse. Movie director Lloyd Bacon, an old friend of Burke's father, got him his first role in an uncredited bit part in the 1951 Betty Grable musical, *Call Me Mister*. He was then cast in a series of minor roles, including an uncredited part in the Richard Basehart film *Fixed Bayonets* (1951). By 1956, he was landing starring roles. The first was in the short-lived Jack Webb veterinarian series *Noah's Ark*. When the series ended, he battled voodoo in the jungles as the lead of the Allied Artists potboiler *The Disembodied* (1957) and then returned to television as a costar opposite Barry Sullivan in *Harbormaster*.

The abrupt cancellation of *Five Fingers* freed Burke to accept his most famous role, NYPD detective Adam Flint on *The Naked City*. Burke replaced James Franciscus in the series' second season, when the show expanded from thirty minutes to an hour. Burke received two Emmy nominations for his work on this show.

Burke was cast in the starring role of Captain (later Major, then Colonel) Joe Gallagher on *12 O'clock High* in 1964. It was his last major television role. In 1967, he made his first misstep by starring in the critically panned *Valley of the Dolls*. Although his role was one of the few solid performances, the taint of the film's failure finished his film career. He did two minor films in 1968 and was forced to concentrate on television.

His best known film was *The Thomas Crown Affair* (1968) in which he played a cop obsessed with catching art thief Steve McQueen.

Burke guest starred in a number of television series as well as having a brief stint on the soap opera *Santa Barbara*. He had a recurring role in *Dynasty* (1982-1988) as Congressman Neal McVane, who memorably disguised himself as Krystle Carrington (Linda Evans) to commit murder and frame Alexis Carrington (Joan Collins).

In 1989, Burke and Harry Connick, Sr., the New Orleans District Attorney, were indicted in federal district court on racketeering charges. Burke was accused of having interceded with Connick, a childhood friend, on behalf of a bookie and therefore had aided and abetted a gambling operation. After a six-week trial, Burke and Connick were acquitted by the jury. Burke returned to Hollywood and found no work. Innocent or not, Burke was damaged goods. He retired soon afterward to Palm Springs.

In an *Associated Press* interview in 1992, he noted that "[b]efore the trial I was just getting into roles playing older men, and suddenly I get back to California and there's no work. I can't definitely correlate it to the trial, but I couldn't get a job, so I said the hell with it."

Now we turn to the filmed episodes of this series, to provide even more history for your enjoyment.

Paul Burke from the Television Series *Naked City* (1960).
Copyright ABC Television Network.

CHAPTER 7

EPISODE SYNOPSES: EPISODES 1, 2, AND 3

Episode 1: "Station Break" (the pilot) #3701

Air date 10/3/1959

Location: The French Riviera; Cannes

Twenty-eight minute (pilot) version directed by Robert Stevens.

With five minute epilogue by stars Hedison and Paluzzi. According to the *New York Times* (1/3/58) Stephens was supposed to direct four additional episodes, besides the pilot, but he never did. He apparently took a better offer to direct two episodes of *The Twilight Zone*, which also aired in October 1959.

The fifty minute first episode that was expanded from this pilot and directed by Andrew McCullough was unavailable for preview.

TV Guide [On-line] Listing for the fifty minute version: Sebastian (David Hedison) tries to break the code used by a Communist radio station. Micheline: Greta Keller. Simone: Luciana Paluzzi. Leslie: Eva Gabor. St. Croix: Theodore Marcuse. Gorog: David Opatoshu. Robertson: Paul Burke. Blanc: Michael Romanoff

Paul Burke (Robertson) is not in the twenty-eight minute pilot version, but his trademark of leaving a message in a glove for Victor to find is established there. Eva Gabor is also not in the shorter version.

Credited cast:
David Opatoshu (Gorog)
Theodore Marcuse (St. Croix)
Greta Keller (Micheline)
Tyler McVey (Government Official)

Recurring:
Michael Romanoff (Prince Dimitri Blanc)

Uncredited:
Ron Howard (Kid on Beach)
Government Official #2

Episode synopsis: Twenty-eight minute pilot.

We are shown Washington DC at night. The lighted Capitol building is plainly visible. A man walks into a government official's office and lays down a briefcase. He opens it and takes out a file that he hands to the official. A voice over begins:

Episode Synopses: Episodes 1, 2, and 3

"This is the dossier of an American. His name: Victor Sebastian. Only one in every three people survives in his line of work. His occupation: Counterespionage. For the Government of the United States. I know these facts because I am Victor Sebastian. My Code name: Five Fingers." Music and Morse code spelling out Five Fingers is played while the credits roll. Al Hedison as Victor Sebastian and introducing Luciana Paluzzi.

We are shown another glittering night time scene, identified as the French Riviera. Victor's voice over continues: *"My attachment to Washington is the fact that must remain hidden. To the other side I'm their man, a spy working against them. But to the world at large, I'm a theatrical agent, representing a clientele that extends from Broadway to the French Riviera."*

We are taken inside a night club where a silver haired French singer is auditioning. Seated off to one side, Victor Sebastian is persuading the night club owner, Blanc, to book his blind singer client, Micheline, the voice of the resistance, along with her accompanist, Gorog. Blanc balks at paying for the two of them, but Victor insists they are a pair. Gorog is her eyes, a guide and companion as well as her accompanist. Blanc gives in, giving Sebastian his booking, at the same price as Chevalier.

Gorog is a Communist whose loyalty is being tested by the area party leader, St. Croix. They met on the beach outside the hotel and Gorog confirms that Sebastian has done what was required and installed him at the club, where he can send messages to the Communists.

Gorog is told to further test Sebastian, make him prove his loyalty to the party. St. Croix asks where Sebastian is. Victor has gone to the airport to pick someone up. St. Croix has traced an information leak to the two men and plans to kill whichever one fails the loyalty test.

A beautiful singer/model named Simone Genet has decided to holiday in Cannes, France. She sent a telegram to her new-found friend, theatrical agent Victor Sebastian, after they met at Longchamp Racecourse. He agrees to come pick her up. Sebastian wants a date out of it, only to be told Simone has come south to do a modeling gig and to see someone else. Victor asks for a consolation drink, but is turned down.

Sebastian knows Gorog sends coded messages for the Communists. His mission is to find his code key while passing the Communist vetting process to St. Croix's satisfaction, so he can continue to work within the party to pass information on to the Americans.

Micheline sings beautifully for their opening night. Gorog takes her back to her dressing room for a short rest and finds Victor camped out in his room. Sebastian has microfilm that needs to be sent to the Communists. He forces Gorog to reveal the location of his transmitter and insists he start sending. Gorog is reluctant, Victor keeps pressing. Gorog finally refuses to do it, saying he wants out. Victor slaps him, calls him a traitor and storms out, vowing to expose him to the Party for the coward he is.

St. Croix walks in from the adjoining room and commends Gorog on his performance. Now they wait to see if Sebastian makes the necessary phone call to report Gorog.

Victor heads for the phone booth in the club foyer. He dials a number. Simone walks into the club, looking for Victor. He hangs up the phone and comes out the booth, pleased to see her. She says her aristocratic date turned out to be a royal bore. Victor promises to do better. They return to her hotel room to do a little dancing and some kissing.

Simone tells Victor she knows he's an agent and she wants to audition for him. She thinks she will be a wonderful singer, if he will only give her a chance. Their kissing is interrupted by a knock on the door. A waiter is there with a tray of champagne. Victor says he didn't order it. The waiter apologizes and asks Victor if he dropped his glove outside the door. Victor says yes and retrieves the glove. He looks inside and then pockets the glove.

Simone wants to resume kissing, but Victor tells her he has to go and asks her to wait up for him. She is put out and won't promise him anything, telling him his timing is lousy. Victor finds the message he is

Episode Synopses: Episodes 1, 2, and 3

looking for in the other glove that is in the glove compartment of his car. He is told to get the code now.

Micheline finds out Gorog is a Communist. She heard them talking in the adjoining room. She interrupts their meeting and learns St. Croix is also in the room. The party leader kills her with scissors when Gorog is unable to silence her cries for help.

St. Croix and Gorog dispose of Micheline's body, not knowing that Blanc witnessed them taking her out the back of the club. St. Croix tells Gorog Victor never called him in.

Victor totally ransacks Gorog's dressing room looking for the code. He finally finds it (in Braille) hidden among Micheline's music. He tries to take a picture of it with his camera. He finally does, right before he is discovered in the dressing room by the returning murderers. Victor does some very fast talking and fortunately St. Croix believes him over Gorog. St. Croix then shots Gorog as the traitor, after telling the Communist that Victor did call and turn him in.

Victor turns over the coded music to St. Croix to preserve his cover as a good Communist. Sebastian wants to take it to the next link up, a party member named LeGrand, but the other Communist refuses to let him. St. Croix says it will be delivered through the regular channel.

The next thing we see is Simone burning some Braille sheet music. How it was recovered from St. Croix is never stated. A cable is sent to Washington by Victor, stating that microfilm he took of the code is being sent to the United States Government. St. Croix has been arrested for Micheline's murder on the basis of a statement by club owner Blanc. The identity of LeGrand remains unknown.

Synopsis of the promo for the series: David is on a set. He puts out his cigarette. [An affectation for the show. David doesn't smoke. Never did.] Hedison then walks to center stage to talk to the camera: "Now that you have seen our pilot film I'd like to tell you about some of the exciting features that will be projected into our series as part of a great new program for television being launched by 20th Century Fox. For example, our director of photography, Joe McDonald, who was nominated for an Academy Award this year for his work on the film *The Young Lions*. The beautiful dresses worn by the Marquis were created by Charles LeMaire, three time Academy Award winner for such films as *All about Eve, Love is a Many Splendored Thing and The Robe*. And many other important creative talents will be associated with our series.

Each episode of *Five Fingers* will be a complete spy adventure in itself; only two characters will continue forward from show to show. The counterespionage agent, Victor Sebastian, myself, and the very lovely Marquis Simone Genet, played by Luciana Paluzzi. Luciana ..."

Luciana enters the set through a closed side door. "Did someone call?"

David walks over to her. "Definitely," he replies. He kisses her lightly on the cheek and puts his arm around her. "Let's tell the audience about our series."

"All right," Luciana answers. "Their intrigues will take them all around the world, next time to Rome. Yes?"

"Yes," David answers. "To West Germany. London. Cairo. With frequent stops in New York and Hollywood where my main offices are."

"Since Victor is also a theatrical agent, there will be a variety of American and Continental personalities involved in our show. And I will sing and dance, too. Hmmm?"

"Mmm. *Five Fingers* will be an action show. It will operate on the explosive level of international secrets and national destinies. There will be comedy. Music."

"Romance ... but only with me," Luciana adds. "Yes?"

"No promises. There will be lots of excitement and suspense. And now, Marquis, what shall we do?"

"Which do you prefer to do, chéri? To sing or dance or kiss?"

"Darling, you give me no choice." David leans over to kiss her again several times, nuzzling her ear.

Luciana is aware the camera is recording them and gently breaks it up. She guides him out the French door at the back of the set. They close these doors behind them and behind the curtains on the doors we can now only see the silhouettes of them kissing. That ends the promo.

What footage was added to this pilot for the first aired episode of guest star Eva Gabor, variously identified as Countess Leslie or Maria Vodnay, both names are listed for the episode in *TV Guide* and other newspaper listings, remains a mystery. The fifty minute version of this episode is not owned by UCLA Television Library, which now owns everything that was in the Fox Studio Archive on this series and was unavailable to preview from any other known source.

Victor's voice-over chronicled above is also different from what will become the series opening narration, which is as follows: *"To the entertainment world on two continents, I am Victor Sebastian, theatrical agent. These are my offices, but the business I'm about to transact can never appear on the company books. Not if I'm to survive. As it so happens, I'm another kind of agent: counterespionage. My employer: The United States Government, although sometimes I pose as its enemy. My code name: Five Fingers."*

This was spoken by David Hedison at the beginning of each *Five Fingers* show. Having David and Luciana speak to the audience will continue into the series. They will introduce coming attractions for the next episode at the end of each show for the duration of the series. I was only able to view two episode prints with the coming attractions still attached. They were at the end of the episodes "The Man Who Got Away" and "The Emerald Curtain," which are two of the four Fox Archive prints of this series held at the UCLA Film and Television Library. The other two episodes held by UCLA are "The Unknown Town" and "The Search for Edvard Stoyan."

Five Fingers: Elegance in Espionage

Reviews:

Oakland Tribune (California) September 3, 1959, by Bill Fiset:
"*Five Fingers*, the exciting new private eye series, introduced its two new stars, David Hedison and Luciana Paluzzi (an Italian beauty), by having them go into a deliberately long kiss on camera against a background of jazz music. This new series is certain to be a success since kisses and jazz are as necessary to a private eye shows as gunplay, horses and action are to popular TV westerns."

Altoona Mirror September 4, 1959, by Pat Hinton:
"A new international espionage series will be introduced Saturday nights with two new and exciting discoveries, David Hedison and Luciana Paluzzi. They play the leads in this action-adventure called *Five Fingers*."

Hutchinson News October 3, 1959:
"This show's biggest asset is a little but fully developed girl named Luciana Paluzzi, who plays a model to provide star David Hedison with some romantic interest. This girl is an absolute knock-out. While the show is interesting, it is by no means a knockout on story terms. Tonight's entry combines the same old familiar elements of TV's *I Led Three Lives* as David Hedison tries to get a hold of a secret Communist code."

UPI news October 5, 1959, by Fred Danzig:
"The new counter-espionage show *Five Fingers*, starring David Hedison and Luciana Paluzzi, was distinguished only by some of the terrific scenery of our nature's treasures, such as the French Rivera and Miss Paluzzi. The script had a lot of padding. You certainly couldn't say the same for that Luciana girl!"

Mike Romanoff has a role in this pilot that was characterized as "the typecast of the year" because he was playing a nightclub owner and a prince.

"Station Break." Victor and Blanc strike a deal for hiring Victor's clients. Copyright 20th Century Fox Studios.

Episode 2: "Dossier" #3703

Location: Paris; Lausanne, Switzerland

TV Guide [On-line] Listing: Sebastian (David Hedison) learns of a manuscript that would reveal his identity. Simone: Luciana Paluzzi. Heidegger: Edgar Bergen. Constantine: John Williams. Van [sic] Stappen: Kurt Krueger. Robertson: Paul Burke. Vogt: Maurice Doner. Stass: Antony Eustrel.

This episode was shot on Bernadette Street, The Train Shed, Stage 2, Stage B, and The Permanent Gardens.

Five Fingers: Elegance in Espionage

Credited cast:
Edgar Bergen (Joseph Heidegger)
Charlie McCarthy (Herr Vogonagel, His Dummy)
John Williams (Nicolas Constantine)
Kurt Krueger (Von Stappen)
Antony Eustrel (Stass)
Frank Wolff (Rudi, the Butler)
Maurice Doner (Vogt)
William Kendis (Agent)
Ted Otis (European Singing Cowboy)

Uncredited:
Herr Volk
Von Stappen's Henchman [Named Scarface in David Hedison's script.]

Recurring:
Paul Burke (Robertson)
Michael Romanoff (Blanc)

"Dossier": David Hedison (Victor) on the phone to Simone. Copyright 20th Century Fox Studios.

Episode synopsis:

A man is murdered in Lausanne, Switzerland. He is found clutching a fragment of a list of known agents. On that list is the name "Five Fingers," which we now know is the code name of Victor Sebastian.

Robertson is contacted by one of his other agents, a ventriloquist, to help him find the author of the manuscript. The author turns out to be the murdered man's employer, an ex-patriate now living in Switzerland under the name of Nicolai Constantine. Victor is brought into the mission since he is the agent who will be exposed.

The three of them find out Constantine is actually a famous spy named Anton Kula. Victor visits Kula. He makes an offer as an American "literary agent" to buy the manuscript without revealing he is one of the spies in it. Von Stappen, the Swiss police officer in charge of the investigation, is in the pay of the Communists. They are after the manuscript and have orders to kill anyone in order to get it.

Simone interrupts the strategy session between Heidegger, Robertson and Sebastian with a surprise visit. Robbie hides in the closet, but she still realizes something is going on. After Simone excuses herself from the room, Robertson and Heidegger want to use her to get to Kula. Sebastian says no.

In the hotel dining room, Heidegger then recruits Simone to visit Kula by telling her Sebastian needs her help to get back into the villa and will fail otherwise. But she cannot tell Sebastian about it. Heidegger is then killed in a drive-by shooting before he can reveal that Von Stappen is the man who killed Kula's caretaker.

Simone gets in with no problem. Kula is very accommodating. She manages to sneak away and unlock a side gate for Victor to gain re-entry. She calls and tells Victor what she has done. He tells her she should not be there and to get out of there.

She surprises Victor by the side gate and asks what he is doing. Victor lies. He tells her Kula has Heidegger's manuscript and won't give it back. He then tells her to scoot.

Five Fingers: Elegance in Espionage

Kula is waiting, having listened to Simone's phone call. He confronts Victor at the safe and reveals he knows his "Five Fingers" identity, and has since that incident in 1951 Berlin in which Sebastian got what Anton wanted.

Kula has come to realize that writing his memoirs was a bad idea and that he will probably get killed by those fighting to possess it. Sebastian informs him he is about to be raided by the Swiss police. Kula invites Sebastian down to the wine cellar to help him burn the tome. They set fire to the paper version. Victor then asks after the microfilm and Kula is about to burn that when the phone rings. Kula is informed by his butler Rudi that the police have arrived in the person of Von Stappen and that they have fake credentials.

The police inspector comes down into the basement and demands the microfilm at gunpoint. Kula gives it to him and, as he is about to shoot them, Victor breaks the light so he has no one to aim at. Kula is shot in the resulting melee, but Victor hides inside a wine cask. Von Stappen tries to lure Victor out without success.

Rudi comes down to rescue Kula. Rudi is shot, but Victor manages to grab Kula's dropped gun during this confrontation and wound Von Stappen's driver. The Communists decide to leave while they can. Victor can explain Kula's dead body to the real Swiss authorities.

The Communists try to escape by car with the microfilm copy of the list, only to plunge over the cliff to a fiery death. The brake line on their car was cut by Rudi before he was killed.

Kula drags himself up from the basement and then dies of his wounds from the gunfight, but not before he warns Sebastian not to drive his car back, either. With both copies of the manuscript now destroyed the identity of "Five Fingers" is safe once again.

Synopsis of this episode from *Monthly Film Bulletin* (10/61 no. 333): "American secret agent Victor Sebastian goes after a dossier listing the names of international agents, compiled by retired master spy Constantin.

The manuscript is of equal importance and danger to both sides in the cold war. By the end, the evidence, Constantin, and Sebastian's rivals have all been eliminated."

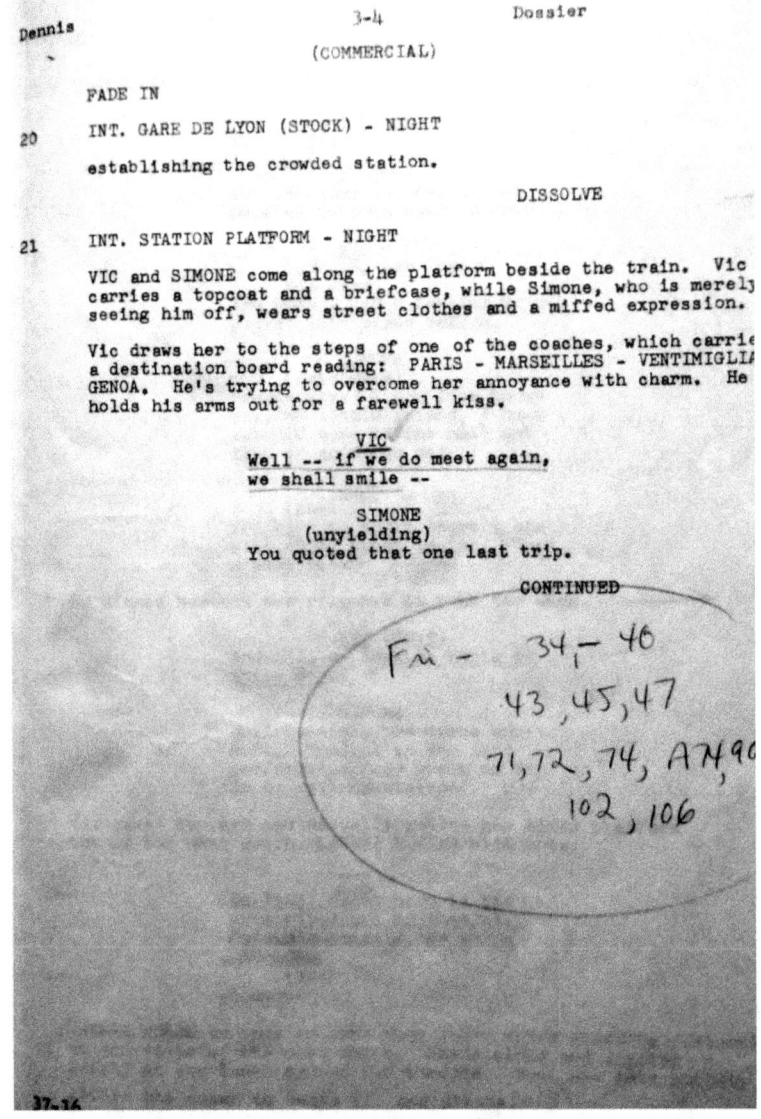

"Dossier" script page with scenes scheduled for Friday.
Courtesy of David Hedison.

Script notes:

The teaser pages of the script (the first murder in Switzerland) are missing from David Hedison's copy. He is not in them. Script begins on page three with Simone and Victor saying goodbye at the train station.

There is much dialogue rewriting and timing notes throughout, with several added explanations and notes to keep track of continuity within the episode.

Dummy is named Wakernagel in the script. Name was changed to Vogonagel in the final aired version. Hedison said he did not remember why this was done. Sounds somewhat dirty, perhaps standards at NBC would not pass their first choice of name.

There is a note in script to keep Simone (tastefully covered) in bubbles while in her bath when she gets Victor's phone call. He is Switzerland and she teases him with a non-existent boyfriend and party. This was done in the aired episode.

"Dossier": Simone in her bubble bath.
Copyright 20th Century Fox Studios.

Bar Exit scene on page twenty-five has a note by David that he doesn't like it, but it is in the show as written. Penciled in dialogue in David's handwriting on page thirty-eight did make it into the aired show. They changed the written lines to sound more "hip" when discussing using Simone. Victor doesn't want Simone involved in his business. Robbie does. Heidegger recruits her for her first mission.

Edgar Bergen's phone number is written with his home address on the top of page forty-eight. David Hedison mentioned that Bergen was very kind to him and would often invite him over to have dinner with him, his wife and young daughter Candace Bergen, who was thirteen years old in 1959, when this episode was filmed.

The word depreciatingly is misspelled by the script's typist on page fifty-three.

Sebastian is named "Five Fingers" by Kula. David crossed this line out, apparently not wishing to have his identity revealed this early. The aired show names him "Five Fingers" here and again a few lines later, with Kula admitting (in the basement) he's known who Sebastian was since 1951 on page sixty-three.

Several lines of script have Sebastian searching the room for the combination of the safe and finding a card with the combination numbers written on it. These lines are not in the aired episode.

Outside, by the wall, Simone tells Victor she is freezing. He very gallantly takes off his trench coat and wraps it around her before telling her to leave. This is not in the script.

There is another whole section of the script that was also omitted later on, where Von Stappen learns Victor's identity from reading microfilm in the dark in a moving car at night, right before they crash. In the filmed version they crash and the film is burned before he can read it so the now dead Swiss policeman never learns the identity of "Five Fingers."

Reviews:

Corpus Christi Times (Texas) September 23, 1959:
"In a very imaginative bit of casting, Edgar Bergen will play a spy who is also a ventriloquist in an early episode of NBC thriller *Five Fingers*. Word is that Bergen's dummy, Charlie McCarthy, may also make a quick appearance."

TV Scout (syndicated review column) by Joan Crosby, October 10, 1959: "*Five Fingers* has a much better story tonight than the one that kicked off its debut show last week. However, this segment is a very strange one. David Hedison, our favorite international spy, gets messed up with a ventriloquist (Edgar Bergen) whose wooden dummy seems to have thoughts of its own. And Luciana Paluzzi, who has already made millions of American fans by being in this show, is back again as David's love interest."

Monthly Film Bulletin (10/61) (unnamed reviewer) had very little good to say about this particular episode. He had a very low opinion of the whole *Operation Cicero* series of films, which was the format they were released in the UK in 1961 and 1962.

He calls this episode "slapdash; full of tired old cloak and dagger tactics." He thinks Edgar Bergen is miscast, saying he is an "improbable ventriloquist spy" but he liked John Williams, stating "he plays the cynical Constantin with sufficient flair to suggest could the job properly… in a Hitchcock film!"

```
DIRECTOR: Montgomery Pittman                              July 24, 1959
ASST. DIR: Ad Schaumer

                        SHOOTING SCHEDULE
                          "FIVE FINGERS"
                       "DOSSIER" - PROD. #3703


       EXT. EUROPEAN STREET, STAIRS        HEIDEGGER    BERNADETTE
       AND BRIDGE                          SCARFACE     STREET
7/29/59 SCS. 1,2,3,4,5,6,7,8               VOGT
1st DAY (NITE) (1-1/2 Pgs.)                SCARFACE'S PARTNER
TOTAL  Vogt confronted by Scarface.         (SIL. BIT)
PAGES  Heidegger spots Vogt's body
10-7/8 in well.                            VOGT'S CAR
       ---------------------------------------------------------------
       EXT. STREET - PHONE BOOTH           VIC
       SCS. 103,104,105,107,108,109,110    HEIDEGGER    BERNADETTE
       (NITE) (1-1/2 Pgs.)                 STAS         STREET
       Heidegger shot by Van Stappen and   ROBERTSON
       found dead by Vic and Robertson.    SCARFACE
                                           STAS' CAR
                                           VIC'S CAR
       ---------------------------------------------------------------
       INT. WELL                           VOGT         BERNADETTE
       SC. 9 (NITE) (1/8 Pg.)              HEIDEGGER    STREET
       Cut of Vogt crammed into well.
       ---------------------------------------------------------------
       INT. STATION PLATFORM               VIC          TRAIN SHED
       SCS. 21 thru 29 (NITE) (6-1/2 Pgs.) SIMONE
       Simone sees Vic off - He meets      STAS
       Robertson.
                                           LADY (SIL. BIT)
                                           VILLIAN (SIL. BIT)
                                           EXTRAS
       ---------------------------------------------------------------
       INT. TRAIN PLATFORM                 VIC          TRAIN SHED
       SCS. 31,32,33 (NITE) (1/2 Pg.)      SIMONE
       Vic catches train on fly.           EXTRAS
       ---------------------------------------------------------------
       INT. LAUSANNE STATION               VIC          TRAIN SHED
       SC. 142 (NITE) (3/4 Pg.)            SIMONE
       Tag.                                EXTRAS
       ================================================================
7/30/59 INT. LE COCHON JAUNE               VIC          STAGE 2
2nd DAY INT. YELLOW PIG                    HEIDEGGER
TOTAL  SCS. 55,56,57,58 (NITE) (4-1/8 Pg.) WAITER (SIL. BIT)
PAGES  Vic meets Heidegger - song by       LADY PATRON (SIL. BIT)
9-5/8  cowboy. (playback or standard?)     COWBOY SINGER
                                           EXTRAS
       ---------------------------------------------------------------
       INT. WINE CELLAR                    VIC          STAGE 2
       SCS. 125,B125 thru T125,127,A127    SCARFACE
       (NITE) (4-1/2 Pgs.)                 VAN STAPPEN
       Burn manuscript - shooting fray.    CONSTANTINE
                                           RUDI
       ----------------------------------------------------- CONTINUED
```

"Dossier." Shooting Schedule. Courtesy of David Hedison.

FIVE FINGERS: ELEGANCE IN ESPIONAGE

Episode 3: "The Moment of Truth" #3702

Location: Mexico City

TV Guide [On-line] Listing: The search is on for a list of Trotsky's followers who are still living behind the Iron Curtain. Sebastian: David Hedison. Fitzgerald: Jack Warden. Hidalgo: Nehemiah Persoff. Tucumcari: Linda Lawson. Simone: Luciana Paluzzi. Blanc: Michael Romanoff

Sets: Stage Two (Fitzgerald studio); Stage Fifteen (Simone's Hotel room and the supper club); Stage Fourteen (Café Escobar); New York Street (outside of Hotel); Adano Square (outside of Fitz's house and Grandstand for Bullfight); Fox Stables (bull holding pens)

Credited cast:
Jack Warden (Fitzgerald)
Nehemiah Persoff (Hidalgo)
Edward Atienza (Nicolai)
Linda Lawson (Princess Tucumcari)
Lou Krugman (Trotsky)
Charlita (Nina)

Recurring:
Michael Romanoff (Blanc)

Uncredited:
Carlos, Comrade Jackson/Trotsky's Killer, and scads of extras: Waiter, Matador, Matador's Assistant, Flamenco Guitarist, Boy, Two Mexican Soldiers, Hidalgo's Children, Party and Nightclub extras, Bullfight spectators.

```
REVISED - "THE MOMENT OF TRUTH" - 7/16/59                    24

42 Cont.
                         VICTOR
            Why not?
                         HILDALGO
            It's a matter of talent.
            They have none.         → why do you teach them
            Victor raises his camera.
            you execute the veronica so perfectly.
                         VICTOR
            May I take your picture, Senor?
                         HILDALGO
                    (pauses and
                    eyes Victor)
            I would be flattered.

            Victor holds the camera to his eye and snaps the
            shutter.
                         VICTOR
            Thank you, Senor.

            Hildalgo walks to the fence and leans against it.

43-      OUT
44
45       TWO SHOT - HILDALGO & VICTOR
                         HILDALGO
            Now, I suppose we talk?

                         VICTOR
            That's why I'm here. Do you
            have the list of names?

            Both men watch the novices work during the following.
                         HILDALGO
                    (shakes his head)
            I only take the bids.
                         VICTOR
            Who is the principal?
                         HILDALGO
            A man once close to Trotsky.
                                                      Cont.
```

"Moment of Truth" script page. Courtesy of David Hedison.

Episode synopsis:

Victor and Simone try to have a romantic getaway in Mexico City while she is booked to sing there. Victor is given a mission to buy a list of former Trotsky supporters from a shady crippled ex-bull fighter. Aiding Victor in this purchase is his old pal Fitzgerald and his Aztec princess girlfriend, who also work for Robertson. The Princess makes Simone quite jealous. Mexico City may be Fitz's station, but Victor is the Trotsky expert.

Hidalgo does not want to give up his Trotsky contact with the list and leads Victor on a lengthy chase. When he finally arranges for Victor to meet the former Trotsky loyalist to pay for the list, Hidalgo attacks Victor and the contact with his cane. He knocks both of them unconscious and takes off with the money and the list.

The Princess comes to Victor's aid. Simone finds Sebastian lying on the floor with his head in the Princess' lap. That sends Genet back to the hotel in a rage.

In the morning, Victor tries to explain he was mugged and the Princess was only trying to help. He throws himself on top of her suitcase and will not budge, despite Genet's vain attempts to remove him. Simone will have none of his excuses. She grabs her bag and storms off to drive herself to the singing gig at the private ranch that Victor has arranged.

Vic gets a phone call from Fitz saying Hidalgo is also at the ranch party, flashing Victor's money around. Sebastian chases after Simone. He whistles for a cab to block her exit from the hotel so he can catch up to her and get a lift out to the party. Sebastian gets several cabs to respond. So many respond, they can't move the car at all.

Vic confronts the ex-bullfighter at the ranch. Hidalgo would rather keep Vic's money and sell the list again to the other side. Sebastian demands the list he paid for. They go out to Hidalgo's car where Victor is finally given his list.

Still determined to resell the list, Hidalgo tries to kill Victor by trapping him inside a live bull pen. Victor manages to evade the charging bull twice, but before the third pass he climbs up and out, knocking Hidalgo down into the bull pen as he escapes. Being crippled, Hidalgo cannot escape the bull and gets trampled to death.

Victor delivers the list to Fitz. He finds Simone there, modeling for Fitzgerald's large sculpture. Vic graciously agrees to let Fitz borrow her, but then makes sure Simone knows she's his by giving her a very long kiss.

Synopsis from *Monthly Film Bulletin* (3/61 no. 326): "Twenty years after the assassination of Trotsky, American agent Victor Sebastian arrives in Mexico to bargain for a list, held by the one-time assistant of the dead man, containing his follower's names. His go-between is Hidalgo, an ex-matador, who suddenly makes off with the list and some American money. Sebastian tracks him down, recovers the list, and sees Hidalgo die the horrible death he had planned for the American."

Script notes:
There are very few, mostly dialogue has been scratched out. There are several blue (revised) script pages, mostly exposition of the Trotsky history.

Scriptwriter wrote this very tongue-in-cheek, naming the Warden character Fitzgerald (as in F. Scott) when it's painfully obvious by dress and makeup that the character is Ernest Hemingway.

Princess Tucumcari is an Apache legend (attributed to Geronimo) about star crossed lovers and a duel to the death on a mesa somewhere in northeast New Mexico that people are always asking for directions to. You take a left at Albuquerque, according to Chuck Jones. What this legend has to do with Aztec princesses, well, only the script writer knows that.

David has his wardrobe written on the shooting schedule: what he is supposed to wear in each scene. He lists a brown and yellow diagonal stripe tie or a blue, black, brown and tan diagonal stripe tie. Also listed are a black and white patterned sport coat, a white dinner jacket and a dark grey suit. David's added dialogue on p. twenty-four made it into the aired episode.

"Moment of Truth." David and Luciana with Director Lamont Johnson. Copyright 20th Century Fox Studios. Photo Courtesy of David Hedison.

Back of page twenty-nine David wrote "It's been twenty years and some of the Trotskyites must be dead." This correction makes it into the episode.

"Moment of Truth." David and Luciana in one of their end of the episode embraces. Copyright 20th Century Fox Studios.

On page fifty, David wrote "headache" and played the scene very differently than was written for him in the script.

Simone's escape from the hotel on page fifty-nine was also modified from what is on the script page.

Reviews:

The *Monthly Film Bulletin* reviewer (3/61 no. 326) is kinder to this episode. "Another crowded episode in the *Operation Cicero* series and with its Mexican backdrop, its hero's outrageously transparent theatrical agent pose and its phony Bohemians, including an Aztec lady named Princess Tucumcari, the most bizarre yet. The plot is by no means clear, but the players (notably Nehemiah Persoff and Jack Warden) are resourceful, the climax is showmanlike [sic] and the whole thing is, in its absurd way, spirited."

In these first three episodes, a tone is set for the series and the relationship between Simone and Victor begins to build. Simone has been inadvertently introduced to the "spy" side of Victor's clientele, but it is Sebastian's choice to keep her in the dark as what it is he really does, besides being a very annoying theatrical agent who is never there for her. This scenario in terms of their relationship will continue as we look at the next three episodes.

CHAPTER 8

EPISODE SYNOPSES:
EPISODES 4, 5, AND 6

Episode 4: "The Unknown Town" #3707

Locations: Rome; Middletown (the unknown Russian town); Idlewild Airport, New York City [now known as JFK airport]; Frazee, South Carolina

TV Guide [On-line] Listing: Sebastian is trained as a Soviet spy in a Communist camp that is an exact replica of a U.S. town. Sebastian: David Hedison. Robertson: Paul Burke. Sientani: Salvatore Baccaloni. Simone: Luciana Paluzzi. Tatum: Gavin MacLeod. Davey: Michael J. Pollard. Doliak: Robert Emhardt.

Five Fingers: Elegance in Espionage

Original TV Guide Listing, October 24, 1959: Pretending to work for the Communists, Victor Sebastian is assigned to spy on a US missile plant. As he leaves Europe, he is drugged and wakes to find himself in a very strange American community.

Studio sets: Frazee is N. E. Street [New England] with a church.
Rome Airport was filmed at the Pico Gate (Studio Entrance) aka the *Hello Dolly* Street.
Stage Seven, Stage Three and Stage Two.
Trevi Fountain and the Rome Ruins are Process shots.

Credited cast:
Salvatore Baccaloni (Sientani)
Robert Emhardt (Mayor Doliak)
Michael J. Pollard (Davey)
David Lewis (Staatz, the Vice Mayor)
Jack Albertson (Frazee Desk Clerk)
Gavin MacLeod (Richard Tatum)
Evan McNeil (Peggy Hart/Waitress)
Carol Hill (Phone Operator)
William Schallert (Middletown Desk Clerk)

Recurring:
Paul Burke (Robertson)
Alan Napier (Wembley)

Extras/Day Players from the episode call sheet:
Ben Parker (Clerk Number one)
Hank Vespia (Plane Steward)
Hald Swenson (Porter)

Episode Synopses: Episodes 4, 5, and 6

Earle Hodgins is credited with being in this episode but no character name is given for him. Uncredited players: Ned Lawson, Auctioneer, Mr. Johnston (Davey's grandfather), Townspeople and kids, Waiter, Driver, Cop, and Guard.

Production Requirements. "Unknown Town."
Sheet Courtesy of David Hedison.

Episode Synopsis:

A man is being chased across an electrical power plant in America. Desperate to escape after being shot at, he tries to climb an electrified fence and the voltage kills him.

Victor and Simone are in Rome. They are about to leave for business in America. Simone is giving Victor a really hard time. She is convinced he will be called away at the last minute for one of his mysterious casting trips. Sebastian assures her he is going with her. He does, however, have one little appointment in the morning. Simone remains unconvinced and threatens not to wait for him if he doesn't show up on time at the airport.

Sebastian meets his Communist contact and is told he is going to Frazee, South Carolina. He is given his contact phrases and told to look for a white pencil. The Communist insists he travel on their plane. Vic tries to get out of that, but in the end he has to agree to it. He then meets with Robbie. He is given a silent coded message that Washington is aware of his mission.

As promised, Victor meets Simone at the airport. She is ecstatic they are finally going someplace and will be together to celebrate her birthday in three days. Victor then exits the plane at the last minute. Simone is livid when she sees him out on the tarmac and yells at him out the closed window as the plane taxies away. Sebastian waves an unrepentant goodbye to his lover.

Victor calls his partner, Wembley, to send Simone a cable to meet him in Frazee. Wembley is not happy about being drafted as a messenger boy. Victor consoles him with all the money their agency will make booking both the tenor and the hillbilly band. Wembley wants nothing to do with a hillbilly band.

Victor boards a different plane where he is the only passenger. He is served a knockout drug in his drink and wakes up in South Carolina. At least that is where he thinks he is. Then little things start to get strange. The residents' Southern drawls change to New England accents, none of the dates and states on the license plates on the cars match, and Victor discovers that the town dead ends at a fence with occupied guard shacks on top of it.

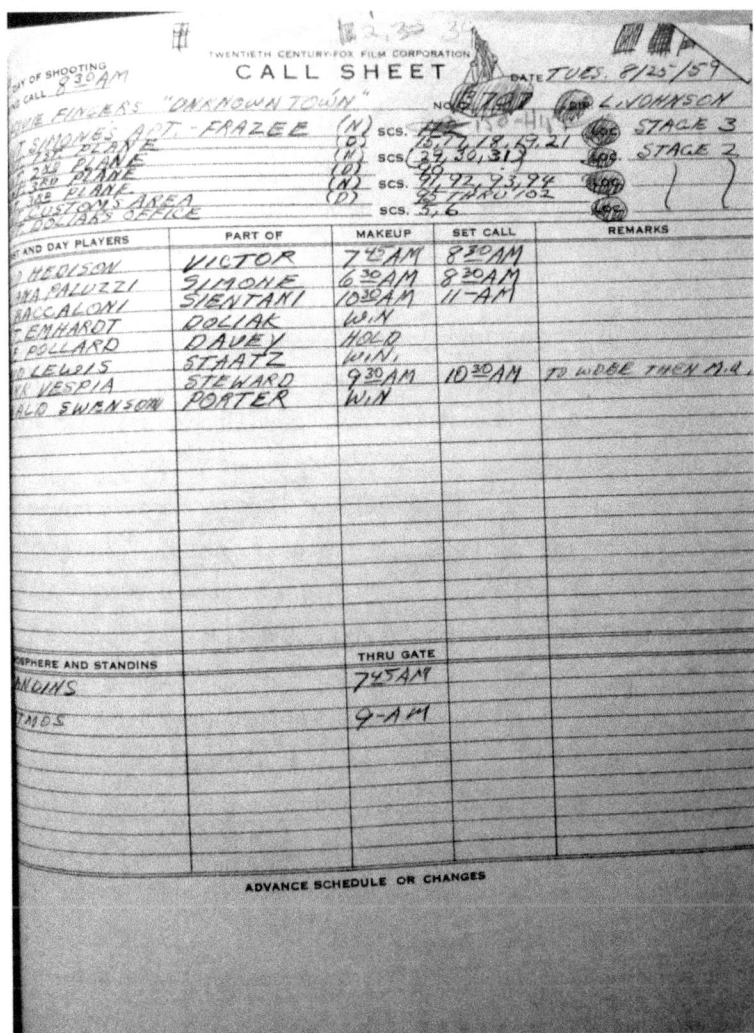

Call sheet. "Unknown Town." Courtesy of David Hedison.

Brought before the mayor, Sebastian learns he is in Eastern Europe at a model town for Russian agents training to pass as Americans. He is briefed on his mission. The Communists are sure they have a leak in Frazee. Two of their recent graduates were picked up by the Americans. Now their contact agent has gone out of touch. Victor is to find the leak, eliminate it and restore Frazee back to sleeper cell status.

While they are talking Mayor Doliak silently gives Victor the five fingers signal while telling him he only has three children and then hands him a cigar "too good to smoke" for his newborn. Later, when he is alone, Victor cuts the cigar open. He finds a roll of microfilm that he assumes he must smuggle out. Victor hides the film in the empty bottom of his cigarette lighter.

At the town auction they both attend, Doliak confides to Victor he is a mole who works for Robertson. It is imperative that Victor get the microfilm of the town's residents to Washington. Unbeknownst to them, they are observed talking together by deputy mayor Staatz.

Flown back to Rome, Victor finds out Sientani will to accompany him to Frazee as the new Italian talent agent assigned to Wembley and Sebastian. Vic asks why, but he won't tell him. Sientani does tell Victor, however, that he knows all about his visit to the Russian training town.

Later, on the plane to America, while Victor is sleeping, Sientani swipes his lighter out of his pocket. Victor isn't really asleep. He is amused when the Communist finds he is indeed out of lighter fluid as he said and doesn't find the microfilm he is so obviously looking for.

They pick up Simone in New York. Sientani is introduced to her as a "great Italian agent." Victor passes Simone the microfilm for safekeeping at the airport. They rent a car for the drive down. Sientani tries to steal the film again during the drive, this time from Simone's purse under the guise of searching for a tissue. Simone has it hidden in the lipstick she has in her hand and lets Sebastian know this. By the time they reach Frazee, Simone has had it with the Italian's singing and apple peeling. Three is definitely a crowd.

Episode Synopses: Episodes 4, 5, and 6

Sientani leaves the hotel, finds his Communist contact and they plot to trap Sebastian. Doliak has been exposed back in Middletown and subsequently shot. They think Victor was given the film as his last known visitor. Tatum is told to pose as an American agent and persuade Victor to pass him the film, thus exposing Victor as the double agent Sientani believes he is. If Victor does hand it over, Tatum is to kill him.

Tatum approaches Victor at dinner and asks for an audition. Victor sets the meeting for the next morning. Tatum tries to convince him to give him the film to send to Washington, but Victor is wary. He pretends not to know what Tatum is talking about.

Simone decides to get all her film, including Victor's, developed in Frazee, setting off a mad scramble by everyone to try to pick up the printed photos. Davey, the camera shop assistant, hand delivers the pictures to Simone. Simone gladly shows Sientani what he delivered. They are pictures of her family from a different roll. The Italian remains determined to get the microfilm photos.

Davey and Victor go for a ride after Davey gives Victor the correct code response in the camera store. Davey confesses he is from Middletown. He says he kept the pictures Sebastian wants. Davey has burned them to protect the Communists' identities. He then scatters the ashes out the window of the car.

Back at the hotel, Davey brings another set of the photos to Simone. He didn't want to give them to Sebastian, because he wants Victor to think they are destroyed. He comes to her because he wants to defect to America. Simone has no idea what Davey is talking about and tells him he has to talk to Victor. She offers to go get Sebastian for him and leaves the room.

Sientani has been listening from the balcony. He comes into the room for the photos. He has his apple knife in his hand and swears to kill Davey for betraying Middletown to the Americans. He advances.

Victor bursts into the room, tackling Sientani. The Italian tries to kill Victor with his knife during their fight. Ultimately, Sientani is thrown from the balcony by Victor's final judo flip and killed. Sebastian takes custody of the photos. He calls Washington. Davey is granted asylum and Victor has to make a trip to Washington to deliver the pictures.

Three days later, Davey, Victor, and Simone go off to listen to *Happy Hemingway's Hillbilly Seven Band* for Simone's birthday. Simone notes that for her last birthday she was given a masked ball, but she does not seem that unhappy to have Victor with her for this celebration, even though three is still a crowd.

Script notes:

The cover page of David's script is quite interesting. There is Brett Halsey's phone number; apparently Luciana has moved in with her fiancé. There is another phone number with no name and a note to write to David Tebet. David, when asked, said Tebet was an NBC executive.

David W. Tebet was a Vice President of NBC at the time and for long afterward. His title was Director of Talent Relations and he took care of whatever the actors wanted to sign with NBC. He was very good at this. Tebet was the first husband of actress Nanette Fabray. Nanette was the aunt of David's frequent co-star Shelly Fabares.

The title page is half filled with Italian phrases and their English equivalents, apparently one of "Luci's" lessons in Italian that she was giving David, as mentioned in publicity for the show. David went to Rome on holiday later that year.

In a case of casting versus whatever contract player was available, Sientani is written as a slender, blonde Italian in the script. Baccaloni is neither. There was a female auctioneer in the script who became a male auctioneer in the aired episode. Gavin MacLeod's character is supposed to be wearing glasses; he wears sunglasses in the horseshoe scene, but no glasses later on. Davey is supposed to be thirteen. Pollard says he's sixteen in the episode, sent out into the field at fourteen.

Episode Synopses: Episodes 4, 5, and 6

Other script revisions: The "Old Pianist from Paraguay" bit is in the episode but totally retyped and pasted over in the script. The pasted version is what aired. David takes credit for rewriting this bit and the line of Wembley's, "And you, dear boy, are square!" Victor tells Robbie he is, "going to kill them with that hat." This line is also not in the script. David said the ad lib was his.

Victor tells Wembley he is after a tenor. Script says Vic is supposed to be scouting for a basso. Swope made this change, according to Hedison. Victor Sebastian's drink of choice is scotch and soda, changed twice in the script by Hedison from this scriptwriter's choice of brandy and soda.

Victor and Sientani arrive in Frazee singing a really bad version of *Dixie* in the episode. It looks like they are doing this to drive Simone nuts. This was not in the script. When I asked whose idea it this, David said he could not remember, but it played like he was in on this gag.

Happy Hemingway's Hillbilly Seven Band. This is the second Hemingway reference in as many episodes. Ernest must have been very popular in 1959 or whoever wrote the scripts for these two shows were Hemingway fans.

Missing Scenes: In the script, not in the aired episode: Doliak asks Staatz to recruit Sebastian (in Rome) to plug the leak in Frazee. Three page scene with (revised) blue pages.

Arthur Halsey, the regular piano player, is killed so Chatham [renamed Tatum in the episode] can take his place. Robbie was supposed to tell Victor to meet Halsey in Frazee. Two mail clerk scenes setting up the Halsey murder and the whole Halsey subplot was dropped from the aired episode. I asked David if naming the character Halsey [after Luciana's fiancé] in this script was an inside joke. He said no.

The aired version of this episode is quite different from script, which is full of revised blue pages. Someone didn't like this script. It was extensively re-written before and during filming. David said, "NBC didn't like it."

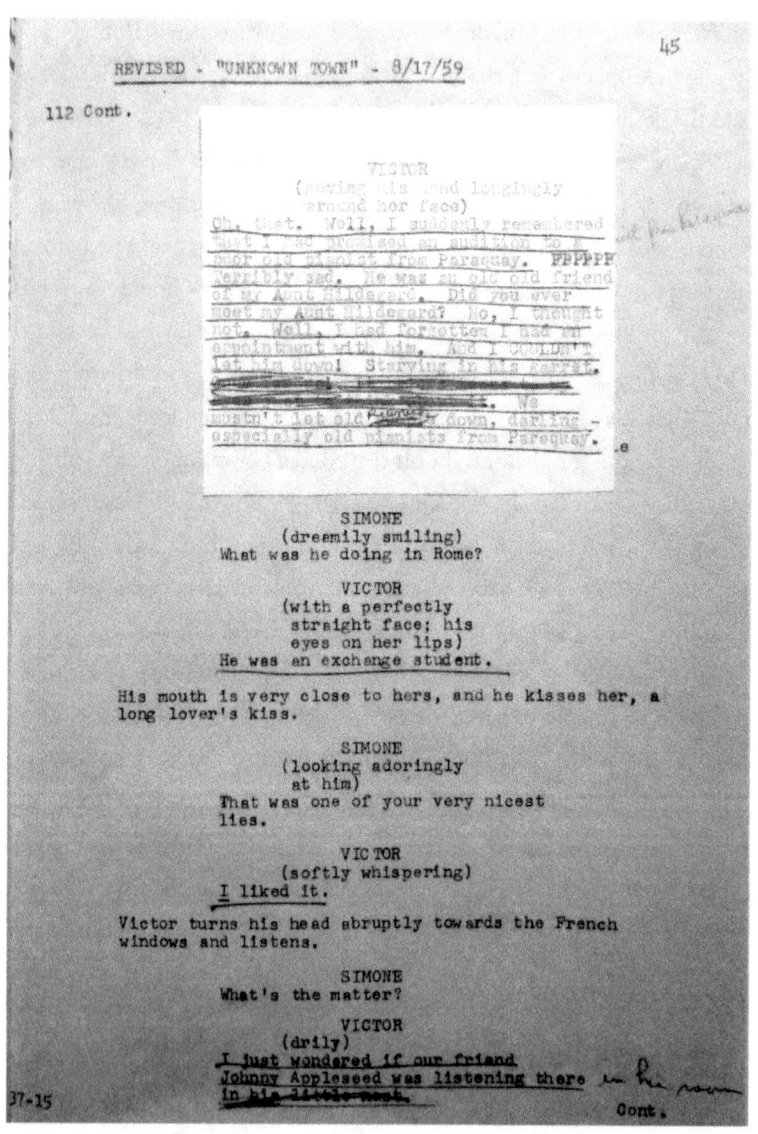

The rewritten Old Pianist from Paraguay bit. Courtesy of David Hedison.

Episode Synopses: Episodes 4, 5, and 6

The following item appeared in the *Independent Star News* (California) by Mike Connolly in 1959:

"Ex-Chicago Civic Opera bass singer Salvatore Baccaloni is down from 310 pounds to 255 pounds. The weight loss is all for a segment of his upcoming appearance on a *Five Fingers* segment."

David told me that Agnes Moorehead (*Bewitched*) threw a party for him during the filming of this episode. They were great friends for many years. Moorehead was at the wedding party that Debbie Reynolds threw for David and his new wife when they returned to Hollywood after spending the summer of 1968 honeymooning in Europe.

Agnes Moorehead, David Hedison, Dorothy Strelsin and Gordon McRae. Photo Courtesy of David Hedison.

Episode 5: "The Men with Triangle Heads" #3704

Location: Berlin, Paris, Versailles and an unnamed French Provincial Town [Song of Bernadette set]

TV Guide [On-line] Listing: Sebastian (David Hedison) tries to prevent Communists from getting top-secret NATO defense plans. Director [sic]: Monty Woolley. Count: Alfred Ryder. Mme. Du Bois [sic]: Estelle Winwood. Simone: Luciana Paluzzi. Robertson: Paul Burke. Marie: Pamela Mathews.

>Credited cast:
>Monty Woolley (Monsieur Le Director)
>Alfred Ryder (The Count)
>Estelle Winwood (Madame Dubois)
>Jason Wingreen (Dentist)
>Pamela Matthews Danova (Marie Camus)
>Robert Brubaker (Colonel Matthews)
>Bill Couch (Sgt. Davis)
>David Hoffman (Henri)
>
>Recurring: Paul Burke (Robertson)
>Uncredited: Helene, Pierre

Episode Synopsis:
A woman returns to a ransacked hotel room and starts packing frantically to leave. A gloved man walks up the stairs to her room, uncorking a vial of steaming acid outside her door. As she wrenches open the door to leave the masked assailant throws the acid in her face, disfiguring her badly.

Episode Synopses: Episodes 4, 5, and 6

We find out at SHAPE [NATO] Headquarters in Versailles, France, that she was working with the top American spy in Berlin. His cover was blown. They were able to extract the agent, but not the woman, Helene, who had worked with him. Now, SHAPE is worried that a vital shipment of Lantern slides [alternate name for Kodachrome as they (obviously) did not have permission to use the Kodak trademark] might be intercepted. Security on the shipment is increased.

A sergeant and two armed guards are dispatched to pick up the slides. They stop for lunch on the way, where they are overheard, and the information about their run is relayed to a dentist who reports the delivery to Monsieur Le Director, the district party supervisor. He dispatches a female agent, Marie Camus, to relieve the Americans of their slides.

Camus comes to Paris and to the office of Victor Sebastian. She barges in, demands an audition using the alias Babette, the bird girl, and puts on a tape of bird calls. Victor tells her he's not interested in her novelty act, but she says it is a cover for their conversation about a task Monsieur Le Director wants Victor to perform. A car will pick him up outside. Victor mentions the acid attack and does not approve. He is told not to question the style of Le Director and do what he is told.

Simone barges into the office with ski equipment and demands to know when they are leaving. "Babette" packs up her tape as Victor rejects her "act." He tells Simone he had car trouble and asks for ninety more minutes. She is not happy but lets him go take care of his car.

Victor is picked up by Marie Camus. He says he was expecting a man. She asks him if he has a gun. Sebastian shows her he is armed. They drive to Versailles and pull over behind a blind of bushes and wait. Victor asks why they are there. She tells him they are stealing the slides that are on their way to SHAPE because they contain the plan of attack for the next war.

The jeep carrying the slides drives past. Marie pulls out and gives chase. She uses her heavy sedan to force the jeep off the road. The two soldiers jump out before they crash. Marie pulls up beside the wrecked jeep and tells Victor to grab the box of slides.

He runs over to the open jeep, takes the slide box and leaves a glove behind for Robbie. One of the soldiers rouses and fires at Victor, hitting the car. Victor slides under the car and out the other side, using the vehicle as a shield to get into the back seat. Marie hits the accelerator as soon as he is in and they make their getaway.

Victor is taken to Monsieur Le Director, who is hiding behind a wall so Victor can't identify him. Victor turns over the slides, but the box is empty. Le Director asks where the slides are. Victor says he doesn't have them, that the box must have been empty when he stole it. It had to be a SHAPE plant. He offers to find the slides for the Communists to clear up any suspicion that he stole them. Sebastian is frisked by Marie to make sure, but he does not have the slides. Victor is cautioned to find the slides in twenty-four hours or face the fate of traitors.

Victor's glove is delivered to the SHAPE commander. He makes a phone call and asks if the glove means anything. He is told yes. Robbie meets Victor in a cafe. SHAPE doesn't have the slides. Victor dumped them into the weeds by the car, but someone else picked them up. Victor wants Robbie to guard Simone. He says no, they can't do that. He urges Victor to find the slides as quickly as possible.

Victor goes to pick up Simone, only to find her having a drink with an old friend, the Count. The Count offers Victor a drink, but gives him Rye instead of the Scotch Victor asked for. They want Victor to go away with them for the weekend. The Count had to cancel the jet to Tangiers because Vic was late and now there isn't another one to be had. Victor suggests they take the Count's yacht, but, alas no, his boat is in dry dock. The Count feels sorry for Victor because he always has to work.

Victor wants to talk to Simone, alone, but she insists she has no secrets from the Count. Her friend tells her no, he is a terrible gossip and should leave them. Victor doesn't give The Count a chance to depart. Sebastian declares his love for Simone and sweeps her out of the room with him. The Count laughs at their abrupt departure, shaking his head over impetuous Americans. As the Count puts his glass down, we see he has a scarred wrist, the same scar as the acid-thrower.

Publicity Still. Copyright 20th Century Fox Studios.

Victor stops in a small French town on the way to St. Moritz for skiing in search of his missing lantern slides. He is directed to Madame Dubois, the town collector. She does not have them. He sees a drawing of the little man symbol from the slides on a wall. He questions an old man sitting on a bench near it. The man says he had nothing to do with it.

Victor turns around and Simone has vanished from his car. He finds her sitting a short distance away in the Count's car. The Count wants to whisk her away to dinner in the next town; he personally knows the chef. Victor is about to let him, until he notices the scar on the man's wrist. Sebastian pulls Simone out of the car and tells the Count they will meet him there.

Victor drives by a school letting out and questions the boys leaving the building. He discovers he should talk to Pierre. Vic and Simone spot Pierre leaving the school, but he is afraid of them and runs away into an abandoned church. Victor goes in after him, but he won't come out of hiding. All Victor finds is a dropped slide.

The Count pulls up to the church, questions Simone and says he must go in and have a word with Victor about his slides. Once inside he pulls on his assassin's gloves. The Count informs Victor he must hand over the slides to him as an agent of Monsieur Le Director. He stalks Victor with a vial of acid. Victor fakes him out and the Count throws the acid on a religious statue instead. Victor jumps him and the Count is knocked out in their ensuing fight.

Victor runs outside, afraid the Count may have harmed Simone. She is slumped in the seat, but Simone wakes up when he cradles her close to him. He is very relieved she is okay. They track the school boy Pierre back to Madame Dubois' house. She claims she hated his slides and gave them back to the boy.

Sebastian comes out of her house to find Simone has the box of slides and Pierre is eating an ice cream cone. Simone tells Victor he will have to give her something for the slides, because now they belong to her. He gives her a very long kiss and she surrenders the slide case to him.

Victor reports in to Robbie. Inspecting the slides, Vic finds them out of order and wiped clean, which means Dubois copied them. He goes back to Simone. She says yes, Pierre did come out the dentist's office

Episode Synopses: Episodes 4, 5, and 6

with the slides. Victor insists on seeing the dentist. Simone hits the end of her patience with the whole slide thing and drives off in a huff in Sebastian's car.

Victor tells the dentist he has a toothache. The man agrees to treat him. He takes an x-ray of Victor's tooth. Sebastian tells him Monsieur Le Director wants him to pick up the slides. The dentist pulls a gun on Victor, says Le Director couldn't possibly know he has obtained the slides. He tries to kill Victor by tying him to the chair and leaving the x-ray machine on. Victor fights back, kicking the dentist with his free foot so that the man shoots the x-ray machine instead. The x-ray machine shorts out, electrocuting the dentist. Vic then wrests his way free from his bonds. Sebastian searches the office until he finds the x-ray film of the slides in a locked cabinet that he breaks into.

He has to get past an armed Madame Dubois when she comes over to investigate the noise. Victor hides himself and the dead dentist behind newspapers (as waiting patients) when she walks in. When she comes out of the wrecked office, Dubois only finds one patient waiting. She pulls the newspaper away and the dead dentist falls to the floor. Victor is long gone.

[We never do find out how Sebastian returned to Paris.]

Sebastian picks up a phony slide set and the "doctored" x-ray film from Robbie to deliver to Monsieur Le Director to clear himself. Robbie says the Count has been arrested, but they are going to leave Madame Dubois free to see who else they can pick up when she receives her next visitor.

During Sebastian's visit with Le Director, Marie verifies the slides. Victor asks who the dentist was working for since he wouldn't give Victor the slides. The director says he was working for him, but someone electrocuted him. Victor then asks if the director sent an acid thrower after him, because Victor had to kill him. The director says Sebastian is to wait; they will contact him again now that his loyalty to the party has been proved.

The briefing at SHAPE is held with the original lantern slides and the world is safe once again from the diabolical plans of the Communists. And Simone gets a special lantern slide show, with two of the SHAPE stick figures holding hands in a heart. This is Victor's way of saying he loves her. He draws them together in a heart.

Publicity photo. Copyright 20th Century Fox Studios.

Episode Synopses: Episodes 4, 5, and 6

Episode 6: "The Assassin" #3710

Location: The French Riviera, Summer Palace of the Vizier in an unidentified Middle Eastern Country

TV Guide [On-Line] Listing: Sebastian (David Hedison) guards a threatened European ruler whose death could precipitate a war. Bentar: John McGiver. Anderson: Don Taylor. Simone: Luciana Paluzzi. Met: Gregory Morton. Hope: Avis Scott. Robertson: Paul Burke. Carlos: Nico Minardos. Emmett: Alan Caillou.

Credited cast:
Don Taylor (Burr Anderson)
John McGiver (Vizier Bentar)
Nico Minardos (Carlos Olivedos)
Gregory Morton (Colonel Met)
Avis Scott (Hope Von)
Alan Caillou (Emmet Von)
Fritz Feld (Headwaiter)
Maria Medwar (Café Dancer)

Recurring:
Paul Burke (Robertson) also has cameo as "The Arab."

Episode Synopsis:
In a glittering salon on the French Riviera, Simone is singing. The Grand Vizier enters. The maitre d' rushes over, but the Vizier waves him to silence. He stands transfixed listening to the lovely French song Simone is performing. He is so attentive he does not see the statue being toppled over onto him in an assassination attempt. The maitre d' shoves him out of the way and the statue shatters into pieces on the floor.

The Vizier is unharmed. After he is seated and looked after, he tells everyone to go back to their table. All he wants is for Simone to finish singing her lovely song. While Simone is singing, the Vizier's new head of Security, Burr Anderson, an old agent colleague of Victor's, comes over.

Burr wants Victor to provide entertainment for the conference the Vizier is holding at his summer palace. Sebastian can bring any one else he wants as long as Simone is there. Burr kids Victor that if he is worried about losing his girl, he can come, too.

Simone is ecstatic about the invitation and can't wait to go. Victor warns her about the fast crowd around the Vizier and his reputation. She is undeterred. Victor draws a heart on the mirror with her lipstick that frames both of their reflections. He tells her she is his girl.

The maitre d' brings an orchid in a bowl. Victor again warns Simone about getting in over her head. The phone rings. Simone thinks the phone is for her, but it turns out to be Robbie calling for Victor. Victor passes the call off as another client, a guitarist that he has to go take care of. He makes Simone promise to wait for him. She gives in but only if he tells her she is beautiful. He tells her to stop fishing [for compliments].

Victor heads down to the docks where he finds Robbie fishing. They discuss the Vizier and why is it important that Victor go to the Palace to make sure the Vizier stays alive to award the water rights of his desert country to the Americans. Victor is to stop the plot to kill him before he can announce his decision. The Communists also want him killed because the Vizier is pro-American. Whoever gets the irrigation contract will control the country's oil pipeline as well.

Victor catches up with Simone on the beach the next morning. She hands him her suntan lotion bottle and he obligingly rubs it in as he questions her about where she was all night with the Vizier. He says he waited up until 3:30 a.m. She claims she came home at 4:00 a.m., right after the Vizier stopped being a gentleman. Rubbing turns into kissing when she tells Vic he can do her face, and they make up. He tells her he

Episode Synopses: Episodes 4, 5, and 6

John McGiver guest stars as Vizier Bentar.
Photo Copyright Estate of John McGiver.

has accepted the invitation to the palace and is going with her. Simone is very happy to have Victor there to protect her.

They fly to the palace and are driven out to the estate. They are welcomed in grand style, their bags are put in their rooms and they are brought into the great room where they meet Colonel Met, the Vizier's right hand man, and his guests.

Emmet Von is an irritated Englishman who is livid after being cheated at cards by a bogus Turk. His languid wife, Hope, immediately puts the move on Victor. She says he has passionate eyes. Carlos Olivedos remembers Simone from the club and wants to pursue her. Burr Anderson wants to get Victor drunk.

The Vizier only has eyes for Simone. He asks her to sing. She claims she has no accompanist. Carlos volunteers; apparently he can do everything. Simone says she must go get her music. The Vizier says nonsense, her man can go get it (Victor). Simone almost winces, and then asks Victor if he would mind. Victor goes and brings back the music, almost running into Emmet who is skulking around where he doesn't belong.

Everyone has a drink and then they gather around to hear Simone sing. Victor seems to be the only one listening, until Hope puts the move on him again. Burr, sitting behind her, tells her to slow down; she's embarrassing Victor. Simone finishes her song and everyone applauds, except the Vizier, who is passed out asleep or drunk, no one is quite sure. Colonel Met tells them to go back to their rooms and let the Vizier sleep it off.

Back in the room, Simone is pouting. She can't believe Bentar fell asleep on her singing. Victor laughing about it doesn't help. He tells her to forget it, the Vizier was sloshed. It wasn't her. They both are hungry. Victor doesn't think he will find any food at this hour. He goes to fetch some champagne for the two of them.

He sees Colonel Met standing guard over the sleeping Vizier. The Colonel sees Victor in the shadows and asks what he wants. Victor asks for champagne. Met promises to have it delivered it to his room. Victor is headed back when a shot rings out, barely missing the Vizier. Met yells for the guards. They spook Emmet out of hiding and he runs for the cars, only to be shot dead.

The surviving guests are gathered again in the great room. Carlos can't help but denigrate Emmet in front of his widow who seems intent on getting drunk and does not defend him. Emmet has to be guilty because he ran.

Colonel Met comes in, shows Avis jewelry taken from her husband's corpse and declares it is the property of the Vizier. Colonel Met then demands Victor come with him. Now! After their departure, Avis admits Emmet wanted a lot of things; respect, money, but he was a very poor thief.

Colonel Met pulls the smoking gun [literally] out of Victor's suitcase and demands to know who is behind the plot. Victor denies complicity and swears it is not his gun and that he is being framed. Met says he underestimated Victor, thinking him only an inconsequential theatrical agent.

Victor defends himself vehemently. He had no reason to kill the Vizier. Met will hear none of it. He orders a car and makes Victor leave, saying his arrest would cause hard feelings and be counterproductive to the conference. Victor is supposed to go stay in town, under watch, until after the conference when his fate will be decided.

Victor charges into the room, grabs Simone and tells her they are leaving. He explains his passport has been confiscated, and he is forbidden to leave the country. Burr objects, says he will straighten it out, but Victor is livid. He stalks out, dragging Simone after him, after telling Metz to have Simone's luggage delivered into town.

Simone goes with him and is upset he's in trouble. He tells her he wants her to leave him, go back to Paris, where she will be safe. Simone knows he didn't do it and vows to go back in the car they came in and find out who did. They are followed into town by two guards in a jeep.

Sebastian stops at the first hotel he sees and is accosted by an Arab, who flashes him the Five Fingers sign. It's Robbie in disguise. They set up a meeting at a cafe, but first Victor has to ditch his watchdogs. Victor takes off; his guards pursue. Sebastian finally loses them by hiding in a well, but he twists his ankle on the rough stones while doing so. The guards pass him by, and he limps off to his meeting with Robbie.

The dancer is very good, but Victor has to pay attention to his briefing. It's safe; the woman doesn't speak any English. Vic tells Robbie that Met is going to kill him after the conference. Robbie tells him the situation in the country has gone from bad to worse. If the Vizier is killed, there will be a riot and there is nothing the US can do to secure the country. There is no time to get another agent. Victor has to go back and try to stop the assassination. Sebastian reluctantly agrees and leaves in the middle of the dance. The dancer is not happy.

Victor limps back to Simone, only to find a very drunk Burr with her. He claims the Vizier sent him into town after Simone, but she won't leave until she knows Victor is safe in the hotel. She is upset Sebastian is limping. Victor tells Burr he's an accomplice now and that he has to smuggle Vic back into the palace to find the real murderer.

Burr is reluctant, but they finally persuade him. He is quite drunk and can't remember where he left his car. Victor stows away in the minuscule back seat, and they cover him with a blanket. Burr and Simone have a discussion about Carlos and how he is all bluster and no substance. Simone uses their talk to tell Victor how much she appreciates a real man.

The blanket works; they drive right by the gate guard. Burr lets Simone out to distract Carlos while he parks in the garage, so no one will see Victor has returned. Victor tells Burr his plan to talk to the Vizier to convince him he didn't try to kill him. Burr loans him a gun. Victor warns Burr not to double cross him. He will name Anderson as an accomplice for bringing him back to the palace if Sebastian is caught.

Carlos tries to charm Simone out some money but fails. Simone goes looking for Victor. She finds Burr, who is really drunk now. He wants to make time with Simone, but she leaves him in his cups. Victor uses his borrowed gun to neutralize Colonel Met.

Burr meets Victor as arranged to get the guard to leave his post so Victor can knock him out. Victor enters the Vizier's empty room. We can hear a shower running. Victor waits with his gun for the shower to turn off.

Burr walks in with a gun and turns it on Victor, making him drop his. Burr explains how it will be so perfect for Victor (an American) to kill the Vizier. Burr has set him up to take the fall since the Riviera. They are going to wait. Then Burr will shoot the Vizier, kill Victor as his assassin and come out the hero. Very tidy. Burr is being paid enough money for this assassination to retire for good.

The shower stops. They wait for the Vizier to appear out of the bathroom. The late Colonel Met throws the door open and shoots Burr dead. Then Met walks over to Victor and thanks him for exposing Burr and saving the Vizier. Victor had pegged Burr as the assassin because he was being too helpful. Met praises him for being a good judge of character.

They go in the other room and the Vizier is trying to put the move on Simone. She looks up at Victor and shakes her head. Met tells the Vizier they have killed the assassin. The Vizier thanks Simone for being such a lovely diversion, but he has to get back to running his country.

Victor and Simone are left alone. Victor claims he was promised some champagne and that he is drowning in broken promises. Simone promises to rescue him and they seal it with a kiss.

Author's note: If this tale reminds you of Agatha Christie's And Then There Were None, *you are not alone.*

TV Scout by Joan Crosby (syndicated column), November 7, 1959:
"A TV highlight tonight is *Five Fingers*. David Hedison, as Victor Sebastian, our chief spy, is up to his handsome ears in an assassination attempt story, while Luciana Paluzzi makes her public debut . . . in a bathing suit!"

Publicity photo. Copyright 20th Century Fox Studios.

CHAPTER 9

Episode Synopses: Episodes 7, 8, and 9

Episode 7: "The Man Who Got Away" #3708

Location: Los Alamos, New Mexico; Canada; Paris

TV Guide [On-line] Listing: Sebastian (David Hedison) must stop a defecting U.S. scientist (Bill Phipps) from reaching Moscow. Mlle. Cardin: Arlene Francis. Simone: Luciana Paluzzi. Lenska: Leo Gordon. Robertson: Paul Burke. Kane: John Hubbard. Phil: Arthur Hanson. Spy: Dolores Donlon.

Original *TV Guide* Listing, November 14, 1959: A scientist who has defected from the West is en route to Moscow. Counterespionage agent Victor Sebastian is assigned to delay the man.

Other TV listing from *The Press Telegram* (California), November 14, 1959:

"Tonight, Arlene Francis guest stars in an exciting cloak and dagger tale about an American scientist who defects for Russia. Our agents must halt his flight."

Credited cast:
Arlene Francis (Cardin)
Leo Gordon (Captain Lenska)
John Hubbard (Major Kane)
Delores Donlon (Nina the Blonde Spy)
William Phipps (Turnbull)
Arthur Hanson (Phil)

Other cast: (as listed by UCLA)
Rachel Stephens
Nick Dennis
Albert Carrier
John Morley
Michael Keith
Pete Jolly

Episode Synopsis:

Victor and Simone are out on the town in a chic Paris cafe. It is the hang-out for spies. Victor knows all the players, including the sophisticated female owner who works for the other side. Victor is there to get Simone a job singing, if he can talk Madame Cardin into it. Simone tells Victor to stop flirting with all the women there, in particular, the platinum blonde at the bar. He swears he is not.

After her piano set ends, Madame Cardin, the cafe owner, grants Victor a meeting at her special reserved table. Victor tells Simone it is to get her a singing gig. After he sits down, Victor is told his new job for the Communists; deliver a defecting American to Moscow. The party definitely thinks it will look better if he is brought over by a fellow American. Cardin is very close with the details of the pick-up. Victor is to wait to be contacted.

On his way back to Simone, Victor catches the attention of the sexy blonde at the bar. She works for Robertson. He tells her sotto voce, while they flirt, to tell Robertson to check all top level scientists back in the states. She kisses him, causing Victor to remark, "what a way to fight a cold war." He then has to take off after Simone, who has stormed out in a rage over his non-stop womanizing.

The scene shifts to Los Alamos Laboratory in New Mexico. A scientist enters a top secret file room and removes a file folder. He is caught on surveillance tape, since the base is on alert that an action like this may happen. Major Kane, in charge of base security, finds his late night activity suspicious and starts checking Turnbull out. The scientist has left New Mexico and is on his way to Canada for an all too convenient fishing vacation.

The US sends the Mounties after him. The RCMP tracks him to a fishing camp where he is nowhere to be found. The Mounties comb the area and finally find the "vacationing" scientist floating face down in a lake. All they can identify is his clothes, which makes everyone suspicious.

Victor and Simone are having publicity photos made. The photographer doesn't like Simone standing there like a statue, but Victor is taking full advantage of the view. Madame Cardin walks in. She could care less about the argument Simone is having with the photographer about how animated she looks in the photos. Cardin wants her pictures. The photographer tells her to help herself. Victor follows her behind the curtain.

Cardin gives Sebastian a picture of the defector he is supposed to pick up at Orly Airport. His name is Oscar Strang. Victor tries to get a date with the club owner, but she tells him to stick to business, she is not the least bit interested in his callow advances.

Victor uses Nina once again to get the new information to Robertson. Simone leaves in a huff because he is still flirting with that blonde! Victor sighs dramatically about the things he has to do for his country.

Victor and Simone are sitting in front of the cafe. She is still mad at him. A cowboy saunters by their table and tries to pick up Simone. It is Robertson, but Simone doesn't know that. Victor objects to this. Simone can't believe it. Sebastian is flirting all over place and the minute someone pays attention to her, he can't stand it.

Victor and the cowboy trade insults, then Sebastian punches him for being so forward. They get into a fight, wrestling with each other in the street. Robertson lifts the photo from Victor's coat pocket before their fight is broken up and the combatants are forced by others to go their separate ways.

Robertson uses the photo to identify the scientist, who is supposedly dead in Canada. He says the name Victor was given belongs to a double agent who is now missing. The defecting scientist must have traded identities on his way over and the disfigured body they found (done deliberately) is the dead agent. Nina passes the picture back to Victor at the cafe while once again they flirt, which does not go unnoticed by Simone.

Madame Cardin calls Victor over to her special table and gives him more instructions about the pick-up and a new companion, a hulking Russian Captain named Lenska. Victor is to stash him in his apartment until the defector's plane comes into Orly.

In the meantime, Victor tries to placate Simone by introducing her to Madame Cardin. He asks if Genet can sing at the cafe that evening. Cardin tells Simone to wear something modest. Cardin and Sebastian confer again. Victor wants her to give him a car to do the pick-up, to protect his cover. She refuses that request and his advances once again. She is not interested in him, at all. He needs to stop trying to pick her up. It will never work. Sebastian tells Cardin he will take Simone's car.

Episode Synopses: Episodes 7, 8, and 9

Publicity Still. Copyright 20th Century Fox Studios.

Victor takes Simone home to get ready. He comes back to his apartment to find the Russian Captain half drunk on his bottle of vodka and singing. Victor plays along and sings with him. He then angrily tells the Captain he is a disgrace to the party! Sebastian decks the larger man with a sucker punch and then tells the Russian he has to shine his shoes. The Captain does so grudgingly, with new respect for the boss.

At the cafe that evening Simone is singing, with Victor seated almost under her elbow, where she can see him. All is well until Victor gets the signal from Cardin to go get the defector. He leaves in the middle of her song. She runs out after him, only to see Victor drive away in *her* car. Simone is very upset about being deserted, plus she now has to find a ride home.

Lenska and Sebastian meet the defector at the airport. He is upset and scared. Someone stole his briefcase of top secret files while he was in Spain and he had a terrible trip over on a tramp steamer. Turnbull is not sure he wants to go through with the defection now. Victor tells him to stop sniveling; it's too late to back out. He is told to get into the car. Lenska's hulking menace convinces the scientist he'd better cooperate.

They go back to the apartment where Victor tells the wavering defector what he can expect in his new life as a Communist. The scientist becomes even more wretched at Victor's deliberately graphic descriptions of his new life. He wants to leave, call the whole thing off. The Russian Captain won't hear of it. He tries to beat some sense into the scientist.

Victor leaves Lenska guarding the jittery defector with orders not to let him leave for any reason. Sebastian goes out to mail a letter. Robertson meets him at the postal box. Robbie confirms that the stolen file was sold back to America in Spain. Victor must not let this defector fall into Russian hands. The penalty for treason against the United States is death and Vic can mete out that sentence if he has to.

Sebastian comes back to find the scientist cowering in a chair. Lenska swears he tried to escape again. Victor is not at all sympathetic, telling the scientist this is what he can expect if he does not toe the party line.

Cardin arrives to check on the defector and tries to soothe his fears, but Turnbull only becomes more hysterical. Cardin chides Sebastian for not making him feel more welcome as a new party member. Victor continues to be very hard line.

Simone arrives at the apartment complex with the French Police.

She points out her "stolen" car and encourages the gendarmes to go ask the man upstairs why he took it without her permission.

The police enter the building, only to have Turnbull come flying out of Sebastian's upstairs rooms with Lenska in hot pursuit. The scientist is shouting for help, until Lenska shoots him in the back and he tumbles down the remaining stairs, dead.

The French police fire back at Lenska and he runs down the second floor hall to escape out the window. They pursue him across the roof, firing their pistols at the Russian until they kill him.

Sebastian and Cardin escape down the back stairs during the commotion. They come around the front arm in arm as a couple and hop into Simone's car as if they own it. The remaining policeman lets them drive it away.

Simone comes out the foyer to find her car has been taken once again. She takes out her anger on the hapless French policeman standing there, who has no idea why she is so upset.

Victor drives Cardin back to her cafe. They talk about the reports that they will have to send in to the party. They decide it is best to cover each other. They will blame the whole debacle on the now dead overzealous Captain Lenska and the extremely uncooperative and equally dead defector.

Cardin also tells Sebastian that his advances were not that unwelcome and he should keep trying. If he does, she might finally respond to him as a woman.

Victor brings back Simone's car. She finds him dining on chicken. She tells him how infuriating he is, but that she loves him and forgives him. He offers her chicken. She starts yelling again and threatens to have him charged with stealing her car. He says she can't now, not if she truly meant it, when she said loved him. Then he kisses her. Simone starts to melt and says maybe she won't press charges. He kisses her again and they agree they must have champagne together now all is forgiven.

FIVE FINGERS: ELEGANCE IN ESPIONAGE

Author's note: I was only able to view this episode once at the UCLA Film and Television Archive in California. I took copious notes, but any mistakes in this synopsis are mine.

Publicity Still. Copyright 20th Century Fox Studios.

Episode Notes:

Arlene Francis is Armenian. Her signature heart necklace worn as a panelist on the *What's My Line* game show was made by Hedison Manufacturing in Rhode Island, a costume jewelry company run by

David Hedison's uncle, Harry Hedison. She wears two very large heart-shaped pieces in this episode as well; the aforementioned necklace and a heart-shaped brooch. The heart was the watermark for Hedison jewelry. The heart is also used in the series by Victor as a symbol of his love for Simone.

When I asked David if he knew Donlon was a Playmate when she did the show, he said, "Yes, he did and no, that fact didn't have any effect on the mostly male crew filming the episode." At least that he remembers.

David used to read *Playboy Magazine*. It was where he first read the short story that would become the basis of his now classic 1958 film *The Fly*. Donlon's centerfold was published two issues before *The Fly* short story.

This episode also included a promo for the next week's show, "The Emerald Curtain," with selected scene clips introduced by David and Luciana. They describe for us a little about the Irish plot of the next show and the guest stars. Luciana cannot pronounce "debut" when she talks about Michael David and Hedison (very gently) corrects her pronunciation.

Episode 8: "The Emerald Curtain" #3709

Location: Ireland

Sets: Sligon Castle, The Permanent Gardens

TV Guide [On-line] listing: Sebastian (David Hedison) tries to smuggle a Russian novelist into Ireland. Simone: Luciana Paluzzi. Kevin: Michael Davis [sic]. Robertson: Paul Burke. Kishinev: Cyril Delevanti. Denny: J.M. Kerrigan. Starlet: Linda Hutchins.

Five Fingers: Elegance in Espionage

Original *TV Guide* Listing, November 21, 1959: Victor Sebastian agrees to smuggle a Russian novelist from behind the Iron Curtain into Ireland. Before Sebastian can carry out his plan, he, Simone and the author are seized by Soviet Agents.

Actual plot: Film maker Kevin O'Neill is trying to smuggle the novelist in so he can option his famous novel for a movie. [Likely based on author Boris Pasternak, who wrote *Doctor Zhivago*, which was smuggled out and published in 1957.]

Victor is tasked (by Robertson) to make sure the Communist's defection is not thwarted by Russians agents sent to intercept him before Kishinev can ask for asylum from the Americans. The episode is done very tongue in cheek. O'Neill, not Sebastian, is the one captured by the Soviets, but he is let go and they only keep the author, Kishinev, and Simone.

The beginning of this episode plays very much like a Halloween episode. That was where it would have fallen in the air date order, if the premiere of the series had happened in September as originally planned, instead of debuting the first week in October.

Credited cast:

Michael David (Kevin O'Neill)
J. M. Kerrigan (Danny O'Neill)
Cyril Delevanti (Kishinev)
Jimmy Murphy (Jingo)
Linda Hutchins (Margo the Starlet)
Bern Hoffman (Hulk)
Francis Bethancourt (Camera Crew)

Episode Synopses: Episodes 7, 8, and 9

Recurring:

Paul Burke (Robertson)

In reply to an urgent summons from an eccentric film director, Kevin O'Neill, theatrical agent Victor Sebastian and client Simone Genet arrive at Coppell Castle in Ireland, in a horrible thunderstorm. They ask for directions on the way, but the locals are very unhelpful. They talk of banshees and wild men and tell the couple the castle is haunted.

David Hedison, Michael David and Luciana Paluzzi. From the episode: "The Emerald Curtain." Copyright 20th Century Fox Studios.

Victor and Simone finally arrive only to be met by a creepy looking butler. O'Neill finally shows them in, and explains his butler is right out of central casting; he was once in a horror movie. Kevin introduces his guests to his father Denny, late of the IRA, and his latest conquest, Margo. He won her at Cannes. *She* wants to know if Victor is Mr. Preminger. And finally, the last introduction is made to his guitar playing assistant, Jingo. Kevin asks Victor to line up two of Hollywood's biggest stars for his next picture, the plot of which cannot yet be disclosed. When Victor explains how impossible this makes the deal, Kevin confides that he has arranged to smuggle leading Russian author Kishinev from behind the Iron Curtain in return for exclusive film rights to his latest award-winning novel.

Victor realizes that Kevin's coup, if successful, would prove of tremendous propaganda value to the west. He tells Kevin he will certainly obtain the services of the two [Fox] stars he wants, Greg [Peck] and Deborah [Kerr], if everything goes according to plan. Leaving Simone to entertain their host, Victor slips away to the village and telephones Robertson in Dublin. Robertson tells Sebastian that rumors are circulating about Kishinev's disappearance. He warns Vic that Russian agents are known to be in the vicinity and will definitely try to stop any attempt at defection.

Simone takes a shine to Kevin and he enjoys playing lord of the manor to his "delicious" guest. He wants to cast Simone as Ann Boleyn. They go riding together. Simone is trying her best to make Victor jealous, but he doesn't bite. He drives to Dublin to meet with Robbie to be updated on the Kishinev defection. The Russians are claiming the Author is "resting" at his summer home.

Returning to the castle, Victor finds a camera crew there, ostensibly filming Kevin at home. Victor strikes up a friendship with the father, Denny, and invites him down to the village for a drink. Unfortunately, Denny wants Victor to "go down to the pub" right when he has finally found time to spend a quiet evening with Simone and he is forced to stand her up. Simone is not happy, but Kevin is there. He asks Simone to go out with him.

Victor's efforts to pump the old man for his son's plans are foiled by the wily Irishman's capacity for whiskey. Victor does learn that the camera crew that has been filming Kevin is bogus. He leaves the bar to warn Kevin, but is knocked out by Jingo before he can get to his car. Denny finds Victor unconscious by the front door, rouses him and then

"The Emerald Curtain": David Hedison and Luciana Paluzzi on the set during this episode. Copyright 20th Century Fox Studios.

chides Sebastian that he shouldn't go drinking with him, if he "can't hold his liquor." Back at the castle, Kevin seeks Simone's help in picking up Kishinev. The defecting author is being landed that night from a Russian tanker off the shore at Waterford. Their plans are overheard by Jingo, who is really a Russian agent. He alerts his confederates, the bogus photographers. They allow Kevin and Simone to drive away, and then follow them. Victor and Denny return to find Kevin's bodyguard, Hulk, imprisoned in the dungeon. Denny, realizing at last the danger his son is in, accompanies Victor on a furious drive to Waterford to try and stop the pick-up of Kishinev before Kevin is ambushed. Meanwhile, Kevin and Simone have driven to the waterfront. Simone is left alone in the car and has some tense moments before Kevin returns with Kishinev. On the drive back to the castle they're overtaken by the Russian agents. Kevin is forced off the road. Simone tries to run and is brought back. The Russians drive off with Kishinev. Simone is taken along as a hostage.

Victor and Danny are flagged down by Kevin as they make their way to Waterford. They run into Robbie in another car at the crossroads. He tells them the Russians are heading back to Waterford. Denny is asked if he is still in contact with his old comrades in the IRA.

Victor finds him a phone. Denny telephones those who live along the route taken by the kidnappers. In a series of seemingly innocent mishaps involving a hay wagon, a fallen tree, and finally a flock of sheep blocking the road, the Russians are delayed incessantly.

Their car is ultimately stopped by a small army of fierce Irishmen under the direction of Victor and Denny. The captives are liberated. Victor runs to Simone and crushes her in a hug. Kishinev is now free to determine his own destiny. He decides to do a live television broadcast to the free world, letting everyone know he has defected. Victor and Simone watch this historic broadcast as arrangements are made for Simone to screen test for Kevin's film in London the following Monday. Victor keeps his girl.

Episode Synopses: Episodes 7, 8, and 9

Author's note: This synopsis matches one of "The Emerald Curtain" episode that was provided by 20th Century Fox Publicity Department. It was included in a Front of the House lobby card set for the release of the episode as a forty-eight minute film in the UK in the winter of 1961.

I was only able to view this episode once at the UCLA Film and Television Library in California. I took copious notes, but any mistakes in this synopsis are mine.

Synopsis from *Monthly Film Bulletin* (6/61 no. 329): "Eccentric director Kevin O'Neill becomes violently involved with Russian agents when he smuggles Kishinev, a noted novelist, from behind the Iron Curtain in return for exclusive film rights to his latest award-winning novel. All ends satisfactorily when Victor Sebastian, an undercover man posing as a theatrical agent, gets O'Neill's father to enlist the aid of old IRA comrades."

His review is short and to the point: "The latest of the *Operation Cicero* series, and sufficiently tame of plot, excitement and phony Irish setting [the castle from Prince Valiant] makes one feel this cycle is beginning to outstay its welcome."

This episode was Michael David's US debut as a Fox Contract player. There was supposed to be another guest star according to the March 1960 *Stardom* fan magazine. "The Luba Bodine now appearing in a *Five Fingers* segment [this item ran with a picture spread on "The Emerald Curtain"] is the newly named Luba Otacevic, who once charmed Cary Grant. She is now dating David Hedison, who stars in the series. Not exclusively, though. She also sees Lili St. Cyr's ex-husband, Ted Jordan, and a well-known producer with headquarters at Universal-International."

This appears to have been the Halloween episode with its very *Macbeth* beginning, but the change in the date of the series premiere pushed the airing of this episode into November. And if Luba is in this episode, I did not know who she was at the time I watched this (once) in order to identify her. I checked the credits, she is *not* listed.

At the end of the episode there is a promo for the next week's episode, "Temple of the Swinging Doll," presented by David and Luciana. The clips show Madame Zapote's secret meeting with her "recruits" for the revolution, where she tells them, "they must wait . . . she has a boat chartered."

Victor is then discovered some place he is not supposed to be, as a "stranger," even though he insists, "you know me." Victor is in a knock down drag out fight by his hotel swimming pool, which ends with him being thrown into it.

The setting is Central America… where anything can happen!

Episode 9: "The Temple of the Swinging Doll" #3712

Location: Central America

There is no *TV Guide* listing on-line for this episode.

Syndicated newspaper TV listing #1: "Sebastian and Genet go on a publicity junket to Central America where things are not all that they seem."

Syndicated newspaper TV listing #2: "Sebastian becomes involved in a revolutionary plot backed by a Mayan princess. He must resort to underwater diving to both stop the revolution and save Simone."

Guest stars John Emery and Arline Hunter.
Photo courtesy of Bruce Schwartz.

Five Fingers: Elegance in Espionage

In *The Press Telegram* (California), November 28, 1959, Terry Vernon writes: "Tonight star David Hedison and costar Luciana Paluzzi get involved in South American revolutionary plot backed by a Mayan princess (Viveca Lindfors)."

Synopsis from *Monthly Film Bulletin* (1/62 no. 336) "Posing as a theatrical agent, Victor Sebastian, an American secret agent, goes to a South American republic with a group of artists to open a luxury hotel. In reality, he is on the track of native revolutionaries, led by the bizarre Madame Zapote, with headquarters in The Temple of the Swinging Doll. Eventually the local police capture a ship-load of revolutionaries and Madame Zapote throws herself into a sacrificial fire."

This episode was unavailable for preview from the UCLA film and Television Archive. I was unable to obtain a copy to preview from any other source, therefore I could not provide a synopsis.

Cast:
John Emery (Norman Kingsley)
Sterling Holloway (Hayden)
Clu Gulager (Larry Dane)
Rodolfo Hoyos, Jr. (Rios)
Viveca Lindfors (Madame Zapote)

Additional Cast from *Monthly Film Bulletin*:
Joan Tabor (Mona)
Casey Adams (Randy)
Johnny Seven (Tupac)
Arline Hunter (Gloria)

Uncredited: David Hedison's scuba stand-in

David told me a story about this episode one Saturday at a con in Orlando in January of 2005. The three of us, myself and two other fans, were sitting at the show table with David. We asked him to tell us some stories in the late afternoon when it was slow.

First he told us the "Irish pub birthday story" from the Roger Moore film, *ffolkes*. After we all finished laughing over *that* one, David told us he was feeling somewhat better. He was fighting off a twenty-four-hour norovirus when he came in on Friday. He mentioned how annoying it was, because he hardly ever got sick. But once on his *Five Fingers* series he was not feeling well and had gone home. David spent most of this episode in the water (from the previews and still pictures I have seen) and he had to do the climatic fight at the end clad only in damp swim trunks. I don't doubt he caught something after a couple of days of constantly being wet.

There was this scene left to film where David was coming out of the water in scuba gear (to rescue Simone), but Hedison was already gone for the day. The director decided to cover the shot as an insert showing a wet-suited back. He called a stand in for David and was done with it.

David thought nothing of it at the time, but when he watched the episode, the stand-in came waddling out of the water walking like a huge plastic bowlegged duck. He wasn't anywhere close to David's gait. David knew immediately it wasn't him and that ruined the episode for him! Hedison was so incensed by this physically bad match, he said, "I never allowed Fox to put *that* stand-in on film as me again!"

Review:

Monthly Film Bulletin Review (1/62) "Despite Paul Wendko's name on the credits, this is a makeshift episode in the *Operation Cicero* series, with a plot as unlikely as they come. Viveca Lindfors and John Emery are strikingly hammy, but fail to dissipate the prevailing dullness."

Victor prepares to rescue Simone from the Temple.
Copyright 20th Century Fox Studios.

I spoke to Clu Gulager about this episode in 2015. He had a remarkable memory of who was in the episode with him, but all he remembered of the episode was that he was in a big cave for the finale. He said he has known David Hedison since the late 1950s, when he was Al Hedison.

Gulager also remembered his co-stars John Emery and Viveca Lindfors quite well. He told me three stories about the two of them, but (unfortunately) they had nothing to do with this episode. I appreciate Clu taking the time to share them with me.

Knowing Fox Studio's penchant for re-using sets, it was probably the cave from their 1959 film *Journey to the Center of the Earth*.

Temple of the Swinging Doll. David Hedison with Clu Gulager, John Emery and Luciana Paluzzi. Copyright 20th Century Fox.

Temple of the Swinging Doll. Madame Zapote (Vivica Lindfors) makes her escape. Copyright 20th Century Fox.

Chapter 10

Episode Synopses: Episodes 10, 11, and 12

Episode 10: "The Final Dream" #3711

Airdate: 12/5/1959

Location: An Embassy in the Middle East

TV Guide [On-line] Listing: Simone (Luciana Paluzzi) is led astray by a U.S. ambassador's French valet (Cesare Danova) who is selling top secret information. Sebastian: David Hedison. Robertson: Paul Burke. Phelps: John Hoyt. Tumarin: Milton Selzer.

Credited cast:
Cesare Danova (Alain Fabre)
John Hoyt (Ambassador Phelps)

Milton Seltzer (Tumarin)
John Banner (Sapani, a Middle East Minister)

Recurring:
Paul Burke (Robertson)

Uncredited:
Mark Bailey (Embassy Inspector)
Cleaning Woman
Marine on Train

This is the plot of the 1952 James Mason film, with some changes for TV. The embassy is now American. The diplomat is the American Ambassador who has employed a French valet. This former French aristocrat and war hero is a childhood friend of Simone. Victor is assigned the task of rooting out the Communist mole selling our secrets. Many of the same plot twists found in the movie are here, such as the cleaning woman finding the removed fuse and screwing it back in, thus turning the alarm to the safe back on and exposing Alain as the traitor. New ending: Alain falls to his death under the train while trying to escape capture. So he never makes it to Rio with his money.

Plot synopsis: A tall shadowy figure accosts Undersecretary Tumarin outside his embassy door. The Communist is alarmed, but he is told not to be, his new "friend" has brought him the opportunity of a lifetime. After warning Tumarin that telling anyone about what they are about to discuss might cost them both their lives, the elegant stranger says he has top secret papers detailing American/Middle East relations and for $20,000 American, the Communist can buy them.

He wants Tumarin to inform his ambassador of the offer. His code name is Pierre and in two days he will call to ask Tumarin if he got his letter. If Tumarin says yes to this question, the stranger will then deliver

Episode Synopses: Episodes 10, 11, and 12

two rolls of film with details of the upcoming "Baghdad Pact" meeting which includes armaments and defense plans. If the information is useful, Pierre will make subsequent deliveries, but they will cost $40,000. Tumarin doubts the stranger is a spy, but is told not to worry about his identity or to have him followed; his men are no good at it. The stranger plans to get out the same way he got in, unnoticed.

At the American Embassy, the Ambassador is preparing to go out. His valet is called in to get him ready. It is the same elegant man who met with Tumarin. The man seems to be in indispensable to the Ambassador, giving him cigars to take to his appointment, telling him tidbits for small talk, and reminding him to take his pill.

As soon as the Ambassador leaves, Alain locks the door, retrieves his special high intensity light bulb, opens the safe and starts taking pictures of the "Most Secret" documents in there. Then we cut to Tumarin viewing the exposed film in his darkroom and seeing the defense plans. He comes back in to talk to "Pierre." He agrees the documents seem genuine and that they want more of them, but the price is too high. Pierre won't bargain down.

Tumarin goes to pay the spy out of his safe, only to find Pierre has already cracked it and is busily loading his money into a special pocketed vest he is wearing. Pierre has guessed the combination: it is the day Tumarin's Communist dictator came to power. Tumarin demands to know more about Pierre.

The spy says he is not in his employ, but he will tell him that he works at the American Embassy, since they will probably find that out anyway. He advises Tumarin to change the combination on his safe. Tumarin tells Pierre they have decided his code name is Cicero. Pierre approves. All of the above is right out of the 1952 movie.

Simone is singing to Victor about eternal love in a nearby cafe. Victor gives her kiss and tells Simone he has booked her for four weeks in Rome at the Lido Club. She is thrilled. They are discussing details when a man approaches. Simone jumps up in joy to greet her childhood friend, former Captain Alain Fabre. She has not seen him since the war, but he asks after her mother and they reminisce.

The cigarette girl approaches Victor and says she forgot to give him matches. The match folder has a message inside. Sebastian is to meet Robertson in the steam room. Victor tells Simone he has to go send a cable about the Rome deal. She thinks nothing of his leaving, but Fabre notices.

David Hedison from the episode "Final Dream."
Copyright 20th Century Fox Studios.

Episode Synopses: Episodes 10, 11, and 12

In the steam room, Robbie tells Vic to be prepared. They have been placed on alert that they may be needed to provide security for the upcoming Baghdad Pact meeting. They know the Communists want to know what is going to be discussed.

The minister from a "friendly" Middle Eastern country comes to visit the American Ambassador. He tells him that at a "trade meeting" he was approached by a representative of a "less friendly middle eastern country" named Tumarin and he was dropping hints about American plans he should know nothing about. The minister knows he did not tell anyone about what he and the Ambassador discussed, so the leak has to be on the American end. The American Ambassador assures him he is aware of the seriousness of the leak and what is at stake and promises to investigate immediately. He does not know Alain is listening at the open door.

Robertson and Sebastian meet at an outdoor cafe. Robbie says they have been charged with checking out the embassy staff at the request of the Ambassador. No one should know any details of what he's discussing for the Baghdad Pact, since the Ambassador has kept all the papers locked in his personal safe. Robbie gives Vic pictures of the staff. Sebastian pulls out Fabre's and tells Robertson he's met him and that he's an old friend of Simone's. Robbie answers, Simone better not get too close.

Alain comes to have tea with Simone in her hotel. She laughs about the crush she had on him when she was fifteen and he was a young lieutenant serving under her father. He admits he still has feelings for her and dreams. When Alain gets enough money, he wants to go back to Rio. He was there once, as a cabin boy on a tramp streamer. He saw a man on a balcony in a white dinner jacket and now he wants to be that man in that villa, with the woman he loves. [This is also lifted from the 1952 movie] He implies it could be Simone, but Genet realizes she is late for rehearsal and rushes him off.

Robbie and Vic meet with the American Ambassador. They tell him the spy's name is Cicero and that he lives on the embassy grounds. They advise him to change the combination on his safe and install an alarm.

They will be investigating, but they have no idea who the leak is yet; it could be anyone. [Hedison is dressed in Rennie's tan trench coat to match movie stock footage. Burke is wearing a dark hat]. The car stops and Victor is let off, while Robertson and the Ambassador return to the embassy.

Alain has retrieved his bulb and is taking more pictures when he is interrupted by the Ambassador's unexpected return. He gets the papers put away and the safe closed before the Ambassador walks in with Robbie, but he has to leave his bulb behind.

He comes back in with the Ambassador's smoking jacket and pretends the bulb is burnt out and takes it away, promising to bring back a new one, but this only brings him to Robbie's attention.

Alain takes his pictures to Tumarin and collects his fee. He tells the Communist he has to quit, that pressures have become too great. Tumarin is dismayed; he wants Cicero to find out what Operation Unity is. He will pay double. The spy is tempted and says he will do it for $100,000. He will be back in an hour.

Robbie shows the Ambassador that the safe alarm has been installed and that when it is turned on and the dial moved, it will go off.

Alain comes to see Simone. He wants to talk to her, but Victor arrives. Alain leaves, but makes Simone promise not to leave for Rome without talking to him. Simone doesn't take him seriously, but promises.

Victor sits Simone down after Alain goes and tells her he doesn't want her to see Fabre any more. She asks why. Victor can't tell her that, so she gets mad and vows to see whoever she pleases. Victor again asks her not to see Alain. She refuses.

Alain retrieves his bulb to take his last batch of pictures. As he is about to open the safe, he notices the new wire attached to it. He traces it around the room and out the door to the bell. He then goes to the broom closet and unscrews the fuse. With the alarm off, he opens the safe, finds the Operation Unity documents and photographs them. He can't use the light bulb with the power off, so Alain leaves the curtains open.

The maid comes to vacuum the hallway. The vacuum won't run, so she goes into the broom closet and screws the fuse back in. Alain finishes photographing the documents, puts them back and closes the safe. The alarm goes off. He runs past the Marine sentry, yelling, "Did you see him?" Alain makes his escape from the grounds before anyone can stop him.

Alain contacts Tumarin to meet him down in the seedy part of town. He has the film Tumarin wants, but won't give it to him. They agree that he can take the film with him to Rome and get paid there.

Alain calls Simone. She is rushing out the door to catch her train to Rome. Now he has verified she is leaving, Fabre lets her go.

The Ambassador is devastated that the spy was Fabre. Robbie has the airport staked out, but so far Alain has not turned up. He asks Vic to ask Simone if she has seen him. Sebastian says Simone has already left, without telling him good-bye.

Robbie gets a call that Fabre has purchased a train ticket on the Rome Express. They now know he is going with Simone. They stake out the train station to catch the valet. Alain waits until the train is pulling out the station to board it. Victor and Robbie also manage to get aboard as the train pulls away. [Stock footage from the film.]

They split up to search the train for Fabre. Fabre finds Simone first and enters her compartment. She is glad to see Alain, but less glad when he says the champagne and flowers are from him. Simone wanted them to be from Victor. Fabre declares he's on leave and wants to go to Rome with her. There is a knock on the compartment door. He tells her not to tell whoever it is that Alain in the compartment with her.

It's Victor. He breezes in, claiming to Simone that this is "where you hid out on me." Sensing they are not alone, he turns and Alain knocks him down and flees the compartment. Vic chases after him. Simone has no idea why and follows.

Alain's escape is cut off by Robertson coming the other way. He goes out the side door and hides between the cars. His feet are resting on a hydraulic line and it cannot bear his weight. The line breaks and he's left hanging on the ladder. Alain cannot hold on and falls under the train to his death. Simone leans out the open door in time to see him fall. Victor tries to shield her from seeing him die, but is too late.

Afterward, when they resume their journey to Rome, Simone feels guilty that Alain was stealing to impress her, but Victor tells her his original plan was for one passport, with one ticket to Rio. At least until he met Simone again. He wanted her to be part of his dream: to run away with enough money to live in luxury with a woman he loved. Victor says that could be any man's final dream.

Monthly Film Bulletin (1/61 no. 323) Synopsis: "Alain, a valet at the American Embassy, is photographing secret documents pertaining the Baghdad Pact and selling them to an Iron Curtain country through a diplomat named Tumarin. He reaches a point where he considers it unsafe to continue, but is swayed by a large fee offered for one last job. Alain spots the fact that the safe has been fitted with an alarm by Secret Service [sic] agents, but dismantles it by tampering with a fuse box. Unfortunately, a maid restores it to order to use a vacuum, so that the alarm goes off when Alain closes the safe. Nevertheless, he makes his getaway from the Embassy and succeeds in boarding the Rome Express, but is spotted by two agents, falling to his death while eluding them."

Monthly Film Bulletin Review: "Evidently part of the *Operation Cicero* series, the film precedes *Counterfeit* [also reviewed in this issue] chronologically, and uses much the same material as the [1952] Mankiewicz film. Again, the suspense is pretty mild, action and character meager."

Episode Synopses: Episodes 10, 11, and 12

David Hedison, Luciana Paluzzi and Cesare Danova, from the episode "Final Dream." Copyright 20th Century Fox Studios.

Episode 11: "Thin Ice" #3705

Airdate: 12/9/1959

Location: London, Casanegra, Akkabar

TV Guide [On-line] Listing: Sebastian must either deliver a young Arab prince (Brett Halsey) to Russia or get him back safely to his own country. Sebastian: David Hedison. Karel: Alan Young. Colonel: Peter Lorre. Simone: Luciana Paluzzi. Wembley: Alan Napier. Matthew: Marc Platt.

Credited cast:

Peter Lorre (The Colonel)
Alan Young (Karol)
Brett Halsey (Ibin Ahmed)

Peter Brocco (Gespard)
Marc Platt (Matthew)
Jimmy Fairfax (Bootblack)
Joe Abdullah (Catto)

Recurring:
Alan Napier (Wembley)
Paul Burke (Robertson)

Episode synopsis:

A foggy night in London. A young bearded man waits by the stage door with a bouquet of flowers. He is waiting for someone, but then thinks better of it, drops the flowers and disappears into the mist. Two shadowy figures watch him from the stairs across the street. One of them has a gun. He wants to shoot the man, claiming he is the prince they are searching for. The other stops him and tells the first one to follow the prince. He takes the gun away from him, remarking there are more clever ways to kill the Prince.

Simone and Victor are in London trying to pull together a revue. Victor doesn't like the costume designs. He is trying to get some new ones delivered, when his partner, Wembley, shows up with mail for him. But first, Wembley wants to know if Simone is one of "their" clients. Victor makes the introductions. Simone is very glad to meet Victor's partner and Wembley is very glad to meet Simone. Simone rehearses for the enthralled Wembley, while Victor opens his mail.

He has to meet two people, Aunt Flora, which is a code name of his Communist contact, and Robertson, who has sent him a glove to meet him at Ascot Race Track. Victor leaves Wembley to "look after" Simone.

Aunt Flora sends Vic to Waterloo station where a bootblack [shoeshine boy] tells him to go to St. Martin's gym and work out until his toes turn blue. Victor is working out on the uneven bars when one of the other men comments on his workout. Victor tells him about his toes and the meet is on.

The Colonel likes the gym; there are fewer prying ears around to hear them talk about Assadan and the country's dying king. The Communists think they can take over there if they can prevent the king's nephew from returning home to take over.

In the steam room afterward, the Colonel tells Sebastian what the party wants him to do. Get acquainted with the prince, travel with him and then turn him over to the party at a designated place and time to be disposed of. Vic doesn't think it will be that simple, but accepts his mission.

At Ascot, Robbie is told about Aunt Flora and while he is sympathetic to Vic's double dilemma, he says it's up to Victor to get Prince Dacquil home safe, because of his American sympathies. The Americans can't be seen to get involved, so they are happy to have "Vic the Communist" take him home, but don't let the Communists have him. Sebastian also needs to watch out for Aunt Flora; he is quite the adversary.

Vic wants to know if he has any slack to make up his play. Robbie says no problem, delivering him alive is all they care about. Victor asks to take the Prince into his confidence and is given the okay.

Victor brings Prince Ahmed (his alias) to the theater to meet Simone. She is all excited about her new tour, but Wembley knows nothing about it. Victor sweeps in and sweeps out with Simone without telling Wembley a thing.

In Simone's dressing room, Vic tells her the tour is through the near East, Morocco, Damascus, Tangiers...She doesn't want to be apart from Victor that long. He says he's going with her, so now she is very happy. Then he tells her he has to see a friend's little brother home. She is not happy about babysitting a schoolboy. Victor says wait until she meets him.

He goes out while she is changing and gets Ahmed. Ahmed has been sheltered all his royal life and doesn't know how to act with show people. Victor tells him to relax, Simone is a regular girl and he'll love her. He pushes Ahmed into the dressing room.

Simone is surprised that the schoolboy is so grown-up. Victor adds he's from Oxford University. Simone asks Ahmed how "big" his older brother is.

Victor goes out to make dinner reservations. Wembley wants to come along. Victor says fine. On the other side of the stage wall the first Communist, Karol, is listening to everything Victor is arranging.

Karol shows the Colonel all the clippings of Simone and Ahmed as an item and how they will be traveling on the cruise ship *Arcadia* to Casanegra. [Casablanca.] Karol thinks Sebastian is doing a brilliant job of following his orders, but that is precisely what makes the Colonel nervous. The plan is too good, too clever.

It is the last night of the cruise. Ahmed apologizes to Simone for all the press coverage and hopes he has not been a bother. She says no and invites him to drink and dance with her in the salon. Karol reveals himself to Sebastian with the blue toes code and they talk. Victor wants to know where to drop off the prince. Karol says he will get word to him once they dock in Casanegra.

Simone and Ahmed on board the ship sailing to Casanegra. From the episode "Thin Ice." Copyright 20th Century Fox Studios.

Episode Synopses: Episodes 10, 11, and 12

Victor checks into his hotel only to find a white glove waiting for him. He calls the cleaning service. Gaspard gives the correct code and they talk about American support for Vic. Unfortunately, Gaspard is it; the Communists have taken out three of his men. He wants to help. He warns Victor against using his radio and gives him his hotel number.

During the show that evening, Karol tells Victor to drive Ahmed out on the Assadan Road where he will be met and he can turn the prince over. Victor agrees to do so. Vic tries to call Gaspard for back-up, but the phone is off the hook. Gaspard is dead.

Victor goes to wake Ahmed and almost gets strangled in the process. He tells Ahmed he doesn't need a bodyguard. He tells him Gaspard is dead and they are in a box, but he thinks he has a way out. Ahmed will be kidnapped by someone else before he can be delivered to the Communists at the oasis.

Victor and Ahmed drive out the Assadan Road. They stop about a mile from the oasis, put on Arabic shoes to make it look like they were ambushed, shoot up Victor's car trunk, and then Ahmed has to shoot Victor. He finally does, in time to hide in the trunk before Karol and the Communists show up, having heard the gunshots.

They find Sebastian, wounded. He passes out before he can tell them anything beyond three men kidnapped Ahmed. Karol has him driven back to town before he bleeds to death from the bullet wound.

The Colonel doesn't like it, as they found no trace of Ahmed or the man who kidnapped him. Karol buys the armed men story, until the Colonel sends him down the hill to retrieve a shoe he has spotted. He matches it to a footprint and immediately suspects Sebastian of being too clever.

Back at the hotel, Sebastian has his shoulder in a sling and Ahmed stashed in his room. He gives the prince his lunch. Simone comes to visit. She is very upset Victor has been shot and was very nearly killed. She wants to help, but Victor says she can't, it's his job to see Ahmed gets home safely. She pleads with him and then Victor has an idea.

One Simone can help with.

The colonel has moved in next door to keep an eye on Sebastian. He is convinced Ahmed is hiding in Victor's room when he sees another man close the door after Sebastian leaves. He decides to pay a visit.

They knock on the door. It is answered by a revue skater who is rubbing off his make-up. He claims he was rehearsing and says Sebastian is over at the hotel and will be back in about half an hour, if they want to wait. The colonel says no, but he is still not convinced Sebastian is in the clear.

Victor watches the cafe fill with Communists, while Simone finishes making up Ahmed to pass as one of the skaters. The skater is not happy that Ahmed is using his costume, but he's been paid, so they tell him to disappear.

The Colonel comes and sits with Sebastian. He tells him he knows Ahmed is in the hotel and he is going to watch Sebastian all night until Ahmed is found. Karol barges into Simone's dressing room, looking for Ahmed, but doesn't recognize the Prince under all the clown make-up. Ahmed gets angry and tells Karol off in his best New York accent and it works. Simone then drags him out of the room before he can deck the Communist.

On stage, they do the act, with Ahmed skating his part until he falls (and fakes) a back injury. Simone calls Victor up on stage to help, and the colonel has to let him go. Victor takes charge (as the agent) and gets his "injured" client onto a stretcher and carried out of the hotel. Sebastian is going to go to the hospital, but the Colonel won't let him. Simone volunteers to go. The injured "skater" is loaded into a cab. There is no time to wait for an ambulance. The cab drives to the airstrip, where a hired pilot is waiting to fly the Prince to Assadan.

The Colonel invites Victor to have a drink and bemoans the fact he has not as yet found the Prince, when he was so sure he would. Victor is restless, but is encouraged to watch his own very good show.

Karol shows up much later with a very long face. His palace contact has checked in and says the Prince has returned. The colonel can't figure out how and apologizes to Victor for suspecting he had anything to do with it.

Simone has returned to do her second set as promised, singing "So good." After the show, Victor comes to her dressing room and tells her Ahmed made it home. She tells him, see, she can help. Victor replies he'd rather help himself. To a kiss.

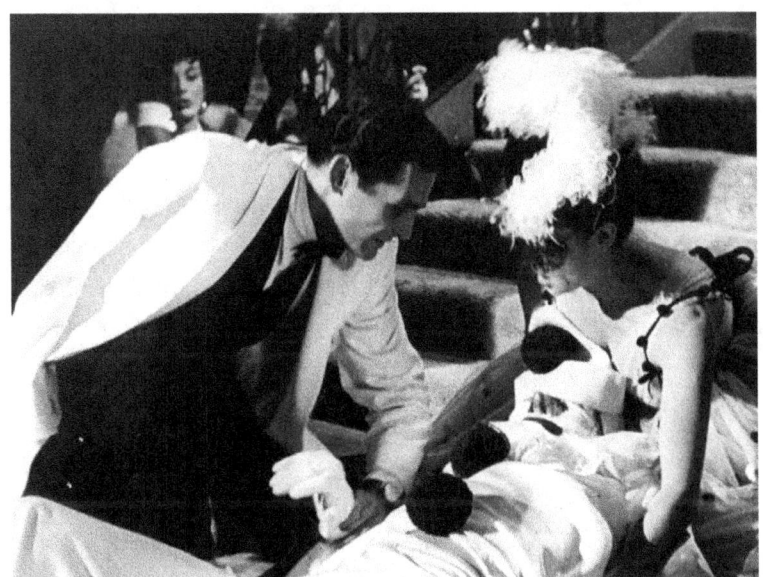

David Hedison, Brett Halsey and Luciana Paluzzi at the Ice Show. From the episode "Thin Ice." Copyright 20th Century Fox Studios.

Monthly Film Bulletin [No date given on-line] Synopsis: Victor Sebastian and his entertainer girlfriend prevent a young Eastern potentate's assassination and, one assumes, world war.

Trivia: *Thin Ice* is a 1937 Sonja Henie skating movie about a Prince, played by Tyrone Power.

Brett Halsey was kind enough to let me interview him on the phone about his memories of this series. Halsey admitted that he was often on the set, watching his fiancée film. One day David and Luciana cooked up a bit of business between them. Herbert Swope, the producer, was in Brett's words "a stick in the mud," always cautioning David and Luciana not to let their "love scenes" get out of hand, because this was television.

So one day there was yet another one of their chaste love scenes they had to film. David and Luciana decided to "go for it" and fell onto the bed and proceeded to do the love scene the way they had always wanted to . . . full out.

The crew stood there, shocked at what they were watching going on in that bed. The panicked director yelled, "Cut!"

At which point both actors came up for air and started laughing. Once the crew realized they had been had and it was a joke, they all cracked up. That scene (of course) never made it into the episode and Herb Swope got a few more grey hairs overseeing his spirited young cast.

Halsey wishes both his future wife's series and the one he did the following year, *Follow the Sun* (1960-61), had been better produced. He blames the executives at the time. He felt they had all the wrong ideas about what should be on television. Those executives wanted snob appeal in a medium that needed to find the broadest audience possible. They should have made less cinematic shows, many of which were over the head of their intended audience.

Halsey blames the famous caviar "episode" that happened during filming of this episode on the director, Lamont Johnson, whom Halsey had known when Johnson was an actor.

The director said, given where they were at the posh Bel-Air Hotel that "Peter should be eating" and "to go ahead and order something."

So Lorre motioned the real waiter over and ordered. The production manager almost died when he got the bill for the dish. Peter was supposed to order something small and cheap, but since he was told to go ahead, he ordered their best caviar. Of course.

Episode Synopses: Episodes 10, 11, and 12

Halsey went on to say that working with Lorre was a lot of fun.

Author's note: David Hedison's version of the "caviar" story can be found in Chapter 6.

Alan Young on working with Peter Lorre: "In 1959, I was hired for a supporting role in a TV dramatic series called *Five Fingers*. I was playing a cockney crook and my cohort was that all-time champion miscreant, Peter Lorre. It seemed as if I had seen Peter in movies forever, always playing the sniveling, sneaky character, never realizing that he had been one of Europe's top dramatic actors in his youth. Only in Hollywood was he typecast as the perennial villain.

Being supporting actors, we had a great deal time between scenes and became quite friendly. I told him I had never had any formal acting lessons and he said, 'have you ever worked "eye-contact" exercises?'

I told him my only expertise was comedic takes, double takes and skulls, so he agreed that we should share our abilities. What he got out of my demonstrations, I don't know, but his tutoring was superb.

His eyes were huge and deep but when he fixed them on you it was mesmerizing. I don't know how many muscles the eyes have, but I'm sure Peter had a few added when he was in Vienna. No matter how he held his head those optics bored into you. And no matter how you turned away, your gaze was invariably drawn back.

Finally, Peter was called to work and I had another opportunity to learn some more tricks of our trade. We were shooting in the magnificent Bel-Air Hotel and Peter's scene took place in the dining room. He had a long monologue to deliver while eating a plate of caviar. He rehearsed with the real stuff and his unctuous dialogue was only surpassed by his licentious, almost sensual enjoyment of the caviar.

The time came to shoot and oddly, though he had it letter perfect in rehearsal, Peter kept forgetting his lines. He didn't seem upset about this, even when they had done over five takes. When they finished shooting, I said, 'Peter, you knew the lines perfectly. What happened?'

He grinned mischievously 'I just couldn't bear to have the scene end. I mean, that that was imported caviar. The best I've had in years.'" From Alan Young's book *There's No Business Like Show Business . . . Was.*

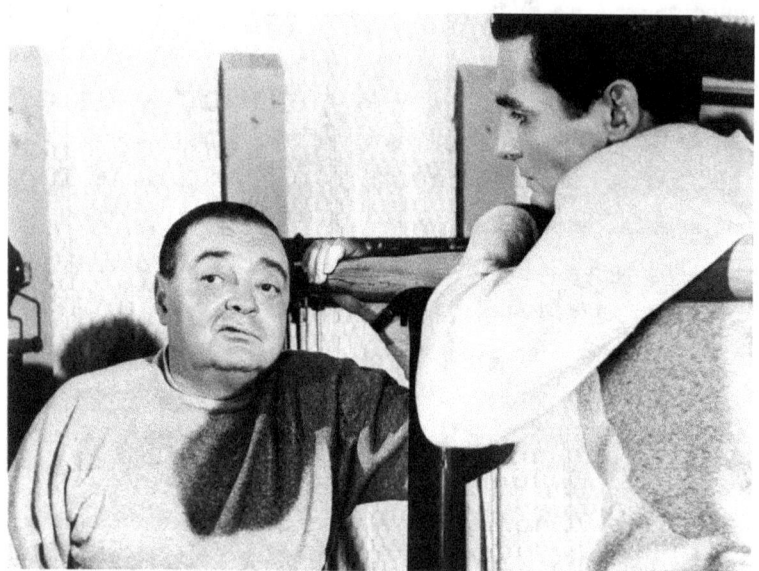

David and Peter Lorre: The Colonel and Victor meet at the Gym. From the episode "Thin Ice." Copyright 20th Century Fox Studio. *TV Guide* used this picture to plug the episode.

Halsey told John Murray in his biography, *Brett Halsey: Art or Instinct in the Movies,* that he had a good part in the episode. He was playing an Arab educated in England, pretending to be an American. His own American accent, which Brett decided to use (after debating over what the part called for), worked for director Johnson and the episode. Brett was believable. He showed the right amount of hesitation when he has to shoot his protector in order to maintain Victor's cover.

Some real life chemistry comes into play as Ahmed and Simone pretend to be an item. In real life the couple was living together, waiting for Brett's divorce from Renata Hoy to become final so they could marry. Her in-show reference to Halsey's height also rings true.

Monthly Film Bulletin Review states "Peter Lorre scores as a Russian Master Spy, but in all other respects this a slipshod *Operation Cicero* episode, badly played and without impact."

Episode 12: "Operation Ramrod" #3713

Airdate: 12/26/1959

Location: Small Mediterranean Town of San Lupo, Paris, Island of La Bruniere

Sets: The "island" is the Sligon Castle set.
The Waterways

TV Guide [On-line] listing: "Operation Ramrod" is ex-President Boska's maneuver to return to power in his small European country. Boska: Oscar Homolka. Chara: Erin O'Brien. Sebastian: David Hedison. Ramrod: Ray Anthony. Marcuse: Carl Esmond. Blanc: Michael Romanoff. Hans: Leonard Bell.

Actual plot: Ramrod is the code name of Victor's "bandleader" partner. Their mission is to rescue Marcuse, the opposition leader, who has been kidnapped by Boska in an attempt to get him to support his coup. The inside joke of this episode is that guest star Ray Anthony really *is* a bandleader.

Five Fingers: Elegance in Espionage

Credited cast:
Oscar Homolka (Boska)
Ray Anthony (Ramrod)
Erin O'Brien (Chara)
Leonard Bell (Hans)
Carl Esmond (Marcuse)
Walter Flanagan (Roque)
Roy Jenson (Carl)

Recurring:
Paul Burke (Robertson)
Michael Romanoff (Blanc)

Episode Synopsis:

Victor is on stakeout in a small Mediterranean seaport town. He is watching a high government official of a friendly country there, who has been kidnapped. They don't know who's behind the kidnapping, so they cannot step in and rescue him, but they do have the name of the boat he was taken on to give to Robertson.

They are sending Morse code when their stakeout is invaded by gunmen. They are overrun and Victor's fellow agent is killed. Victor drives them back with gunfire and barricades the door. He can't escape, so he uses the Morse key to tell Robbie he needs help.

Robertson, in Paris, calls an official in Madrid to send the local cops in San Lupo to the waterfront address. The approaching sirens scare off the gunmen. Victor escapes out a second story window, climbs down and runs for it, as he doesn't want to explain what he was doing there, either.

Victor returns to Paris with his information and holds a strategy session with Robertson on how to rescue Marcuse. Roque, who is the current man in power, thinks Marcuse was kidnapped by Boska in a bid to return to power. They are interested to see what value their current Minister of Information has to the exiled dictator.

Episode Synopses: Episodes 10, 11, and 12

Victor is to go to the closest coastal town to the dictator's island and find out what he is doing. Robbie has sent Ramrod, another agent, ahead to help in this task.

On the island of San Bruniere, Boska comes to see his guest, Marcuse. Marcuse demands to be let go. Boska says no, he needs him to pave the way for his return to power. Marcuse says the country has grown and no longer wants Boska. Boska laughs and tells him he will do it.

Victor takes the train to St. Gatien. He is checking into the hotel when he runs into his old friend Prince Blanc, who is catering a party at Boska's island that evening.

He makes contact with Rolling Stone Jones, a jazz trumpeter, who reveals himself to be Ramrod. Ramrod shows him his recording gadgets and Vic tells Jones about the party.

They agree they need to get Jones on the island and playing at the party to record the next meeting of Boska and Marcuse. They manage to be where Boska can hear "Rolly" playing. He hires him on the spot to play at the party.

Boska leaves his girl, Chara, behind to distract Victor while his thugs search the American's room. Boska has taken a dislike to him. Victor wants to find out what her instructions are, so he goes into the bar to see if she will follow him in. She does. Victor sends the bartender away to get a special cordial so they can talk. She invites him to the party, but Vic says he was going anyway, he booked a client there. She gives him a strange warning about Boska, how he may be in danger, even if he is minding his own business. Victor plays dumb.

Victor goes back to his room and finds it being ransacked. He decks one of Boska's thugs, Hans, and starts yelling. They assure him they are not there to steal. Boska wanted him checked out, being a stranger and all. Victor is not swayed. He picks up the phone to call security. The other thug, Carl, pulls a gun and tells him not to complete the call. Victor puts down the phone.

The shouting brings Rolly to Victor's door. The thug immediately holsters his gun. Victor continues to yell and threatens to cancel Rolly's gig if Boska is going to treat him like that. Rolly protests, he wants to play and he has already hired the band. Victor throws both of the thugs out of his room while he and Rolly continue to argue loudly over whether or not they will actually do the gig.

Down in the bar, Boska is pumping Chara for information she gleaned from Sebastian. She says he is nice. Boska laughs and chides her for not doing what he asked. The thugs come in, saying they found nothing but clothes and booking contracts, which they hand to Boska. He does not have a good opinion of Victor's booking skills.

Everyone goes to the party. Victor thinks Boska threw it to have witnesses that he and Marcuse are collaborating, to ruin his current political career, so Marcuse has to throw in with Boska. Victor tries to flirt with Chara. She warns him that it's not good to bait Boska like that. He won't like it.

Rolly finishes his set and Victor meets him in the cloakroom. They need to set the bugging devices. Rolly sets one in the cloakroom, and then distracts Boska's guard, Carl, so Victor can set the other one upstairs. Vic walks into the wrong room and finds Marcuse there. Sebastian tells him a phony story about checking out Boska and asks Marcuse not to rat him out.

Carl tells Boska Victor is in the cloakroom. Boska checks and finds him gone. He wants him found. He tells Carl to check all the upstairs rooms. Carl checks with Marcuse. Marcuse lies and says he has seen no one but Boska.

Victor leaves, unhappy Marcuse has seen him. He goes into the other room to set up the recorder in the vent. Boska is convinced the American is "hiding" in the castle because he is an agent. He decides to disband the party to flush Victor out. Once he gets the information he needs to return to power out of Marcuse, he is going to kill him.

Boska tells everything to his bodyguard Hans in the cloakroom, unaware he is being recorded.

Boska announces the weather has become inclement on the island and he wants everyone to depart to St. Gatien to continue to party (on him) at the hotel. The guests line up to get on the boat to go back. Chara tells Boska she doesn't like him like this. He doesn't care and is rude and mean to her.

Chara comes back to her room, interrupting Victor placing the recorder in the vent. He hides behind her curtain while she is changing. He can't reveal himself and laments (in the voiceover) that sometimes being a spy means he can't be a gentleman. Finally, she leaves and he climbs up to set the recorder again. Chara hands Boska back his pearls and leaves with the guests.

Boska comes to visit Marcuse after the boat leaves. Victor has turned on the recorder and is still listening at the vent. He hears the entire conversation he's recording. How Marcuse will be named prime minister and get half a million dollars, which Army officers can be bought off. There is only one snag to the plan: Boska's business deal with another country. Boska denies any deal and claims the American Marcuse met told him a lie and he is a spy. Victor hears they plan to kill him.

He extracts the tape and tries to escape out the tower. Carl finds him there and is taking him to the top to kill him. They pass by Rolly, who is also looking for an escape route, and Rolly jumps the big guard. It takes both of them to subdue him, but finally they take him down. Victor gives Rolly his tape recording because he's blown, but Rolly may still be able to get off the island as a member of the band.

Rolly doesn't want to leave Victor, but that's the way it has to be. Victor tells Rolly to remember the names and get out of there. He sends Rolly down to the docks, and then yells to get Hans' attention. Hans runs up the stairs to the tower, right past Rolly, who then continues down.

Vic plays hide-and-seek with Hans in the tower. He has the advantage and is able to shoot the man dead. Victor then runs over the roof and comes back down to the courtyard via the loudspeaker pole. Where he is met by Boska and his gun. It's the end of the line. Boska and

Marcuse will kill him and be on their way. Marcuse wants him dead, but Boska wants to play with him some more.

Suddenly over the loudspeaker, we hear Boska's voice disparaging Marcuse and saying he's going to kill him. Rolly is playing the tape to save Victor. Marcuse is not amused. Boska says he didn't mean it, Marcuse says he does mean it and shoots Boska. The ex-dictator falls and Marcuse steps in front of him to make a new deal with the Americans.

The wounded Boska reaches out for his dropped gun and shoots Marcuse dead. The plot is over as the wounded Boska takes one last smoke and then dies. Rolly pops up from behind the wall and gives Victor a salute. Victor returns it.

Back in the bar on St. Gatien, Victor checks up on Chara. She's heard about Boska's death, but assures Victor she is not romantically interested in him. He has the look of a man already in love. Sebastian admits that he is. This is the only reference to Simone the entire episode.

These episodes are slowly building toward a more involved Simone, which works better for their obvious love relationship than the earlier episodes were she is deliberately and often cruelly kept in the dark about Victor's "other" job.

Erin O'Brien from *John Paul Jones* (1959).
Copyright 20th Century Fox Studios.

CHAPTER 11

EPISODE SYNOPSES: EPISODES 13 AND 14

Episode 13: "The Judas Goat" #3714

Airdate: 1/2/1960

Locations: Paris, Venice, Budapest, a Border Town in Austria

TV Guide [On-line] Listing: In Hungary, Sebastian (David Hedison) searches for a traitor who betrays his people after promising them freedom. Daisy: Margaret Lindsay. Simone: Luciana Paluzzi. Robertson: Paul Burke. Vestos: Vladimir Sokoloff.

Another listing from the *Lawrence World Journal* (Kansas), January 2, 1960, TV Previews: "It is a suspenseful show tonight on *Five Fingers*. Having successfully kept his secret as a government agent from Simone

Genet (Luciana Paluzzi) Victor (David Hedison) finally takes her into his confidence. The reason for this is that he needs her help in searching for a man who recruits families trying to escape from the Iron Curtain."

Credited cast:
Margaret Lindsay (Daisy Cameron)
Kitty Mattern (Countess Schatz)
Frank De Kova (Otto Landau)
Vladimir Sokoloff (Peter Vestos)
Albert Szabo (Bruno)
John Graham (Wilson)
Violet Rensing (Anna)
Bobby Slade (Urchin)
Deborah Sydes (Little Girl)
Greg Dunn (Master of Muse)
Peg Fellows (Greta)
Willy Kaufmann (Max)

Recurring:
Paul Burke (Robertson)

Uncredited:
Refugee Couple, Austrian Police Officers, Street Carnival Revelers

A little girl in an unknown Hungarian town covets a doll belonging to her taciturn neighbor. One day she walks into his apartment and takes the doll while he is dressing. He pursues her. She is finally cornered with the doll. He takes the doll back from her and smashes the doll's head against the brick wall. Frightened, she runs away and does not see him pull the folded paper message out of the broken head of the doll before discarding it.

Episode Synopses: Episodes 13 and 14

Meanwhile, back in Paris, Robbie is trying to convince his mission supervisor that Simone needs to be part of his espionage team. He and Victor have recommended she be hired. After reviewing her file, the boss decides they can give her a small assignment and see how she does. Robbie asks to take her to Venice with him where they will meet Victor.

Simone is waiting outside the office for Robertson. He tells her she's in. She doesn't have to sign or pledge anything; all she has to do is get on a plane with him.

Victor has gone ahead into Austria. He has been given a picture of Otto Landau. The allies want to stop this man who takes desperate Eastern Europeans who want to defect and strips them of their life savings to get them out, then turns them over to the Communist guards at the border. Victor likens it to the tethering of a goat inside the chute that leads the lambs to slaughter, hence the term "Judas goat." Landau must be stopped.

Victor visits the doll shop that he thinks is the mail drop where Landau receives messages from the party. Sebastian goes in and purchases a small doll. He is rebuffed by Bruno, the male shop keeper, when he asks about the custom dolls that are made in the back, to order, by the countess. Victor asks for an appointment to see the dolls. He is told the Countess is sick and that she won't give him one. Sebastian says he will try again tomorrow. The Countess comes out of the back and wants to know who that was. Bruno says he does not know.

While waiting for Simone to arrive, Vic is flagged down by Daisy Cameron, who calls him darling. She wants a date. Vic asks if she knows the countess. Of course, she does. Sebastian makes her promise to get him in to buy one of the fancy dolls, even though Daisy has no idea who he is.

Simone walks in to see Victor being fawned over by Daisy. Victor begs off; says he has to go be with his girl. Daisy lets him go with a promise to call her. He kisses Simone hello. She tells him her good news that she will be working with him. Victor knows already, but he's very proud of her. He asks where Robbie is.

He goes up to Robbie's room and they exchange information. Robbie tells Vic that one of the dolls was traced to Lisbon and they definitely know the doll shop is a mail drop. Vic asks Robbie to hold off on busting the shop. He wants to use the drop to trap Landau, who so far has eluded arrest because he has never crossed the border. Robbie agrees to the plan.

Victor takes Robbie to meet one of the defectors betrayed by Landau. He tells of being taken into the woods at the border and then led right to the border guards, with no chance of escape. He names Otto Landau as the one who took his money and then delivered the rest of his family to the Communists. Victor wants to put Landau out of business for good.

In the meantime, Otto prepares to betray another refugee couple. He gets a list of people they know who want to defect and agrees to take them over the border. After they leave him the list and agree to pay him, Otto sees them out. A man who had been behind a curtain listening takes the list. He will arrest them at the border. The "Judas goat" has betrayed yet another group.

Daisy Cameron is good as her word. When Victor asks her to take Simone to the shop to buy an extra fancy doll, she does. Simone soils her glove with ink so the Countess will have to address the package so they can use her handwriting to get a message to Landau. The countess is distracted by her partner, Bruno, while this is going on. After the women leave, he claims to have found the escapee from Landau's last group. Bruno is going to take care of the stranger personally.

Simone gives the doll and written label to Victor at the festival rehearsal and asks if she did well. Victor gives her a kiss and tells her she's a pro.

They practice writing a fake message until Robbie gets the Countess' handwriting down pat. Robbie then manufactures a note to Landau that they hide under the doll's hair. It tells him it's urgent he come across the Hungarian border to the shop. Victor and Simone take her doll to the post office to be mailed. Bruno comes in after them and Sebastian has Simone distract him so he can't see where Victor is sending the doll.

Peter decides to go for a walk. Anna warns him not to go, that Landau knows he escaped and he should lay low until Landau is captured. Peter says he's only going to down to the square to participate in the festival. He is followed there by Bruno, but does not know it.

The festival has started. The first act we see on stage is an interpretative ballet. Bruno is in the audience. Then Simone is brought out to sing. Her song is interrupted when her spotlight moves across the stage and reveals Peter lying dead on the stage. He has been stabbed.

Victor tries to console Anna. They think they know who did it, but decide to wait until Landau gets his message and comes to town. Victor has been after him for fifteen years.

Landau gets the doll and the message. He then gets a phone call, but tells them he must cancel their trip as he has to go out of town.

Simone is in Victor's room, watching him watch the doll shop out the window. She wants to know what she can do. He tells her to go off to rehearsal. She questions whether or not she's been effective. He assures her he will tell her when he needs her. Simone goes to rehearsal.

Victor sees masks are being delivered to the store for the carnival. Bruno also arrives and Sebastian ducks away from the window so he is not seen. Inside, the countess is very upset Bruno has killed the refugee Peter. She did not sign up for that. Bruno tells her it had to be done. If Landau is exposed, the trail will lead right back to them and they will also be convicted. The countess is not happy about this.

Later that night, with carnival in full swing, Victor sees a man arrive at the shop. It is not Landau. He comes wearing a wolf mask that he ordered for the carnival. Victor and Robbie see he is not Landau. The man with the wolf head mask is also observed by Otto Landau and he follows him into an alley.

Robbie gets a phone call from the Austrian authorities. They are ready to move in and report that Landau crossed the border about an hour ago. The two of them see the man with the wolf head return to the shop.

Inside the shop, the man removes his head. It is Otto Landau. Bruno demands to know why he is there. They did not send him any message. Bruno asks Landau to describe the doll he received. It matches the one the Countess sold to Simone. It's a trap. Bruno has an idea. A trap can work both ways. He makes a phone call.

Robbie sees Simone come to the shop. Victor calls the rehearsal hall and finds out she left to meet him there. Simone enters the shop, looking for Victor. She is led into the back room after being told Victor is there. He is not there, Landau is. They demand to know what she knows about the doll.

Victor wants to go in and rescue her, but Robbie won't let him. They have to wait for Landau. Out the window, they see the shop lights go out. Victor doesn't want to wait any longer. Then they see the first man, who is supposed to be wearing the wolf mask, stagger into the street, holding his head. They run out of the hotel to question him. He says he was mugged and his mask was taken. They now know Landau is inside the doll shop.

Robbie runs for the police while Victor tries to force open the locked front door. The entrance bell alerts Landau. Bruno tells him to go and take Simone. Victor forces the door, but cannot get into the back room; the bolt is too strong. Robbie joins him.

Bruno opens the door and tries to bluff them. He says they are closed and Landau and Simone were never there. The countess won't play along. She tells them Landau took Simone and the masks and is trying to escape. The Austrian police arrive and arrest Bruno and the Countess.

Vic and Robbie wade into the carnival in an attempt to cut off Landau's escape attempt. They finally spot Landau dragging Simone along with him at the edge of town. Landau shoves Simone into them and runs. Robbie catches her as Vic sprints off after Landau. Landau throws off his mask and goes over the side of the bridge. Vic tackles him, and they fight with Sebastian punching him several times until he knocks Landau out. Robbie arrives to help hold him until the police take Otto away. Simone throws herself into Victor's arms and he hugs her tight.

Later, back in the hotel, they have champagne to celebrate her first mission. Simone is ashamed they got her to come to the shop so easily. They both assure her that they could not have gotten Landau without her and that makes her happy. Victor tells her that it always takes new acts a while to break in.

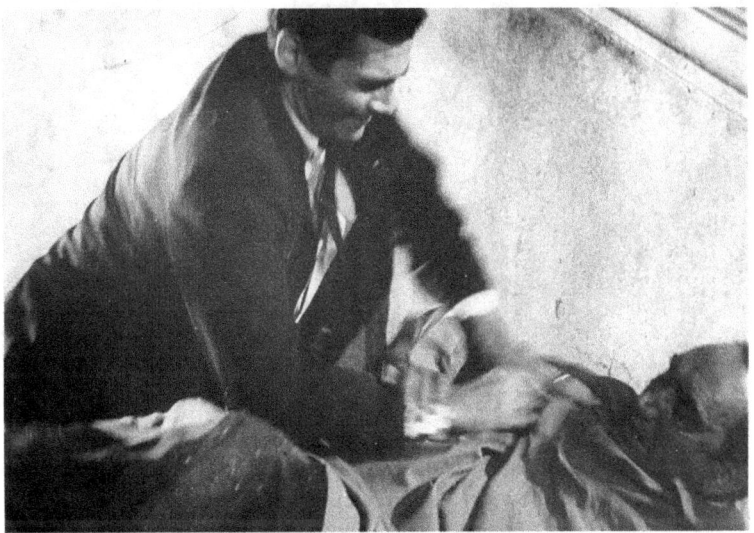

Victor Fighting Landau. From the episode "The Judas Goat." Copyright 20th Century Fox Studios.

Monthly Film Bulletin Synopsis (12/61 no. 335): "A doll shop in an Austrian Border village is the front for a spy ring led by Landau who has turned "Judas," pretending to smuggle refugees to freedom, then handing them over to the secret police. Victor, an American counter-espionage agent, and his fiancée, Simone, send a false message inside a doll to lure the ringleader. The plan misfires. During carnival night Simone is decoyed to the shop, but after a chase Victor rescues her and traps Landau."

Monthly Film Bulletin Review: "The trick title masks just another spy story in the pedestrian *Operation Cicero* series. A makeshift plot carries little conviction or excitement, despite spurts of brisk action. Wooden acting from the stars, one or two neat supporting cameos, including old timer Margaret Lindsey as a dizzy socialite."

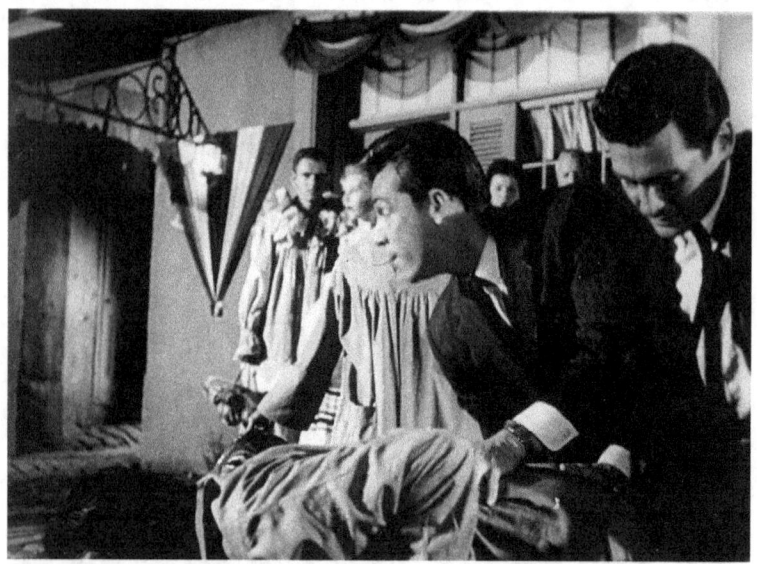
Robbie takes Landau into Custody. From the episode "The Judas Goat." Copyright 20th Century Fox Studios.

Episode 14: "The Search for Edvard Stoyan" #3708
aka Pyrrhic Victory aka Epitaph

Airdate: 1/9/1960

Locations: Yugoslavia (Dinaric Alps), Belgrade, Venice

TV Guide [On-line] listing: When the wreckage of a U.S. plane is sighted in Yugoslavia's Alps, Sebastian (David Hedison) is sent to recover the plane's cargo of gold. Monteverdi: Martin Balsam. Marulic: Hugo Haas. Anneska: Margaret Phillips. Simone: Luciana Paluzzi.

Sets Used:
Stage Three: Venice. Stage Seven: Belgrade. Adano Square: Prozega, Anneska's House exterior. The Waterways: Plane Wreck. French Square: The Donkey Ride to Marulic's. Stage Five: Hoskins' Office, Monteverdi's Suite, Marulic's Hut, Anneska's room and Hallway, Theater Lobby, Vic's hotel room, Balcony ledge and roof chase. Bernadette Street Bridge: Bridge and row boat.

Credited cast:
Hugo Haas (Marulic)
Martin Balsam (Monteverdi/Joseph Cappella)
David J. Stewart (Travik)
Margaret Phillips (Anneska)
William Roerick (Hoskins)
Francis Bethancourt (Pontormo)
Alvaro Guillot (Philippe)
Alex de Naszody (Marco) [from call sheet]
Werner Reichow (Officer) [from call sheet]

Recurring: Paul Burke (Robertson)

Episode Synopsis: A helicopter lands in the Dinaric Alps. On board is a movie crew scouting locations. They discover a crashed American plane, a PBY, out in the middle of nowhere. The plane has remained undiscovered for fifteen years. One of the men, Giovanni Monteverdi, is a flamboyant movie producer.

We find Victor and Simone at the Venice Film Festival. They have seen Monteverdi's latest film. Simone loves it and wants a part in his next film, *King of Epirus*. She asks Victor to get it for her. He suggests they go for a gondola ride. On the gondola she asks him again to get her the part. Victor says he can't, Monteverdi is in Yugoslavia investigating his plane wreck, plus Monteverdi only uses amateurs that he finds on location and Simone doesn't qualify as an amateur. She still wants to make the movie and is quite put out that Victor won't ask. She refuses to have breakfast with Sebastian in the morning after he leaves her at her hotel room.

Entering his room, Victor senses someone is there. A voice tells him not to turn on the light. Victor recognizes it as Robbie's. Robertson comes out from behind the curtains and says the night porter let him in. He says he didn't have the heart to break up their gondola ride and compliments Vic on his instincts. Victor asks if it time to go to work. It is Simone's first official assignment after her recruitment in the previous episode. Robbie tells Victor to call Simone over so he can brief them both. Vic calls her room and she comes over, after he promises to behave.

Robbie briefs them. The Americans are very interested in that plane. It left England with a million dollars in gold for the Yugoslavian partisans and was never heard from again. The cover story (for fifteen years) was that the Nazis captured the plane. Robbie says that isn't true, since the plane is intact and the crew never turned up in a Nazi prison camp. Their joint mission, with the Air Force, is to find out what happened to the gold shipment. Robbie warns Simone that Vic's life may depend on her eager actress portrayal. Victor says she'll be very convincing.

They meet with Monteverdi. He loves Simone. She further cements her audition by telling him she's an amateur. She'd be perfect in *King of Epirus*, only Monteverdi is not making the film. He wants to do a film about the plane, before some American does. He can't get the secret files on the plane. Vic says he knows someone at the embassy and might be able to get him the files, if Simone gets a part. They shake hands on it.

Victor goes to see Hoskins, the man Robbie told him worked in the legation and who will be the primary investigator on the case. They found the missing crew buried in a mass grave about 100 yards from the plane, each one killed by a shot to the back of the head. After fifteen years there is little left to identify. There are five dog tags to match with dental records. One of the crew has steel crowns, which are not used in America, but common in Europe. His dog tags say Major Joseph Capella, which leads Vic to believe Capella survived. They decide to visit the plane themselves to determine who got executed in Capella's place.

Hoskins arranges for Victor to be taken further up the mountain by donkey cart to see the old head of the partisans, a man named Marulic. Victor interrogates him to get the partisan side of the story. The plane passed over the partisans, their signal flares alerted the Nazis and half the partisans were killed.

Marulic doesn't know the plane was found, but he knows the partisans never got the gold. He tells Victor of the other two men who knew about the gold. Victor thinks one of them paired up with Capella to steal it. Marulic tells Vic that one of his men, Edvard Stoyan, also disappeared that night and was never heard from again. He had a girlfriend, Anneska, who might know where he is now.

David Hedison on set. Photo courtesy of David Hedison.

Simone is having lunch with Monteverdi. All he can do is complain how no one will cooperate with him and help him make this movie. Victor comes back and tells Monteverdi he is going to visit Stoyan's old girlfriend in Belgrade and see what she knows. Simone follows him to the door and asks what she should do. Victor tells her to stick with Monteverdi.

Victor goes to the Yugoslavian authorities in Belgrade, a man named Travik. He has to give Victor permission to talk to Anneska. She is a file clerk in his office, but went home early. Sebastian is given her home address after he says he can't stay in Belgrade very long.

He goes to Anneska's house. She lets him in, they talk. She admits Stoyan was her lover and is convinced he is coming back to her. He was captured by Germans and then the Russians took him away, but he will return. While they are talking about Stoyan, a note is slipped under her door. Victor sees it, she doesn't, and when he gets up, Sebastian nudges it back into the hallway, so he can pick it up when he leaves.

Anneska knows about the plane and it has renewed her hope that Stoyan will return. Victor closes the door behind him and picks up the note. It is to Anneska. She is to meet Stoyan at the town bridge at 9:00 p.m. Victor pockets the note.

Back at his hotel, Sebastian is visited by Travik, who takes him to task for encouraging Anneska's fantasy. Stoyan is a deserter who ran away. Travik reveals he is Karil, the commissar to the partisans. If Stoyan is found with the gold, Travik plans to execute him as a traitor. The gold will stay in Yugoslavia. He warns Victor not to interfere. When Stoyan shows, he will arrest him and then inform the Americans. Travik asks if Victor is more than a theatrical agent, but Victor states he is only researching the story for Monteverdi, so the movie will be filmed using the correct story.

Victor returns to Hoskin's office to find out if what Travik said is true. Does the gold belong to Yugoslavia? He wants to intercept Stoyan at the bridge before Travik can capture him. Hoskins won't commit

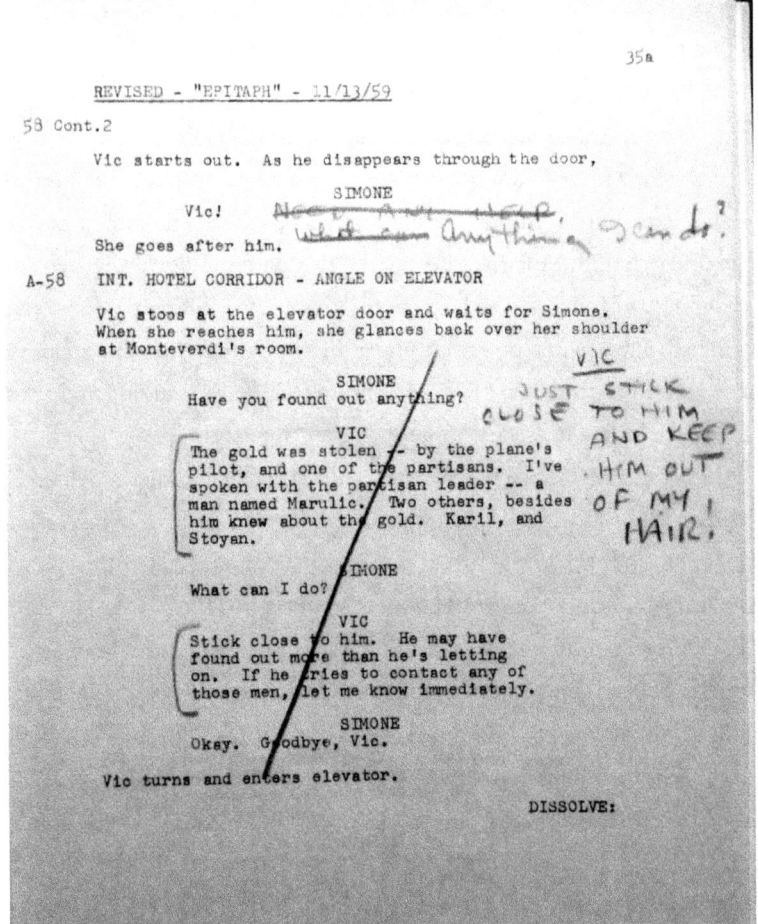

"Search for Edvard Stoyan" Script page. Courtesy of David Hedison.

to anything, he doesn't make policy. Victor asks if he wants the gold. Hoskins says yes. Victor then congratulates him on making a decision.

The phone rings. Marulic has come to Belgrade, looking for Sebastian. Hoskins offers to let them meet in his office. Marulic tells Victor to stop looking for Stoyan, he is dead. Sebastian doesn't believe him. Marulic insists. He doesn't want the gold, it only causes death, death of the partisans that night, the death of Stoyan. He warns Victor to stay out of it. He will deal with the traitors himself. Victor insists he is going to get the truth from Stoyan.

He goes to the bridge at the appointed time. He sees a man walk onto the bridge. Sebastian leaves his cover to go talk to Stoyan. The man on the bridge is not Stoyan and he has an accomplice. They try to grab Victor, but he shrugs out his coat and eludes them, jumping over the bridge rail into the river below. The two men run down the steps to a landing to launch a row boat to go after Victor. They row under the bridge. Victor swims out from under the bridge arch in the opposite direction from the men. He boosts himself up on the landing and runs across the bridge to escape.

Half way across he pauses to check on his pursuers. They are directly beneath him and the bridge ornament he is standing next to. Victor nudges the large concrete ball. It is loose, so he topples it over the side of the bridge and into their rowboat, sinking them.

Victor then runs across the bridge to escape, only to be stopped by Travik. The men in the water are his and Sebastian has blown his trap for Stoyan. Travik vows to find Stoyan by the end of the night or Victor will pay for his meddling.

Simone comes to see Monteverdi. She finds him yelling at Pontormo, who comes storming out of the hotel room. Simone asks what's going on. Pontormo says he was fired for eavesdropping on a phone call promising Monteverdi the whole story. He asks Simone for a job, then tells Simone to come have a drink with him.

Simone phones Victor, who is getting himself back together after his jump in the river. Hoskins is trying to persuade him to leave the country before Travik arrests him for interfering. Hoskins doesn't think he can get Victor out of jail if he is arrested. Simone tells Victor to hurry over to the hotel. Monteverdi is meeting with someone tonight who will reveal the whole story.

Sebastian and Hoskins rush over to the hotel. They are heading for the stairs when a shot is fired. The victim is Monteverdi, who identifies himself as Major Joseph Capella, before he falls down the stairs, shot to death.

Hoskins cannot believe Monteverdi was Capella. Under Tito the border was closed and Capella could not return for the gold until now, using his movie company as a front to haul the gold out of the mountains. Only it was not there.

Victor drops Hoskins at the Agency and goes back to question Anneska. She also tells him to quit, that Stoyan is dead. She knows it now, she wanted to believe, but it is no good. Victor cannot believe her change of story. He wants to know who got to her. He says only three people knew about the gold: Stoyan, Marulic and Travik. Sebastian smells something not there before and finds a man's cigar in the ash tray on the table.

A movement out the window brings him over there. Someone goes around the edge of the window ledge. Victor climbs out the window onto the ledge to chase him up the drainpipe and onto the roof. Once Victor reaches the roof, there is no one there.

Anneska follows him up to the roof through the garret door. She tells Sebastian she knows Stoyan is dead, because he had four steel crowns. He is the unidentified man in the mass grave. Victor now knows Travik took the gold and used it to buy his place in the current Communist government. Sebastian swears he will go home now and call for an investigation.

Travik reveals himself from the shadow of the chimney. He is the man who ran away from the window. He has a gun and is going to kill Victor and Anneska. They are the only two who know he's guilty. Marulic comes out the garret door onto the roof. He tells Anneska to go below, he will handle the traitor. Travik shoots him three times in desperation, but Marulic keeps on advancing until he grabs Travik around the neck and strangles him to death.

Victor catches Marulic as he sags and the old partisan marvels that his hands were still good enough to kill fourteen Nazis and one traitor.

So there is no gold and now everyone who was involved in the theft is dead.

David Hedison's script notes and changes for Episode 14:

Simone is told she's going to Belgrade. This scene is totally rewritten, they are now in Vic's room with Robbie and there is no negligee. Most of David's handwritten dialogue makes it into the episode. NBC (probably) nixed the negligee.

Scene where Hoskins and Sebastian check the plane is rewritten. Again most of David's dialogue makes it in. Extensively rewritten in red pencil on back of script pages. David did not remember why he rewrote this scene, but it definitely plays better than what was originally written.

Donkey cart ride is uneventful. There is supposed to be a sniper shooting at them, but that was cut from the aired version. Simone is told to stick to Monteverdi. This scene is severely cut down from the script and dialogue written by Hedison is used instead.

We are supposed to see a picture of Stoyan and Anneska in Anneska's apartment. We are shown the back of picture frame. We never do see Stoyan, probably because no actor was cast in this role to save money.

David has written in the script that the note he finds slipped under Anneska's door should be written in Serbian. It was not.

Victor is more dressed in the episode after his swim than in the script. He's supposed to be in a towel and then leave the room to get dressed. Victor is already dressed and combing his wet hair when the scene starts in the episode.

When asked, David said he had no objection to being in a towel, but apparently NBC did. Like the negligee above, the director was told to "Cover up his stars. This is TV."

Scene 106: Pontormo tells Victor and Hoskins he knows the name of the partisan, but then he can't remember it. This whole scene has been

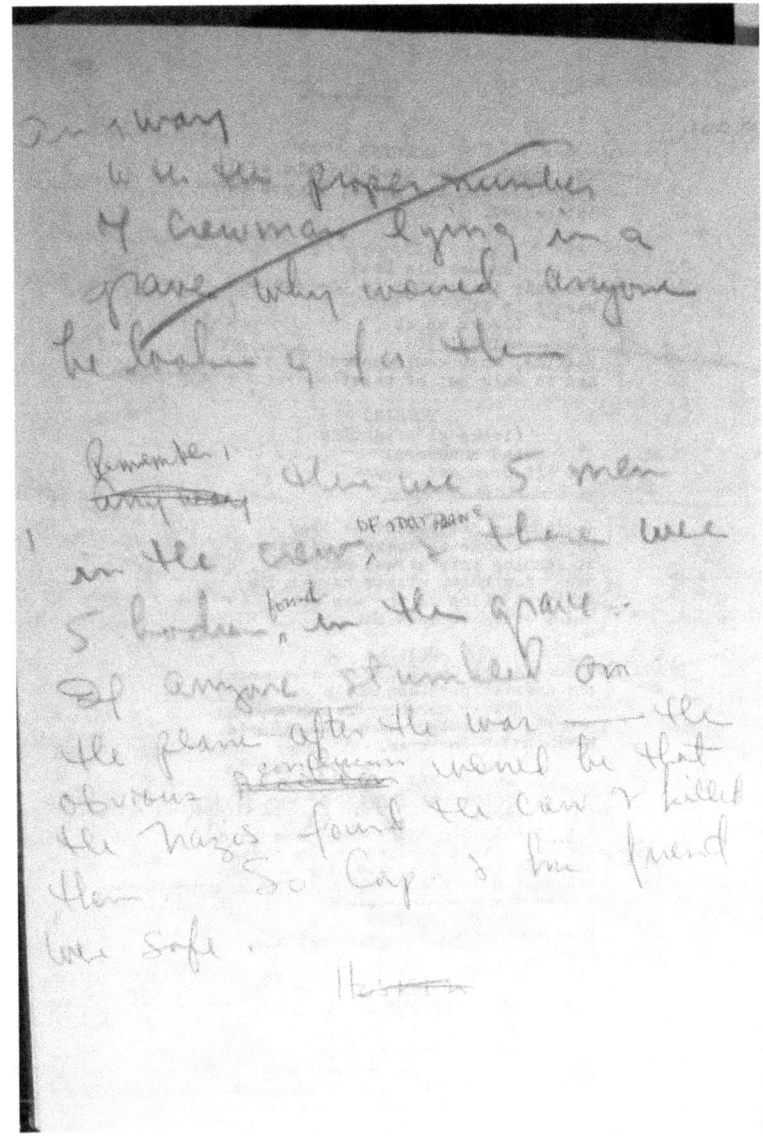

"Search for Edvard Stoyan" Script page. Courtesy of David Hedison.

cut from the episode. For time most likely. David does not remember why it was not filmed.

Scene 107 Monteverdi/Capella's death: It does not take place in his room. He does not answer the door. Victor does not catch him when he falls. Same death line for Monteverdi does, however, remain in the episode.

Capella falls down the stairs to his death? This wasn't written for Balsam. Balsam dies the same way in *Psycho* this same year. (1960). Was this a coincidence or planned?

Anneska is supposed to escape to get help. She finds Marulic. This doesn't happen. Roof scene cut by at least half. Marulic uses his hands, not a gun. Marulic is killed, does not escape.

Ending explanation to Simone in the gondola ultimately cut from episode. Episode ends with Marulic's death. Again, this may have been cut because the episode was running too long.

David mentioned this was filmed late in the season and that there may have been budget cuts that led to all the above trimming. So only about two-thirds of what was written for this episode made it to the television screen.

David Hedison's *Five Fingers* (green) bound Script book.
Courtesy of David Hedison.

Chapter 12

Episode Synopses: Unaired Episodes 15–16; Missing Production #3715

Episode 15: "A Shot in the Dark" #3716
[Only aired in syndication]

Location: South America

TV Guide [On-line] listing: Two agents have been killed. Sebastian's only lead: an alcoholic Englishman (Ronald Howard). Sebastian: David Hedison. Georgia: Joanna Moore. Rita: Neile Adams.

Credited cast:
Ronald Howard (John Dennis)
Neile Adams [McQueen Toffel] (Rita Juan)
Alf Kjellin (Johann Manfred)

Robert Carricart (Dr. Alvarez)
Joanna Moore (Georgia Stevens)
Harold Ayer (Jackson)
Jay Adler (Franco)
Mario Gallo (Waiter)

Monthly Film Bulletin (8/61 no. 331). According to their reviewer, "Victor Sebastian pins down a counter-organization operating in South America."

This episode was unavailable for preview. It is not held by the UCLA Film and Television Library and was unavailable from any other source.

Victor peers out of a car he is hiding in trying to find out who is shooting at him. Copyright 20th Century Fox Studios.

Episode Synopses: Unaired Episodes

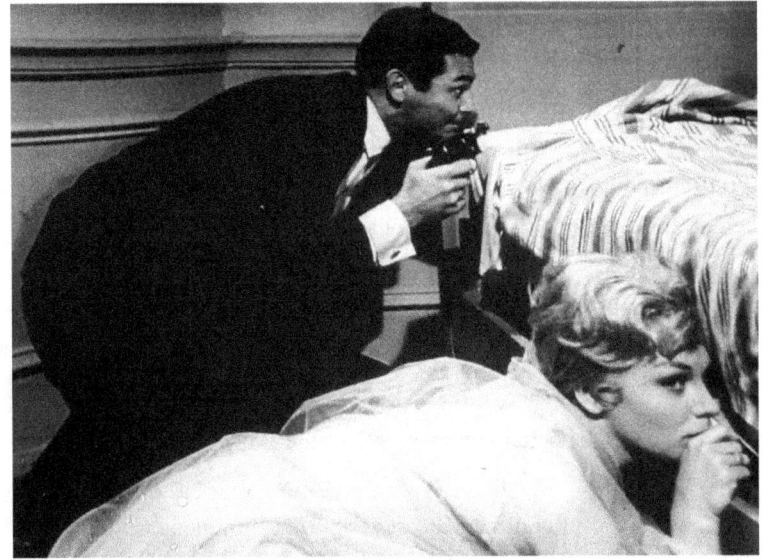

"A Shot in the Dark." David Hedison with Joanna Moore. Copyright 20th Century Fox Studios.

Episode 16: "Counterfeit" #3717

[Only aired in syndication]

TV Guide [On-line] listing: Sebastian (David Hedison) matches wits with the head of a counterfeiting ring. Ferri: Cesar Romero. Mario: Yale Wexler. Simone: Luciana Paluzzi. Robertson: Paul Burke. Alberti: Peter Brocco.

Credited cast:
Cesar Romero (Ferri)
Joseph Ruskin (Lampi)
Yale Wexler (Mario)
Peter Brocco (Alberti)
Montgomery Pittman (Tex Martin)
Eric Feldary (Cashier)

Michael Granger (Police Officer)
Richard Morris (T-Man)
Joseph Waring (Casino Official)

The Team is sent to the Riviera to help Treasury agents find who is behind the counterfeiting of US dollars.

Synopsis from *Monthly Film Bulletin* (1/61 no. 323) "Posing as a millionairess, Simone attracts the attention of a confidence trickster, Tex Martin, who steals [her] money. The forgers kill Martin, discover that [her] money is [a] better counterfeit than their own, and try to come to an arrangement with Simone. Ferri, a journalist, reveals himself as the brains of the outfit and then realises [sic] that Simone is working with Robertson and attempts to kill her. [Simone] is rescued in the nick of time."

This episode was unavailable for preview. It is not held by the UCLA Film and Television Library and was unavailable from any other source.

Episode Notes:
Brett Halsey said: "Charles Rondeau was a good director. He should have done more feature films. I got him his first job in television, directing my (ex) wife Luciana in *Five Fingers*."

Rondeau would direct David Hedison again in the Fox series *Voyage to the Bottom of the Sea* in the fourth season episodes *Nightmare*, *Secret of the Deep* (clip show), and *Death Clock*. *Nightmare* and *Death Clock* were both psychological effects-laden episodes involving Crane thinking he had gone mad. He is tormented by an alien in *Nightmare*, and then travels into the fourth dimension via a time machine in *Death Clock* to an alternate reality where Crane kills Nelson. Actually it's his fourth dimension self that kills Nelson ... but I digress.

David Hedison liked doing *Voyage* episodes with a lot of drama

Episode Synopses: Unaired Episodes

for his character. He really liked directors who welcomed his input and would let him try the scene several different ways until he found what it was he wanted to do in service to what had been written for him.

Episode #3715 is missing from the production order. The show went on to film #3716 and #3717. I asked David if he remembered anything about this missing episode, but he does not remember skipping one. It was fifty years ago.

#3715 could have been the episode seventeen that the cast was supposed to film when everyone came back from the Thanksgiving/Christmas break. David said when he went to pick up his script, they told him, "Don't come in, the show has been canceled." These sixteen episodes were all that were filmed, but they went on to be syndicated in the United States and all over the world. This series is well-liked, but very hard to find.

Paul Burke, Luciana Paluzzi and Cesar Romero. From the episode "Counterfeit." Copyright 20th Century Fox.

Chapter 13

Recurring Guest Stars

Alan Napier as Wembley, Senior Partner in Wembley and Sebastian.

Alan Napier (1903-1988) was a cousin of Neville Chamberlain, Britain's prime minister from 1937 to 1940. Napier studied at the Royal Academy of Dramatic Art, later joining the Oxford Players to spend a decade treading the boards on the West End stage with fellow actors such as Lawrence Olivier and John Gielgud.

His 6'6" height and carefully modulated voice earned him supporting roles in over ninety films in England starting in 1930. His British motion pictures included *Caste, In a Monastery* and *The Secret Four*. However, Napier continued with theater work, as he was unable to break through to lead roles in film.

Napier came to New York City in 1940 to co-star with Gladys George in *Lady in Waiting*. In the US, Napier found his niche performing Shakespeare up and down the Eastern seaboard, but he had his eye on Hollywood, where there was a community of British expatriates who helped each other land roles, a successful maneuver when you consider the group included luminaries like director James Whale. Napier found steady work via this connection, usually playing a lawyer or a doctor. He appeared in such films as *Cat People* (1942), *The Uninvited* (1943), and *House of Horror* (1946). He also appeared in two Shakespeare films: the Orson Welles version of *Macbeth* (1948), in which he played a priest Welles added to the story, and MGM's *Julius Caesar* (1953), in which he played Cicero. In *The Song of Bernadette* (1943), Napier played the ethically questionable psychiatrist who is hired to declare Bernadette mentally ill. Napier also played the vicious Earl of Warwick in *Joan of Arc* (1948).

In 1949, he made his first television appearance, as Sherlock Holmes in the *Your Show Time* adaptation of "The Adventure of the Speckled Band." He took time off from television to try Broadway again in 1952 in *Gertie* starring Glynis Johns, but the show closed after five performances. He would attempt another Broadway show in 1956, but essentially, he had now become a television and film actor.

In the 1951 *Fireside Theatre*'s episode of "A Christmas Carol," Napier played the story's narrator, Charles Dickens. There was some irony in the role, as this episode also featured his wife's only American credit as Mrs. Fezziwig. Although her stage name was Gypsy Raine, Mrs. Alan Napier was in fact Aileen Dickens Downing, Charles Dickens' great-granddaughter.

Napier also appeared in the *20th Century Fox Hour* adaption of "Operation Cicero" in 1956 with Ricardo Montalban as Cicero and Peter Lorre as Moyzisch, playing the British attaché Travers, the role originated by Michael Rennie in *5 Fingers* (1952).

Alan Napier in 1960. Copyright 20th Century Fox Studios.

By 1966, Napier was sixty-three and good roles were beginning to taper off. He was considering retirement and a return to England when he received a call from his agent. He would later retell the story in an interview: "I had never read comics before I [was hired for *Batman*]. My agent rang up and said, 'I think you are going to play on *Batman*,' I said 'What is *Batman*?' He said, 'Don't you read the comics?' I said, 'No, never.' He said, 'I think you are going to be Batman's butler.' I said, 'How do I know I want to be Batman's butler?' It was the most ridiculous thing I had ever heard of. He said, 'It may be worth over $100,000.' So I said I was Batman's butler." Napier was the first cast member hired for *Batman*; his agent had been a colleague of Charles FitzSimons, who had become the assistant to producer William Dozier.

The TV series killed his film career. *Batman: The Movie* (1966) was his final film role. However, the series reinvigorated his television career and he would make guest appearances in a variety of roles for another decade including the miniseries *QB VII* and *The Paper Chase*.

Napier is the grandfather of actor Brian Forster, best known as portraying (the second) Chris Partridge on the television series *The Partridge Family*.

Michael Romanoff as Prince Dimitri Blanc

Michael Romanoff (1890-1971) was a Hollywood restaurateur and actor born Hershel Geguzin in Lithuania. He was best known as the owner of *Romanoff's*, a Beverly Hills restaurant popular with Hollywood stars in the 1940s and 1950s. The restaurant closed in 1962.

In the original version of *Miracle on 34th Street* (1947), a doctor expresses the opinion that Kris Kringle (Edmund Gwenn) is of no harm to anyone despite his insistence that he is Santa Claus. He compares him to a [then] well-known restaurant owner, whose name escapes him at the moment, who keeps insisting that he is a member of the Russian Royal family, but is otherwise quite normal.

Anastasia, starring Ingrid Bergman, was a huge hit for Fox in 1956, and won her an Oscar, so *another* member of the Russian royal family would not be out of place on the Fox lot doing a TV show in 1959.

In *Five Fingers*, Romanoff basically played his "reinvented" self, right down to his character name of Prince Dimitri Blanc. He owns the nightclub in the pilot and caters parties in the episodes "Moment of Truth" and "Operation Ramrod."

Romanoff pretended to be Russian royalty. In actuality, he was a former pants presser once named Harry Gerguson. He eventually became a successful professional impostor known as Prince Michael Romanoff. Harry accumulated an enormous font of knowledge in his numerous travels and occupations around the world and managed to attend, however briefly, Harvard and Oxford.

When Hollywood filmmakers needed a technical adviser for a movie set in Europe, Romanoff claimed to be an expert. He was paid to do this several times. The genial Romanoff was a popular figure in the movie colony, a great raconteur who always amused with his stories of his "royal" life.

When "Mike" finally opened his restaurant in 1939, it was bankrolled and then frequented by many lions of the film industry. Romanoff married his restaurant bookkeeper, Gloria Lister, in 1948.

Romanoff made several screen appearances, but his best role as "Prince Michael" was in *Sing While You're Able* (1937). In April 1957, Romanoff was a mystery guest on the TV panel show *What's My Line?* Romanoff was supposed to be the subject of his own film, *The Instant Prince*, but it never was made, probably due to the turnover of studio heads from Adler to Skouras during the time (1960) the idea was pitched.

After his restaurant closed in 1962, Mike spent his last nine years appearing as an extra, mostly as himself, in several films. Mike plays himself in a re-creation of Romanoff's restaurant (custom built on the Fox lot) in the 1967 film, *The Guide for the Married Man*, right down to the red menus and the signature *Strawberries Romanoff* dessert.

Five Fingers: Elegance in Espionage

In 1982, the episode "Murder in Aspic" of the detective series *Matt Houston* paid homage to Romanoff by having Matt's client, a volatile Russian restaurant owner, as played by Sid Caesar, modeled after the Prince. You have to be in on this gag to catch the references. The French food critic who is trying to frame the Prince is none other than David Hedison. And Sid Caesar was the man who trashed Romanoff's restaurant to avoid getting caught out by his wife in *The Guide for the Married Man* film.

Romanoff claimed he was Prince Michael Dimitri Alexandrovich Obolensky-Romanoff, nephew of the late Tsar Nicholas II. Everyone in Hollywood knew he wasn't, but in a town full of pretenders, it hardly mattered. "Prince Michael" enjoyed great success as a restaurateur. Never mind the Tsar had spelled his name Romanov. The real Prince Michael was killed by Bolsheviks in the Ural Mountains in 1918.

Our "Prince Michael" was actually born Hershel Geguzin in the Jewish ghetto of what is now Vilnius, Lithuania. In 1890, it was known as Vilna, a part of Poland that had been taken over by Imperial Russia. Herschel was the last of six children born to Hinde and Emmanuel Geguzin. His parents ran a successful dry goods store until Emmanuel was killed in Warsaw while trying to break up a fight, six months before Hershel's birth.

Hinde took over the business and over the next decade built it up even more by adding a tailor shop with the help of her oldest children. Her children had a strict routine of going to Hebrew school and working within the business. Her oldest daughter, Olga, was charged with raising the youngest boy, but he disliked school and his chosen trade. Hershel often ran away after he was punished for not going to school or doing his share of the sewing and pressing.

Imperial Russia had no love of Jews. Hershel was not adhering to the Jewish community model proscribed for him that would protect him from the periodic pogroms. At wit's end, Hinde consulted the community elders to determine what his fate should be. It was decided

Hershel should go to America, to New York, where his inclination to be independent would be more tolerated. When Hinde's cousin announced he was taking his family over to the United States, Hinde paid him to take the troublesome Hershel with them.

Geguzin immigrated to New York City at age ten illegally as a child of that relative and came through Ellis Island as Herschel Bloomberg. The cousin ultimately couldn't do anything with him, either, didn't want him and basically let Hershel run away.

The authorities found Hershel "abandoned" as a twelve year old and living on the streets. They put him in the Hebrew orphanage, registering him as Harry Gaygussen. "Harry" behaved no better at the orphanage and was labeled incorrigible, which led to his being placed in the New York Juvenile Asylum. There his name was changed to Harry F. Gerguson in another attempt to anglicize his name. In later years Romanoff would deny the name Gerguson, saying he had never been consulted in the matter.

He was sent to the Children's Village and made to go to school. There he learned English and became Americanized enough to be placed out as an indentured servant. He was sent out to Illinois, which allowed indenture, but he didn't last long on the farm.

Hershel made his way into the nearest town, Hillsboro, and told folks his name was Harry Ferguson. The townsfolk took him in, sent him to school and let him work as an errand boy and pants presser. The oldest in the school, he took a shine to the female teacher and learned everything she could teach him in a year, but ended up being kicked out by his benefactor for not doing the work he was supposed to.

He then moved to Litchfield, found another benefactor, and put himself through high school for another year by stoking furnaces and being a bellhop after school. He ran afoul of the Superintendent for not being the most model student and was kicked out of Litchfield. Hershel was returned to New York, where one more indentured servant placement was tried, and failed, at a ranch in Texas.

At nineteen, Hershel worked off his passage to England on a cattle ship and found work in London as a presser and a valet to Oxford Students. He learned enough about that lifestyle to convincingly pose as an actual student of the University, for which he was arrested and put in Liverpool prison for the duration of World War I and perhaps beyond. Harry turned up in Paris in 1921 and worked alongside two expatriate Russian princes as book shelvers at the American Library. All was well until the police showed up with Harry's suitcase and it was widely assumed they had it because he had been released from French prison. The wife of the librarian saw to it Harry was fired, but not until he had tried out his "Prince Michael" routine, based on what he had learned from his co-workers, on the Left Bank to some success.

Gerguson came back to America in 1922, failed to pass immigration and was detained. He left custody at Ellis Island and went to Minnesota, worked the summer for the Weyerhaeuser family, supposedly receiving a scholarship to Harvard. He was exposed as a fraud there, came back to New York, was arrested for what happened at Harvard, and went to jail again.

His cloudy immigration status and constant lack of funds led Harry (as he was now being called) to spend most of the thirties in and out of jails, when he wasn't being deported for some failed scheme or impersonating someone he was not. During one of these impersonations (on Broadway), *The New Yorker* magazine ran a series of four profiles of his royal highness, starting October 29, 1932, which traced his history from birth until date of publication. Gerguson was then deported to France to serve time for a fraud he had done there.

With New York home to countless Russians of noble birth who had escaped the Bolsheviks, Mike was always being denounced as an impostor Prince, particularly when the real Grand Duke Dmitri was invited to meet his "kinsman." Romanoff made a quick exit stage left at this particular soiree, after saying it would be rude to converse in Russian in front of their non-speaking hosts.

Well into his forties now and tired of being on the lam from immigration, Mike decided to return to Los Angeles one last time in 1936 to try to go straight. He had a modest career playing backgammon or chess for money and usually won, all the while encouraging his Romanoff fantasy and letting the rich pay false court to him. He became widely admired and was often feted and encouraged to entertain as the famous Russian prince.

One actor who enjoyed Romanoff's company was David Niven. He was a frequent visitor to the restaurant. Niven also used Romanoff as a caterer for his dinner parties. He would sit in his booth at the restaurant (Niven gives the date as 1947) and watch Mike maitre d', dismissing Pasadena society people, Texas oilmen and even generals as peasants not worthy of being seated, but who went out of his way to give a "free" meal to a Hollywood writer who had returned from World War II service, only to find he had been forgotten.

By 1947, Romanoff had evolved from an international con man deported from no less than England, France and the US for passing bad checks, and selling object d' art that he had "liberated" from their true owners, into a respectable restaurant owner. Quite a change from someone who had had been twice caught and arrested as a stowaway (in a first class cabin, mind you) on transatlantic ocean liners.

Niven first met Mike in New York, at a speakeasy during Prohibition. Mike operated on a sliding scale of kinship with the murdered czar, sometimes claiming to be his nephew, or his half-brother or, more often, the son of Prince Yusupov, who tried to kill the mad monk Rasputin. In Chicago, Mike passed himself off as a British relation to the Duke of Wellington, a Sir Arthur Wellesley, and liked to refer to the then Prince of Wales (Edward VIII) as "my cousin, David."

He was employed by Fox studios as a reader and/or synopsis writer, when needed, and worked well there and at other studios, even getting paid for what he did. Niven tended to only see him when he needed a bed for the night. Mike would then hitchhike his way to David's house in Santa Monica to find one. Niven did not begrudge him that, as Mike never asked to borrow money from him, *only* the bed.

In 1937, Mike obtained a lease on a defunct building on the Sunset Strip. He threw a party, charged a $50 cover, and had everyone bring their own wine. The hash joint down the street provided the food (from the cover charge) and they raised enough money to install a kitchen.

Mike was in the restaurant business. The first Romanoff's that opened in 1939 did so well that most of his "investors" sold their shares back to Mike. He prospered at that location during the war and by 1945 had moved to a much more upscale location in Beverly Hills, at 326 N. Rodeo Drive, with the Imperial R on the door. He would move once more in 1951, into a bigger and more elaborate establishment at 140 S. Rodeo Drive and his staff and clients went with him. Romanoff's had become the place to be seen.

It started with a friendship with Irving "Swifty" Lazar, who was Humphrey Bogart's agent. Bogart, in the years before his death, would have lunch at Romanoff's. He was always seated at Table Number One in the front, where he could be seen by all.

Bogart's circle of friends was called the Holmby Hills Rat Pack and was the originator of that name. Sinatra became a member, but did not lead the pack until after Bogart's death, when the membership changed to include the more familiar names. The original pack included Lazar, Sid Luft and his wife, Judy Garland, David Niven and of course, Lauren Bacall.

When Sinatra took over, the group traveled more and dined less in Los Angeles, which in turn impacted the expectations at Romanoff's. Only the select few could sit up front in the booths "to be seen" while the rest (and the tourists) had to eat in the dining room that held 170. When Bogart died, table number one passed to Spencer Tracy and so on.

Sinatra did not hold court the way Bogart had and increasingly asked for more privacy and the upstairs room where he and his many friends didn't have to mingle or be ogled by the rest of the diners.

The cachet of Romanoff's had always been "to see and be seen," but the younger stars didn't want to do that with the grace the older stars had and in the end it was the demise of that era and the restaurant. Mike retired and Romanoff's left the stage. Closed in 1962, the building was sold and the restaurant demolished in 1964.

Mike was supposed to write a book about his adventures and apparently attempted to do so, but then asked Gloria to burn the manuscript as he lay dying. Mike lived to be eighty, a rogue and a charmer to the last, who is well remembered by those who knew him. He died of a heart attack in Los Angeles, on September 1, 1971.

Kurt Niklas, Mike's head waiter and catering chief, had learned a lot. He opened a series of restaurants called The Bistro, then The Bistro Gardens, shortly after the third incarnation of Romanoff's closed. Mike, in retirement, was always welcome there and often was, so the most of his clients gravitated to Kurt, as he served many of the same favorite dishes. Kurt's bistros stayed in business for another thirty years. A funny thing happened at the Bistro Gardens in 1988 that brings us full circle.

David Hedison was dining at Kurt's place with his wife, Bridget, when he noticed Cubby Broccoli and his wife Dana were eating at another table. David waved hello. He knew the Broccolis and had attended parties at their home, but he didn't want to intrude any more than that. On their way out, Cubby stopped and spoke to David briefly, saying hello back.

Shortly after that, David's agent got a call to see if David was interested in reprising his role as Felix Leiter in the upcoming Timothy Dalton James Bond film, *Licence to Kill*. The old Romanoff adage "to see and be seen" was in full force *that* night.

Roger Moore recently shared a Mike Romanoff story when he was interviewed on a BBC2 radio program August 11, 2014, to plug his continuing work with UNICEF and to let everyone know he had a new memoir coming out in the UK, called *Last Man Standing*. There is a US edition of this book, titled *One Lucky Bastard*, also published in 2014.

Roger was talking to Frank Sinatra about the 1971 death of Romanoff. Frank was lamenting how much he missed going to Romanoff's and how all his old friends from there were dying. Frank vowed to get some younger friends and asked Roger on the spot to be his friend. Moore credits Frank's friendship offer to "Prince Michael." One of the best characters he ever met.

Mike Romanoff with David Hedison. Copyright 20th Century Fox Studios.

CHAPTER 14

GUEST STARS

Author's note: I have tried to track down anyone who was credited or uncredited, if I happened to recognize them in these sixteen filmed episodes. However, some of these cast members have been lost to time and the death of Fox's contract system in 1962. It's pretty amazing who did show up in these episodes.

Episodes 1-8

Episode 1: Station Break

David Opatoshu (1918-1996) was an American film, stage and television actor. He was born David Opatovsky in New York City. His father was the noted Yiddish writer Joseph Opatoshu. Opatoshu's career in television began in 1952 and spanned five decades. He also appeared in forty-five movie roles. His education and ethnicity led to frequent roles as Jewish or Arabic characters such as in *Raid on Entebbe* (1976) and the 1980s miniseries *Masada*. He adapted his father's 1917 novel *Romance of a Horsethief* into a 1971 film starring Yul Brynner and Eli Wallach. He said the role he was most identified with was an appearance on the original *Star Trek* episode "A Taste of Armageddon," in which he played Anan 7.

Theodore Marcuse (1920-1967) was classically trained to specialize in Shakespearean roles. He appeared on Broadway in "Medea" in 1949 with Dame Judith Anderson. In Hollywood, his training was usurped by his appearance. His sinister countenance was enhanced by a shaven head that accentuated his elephantine ears that made him a staple for villain characters on television. Marcuse was later cast as Dr. Gamma in the pilot of *Voyage to the Bottom of the Sea*. Gamma was originally conceived to be a recurring villain role, but when Marcuse was asked to return to studio to loop his lines, he was under contract to another series and unavailable. His part went to air with the voice-over done by Werner Klemperer.

Author's note: Marcuse served in World War II as a lieutenant (j.g.) on the famed submarine Tirante. *Other officers onboard included future Massachusetts governor Endicott Peabody and author Edward L. Beach, Jr. Beach was the sub's XO. The* Tirante *was the subject of an episode of the syndicated television anthology series* The Silent Service *during the 1957-1958 season.*

Greta Keller (1903-1977) was born in Vienna where she studied dancing and drama. By 1929, she had a record contract with Ultraphon. Her career as a singer took her from Vienna to Prague and Berlin. In the

1930s, she became a star in America as well, appearing on Broadway with Marlene Dietrich, making film appearances with Fox and as a frequent guest vocalist on radio. Rod McKuen wrote the classic chanson "If You Go Away" for her. Keller spent many years performing a lounge act; it became de rigueur to see her at the Waldorf and, later, the Stanhope in New York City. Her show always included the song "My Way," by Paul Anka, and several Noel Coward numbers. Returning to Austria often, she died there in 1977.

Eva Gabor (1919-1995) was a Hungarian-born socialite and actress. She is most remembered for her role as Lisa Douglas, the society wife on the 1960s TV series *Green Acres*. She also had success as an actress on Broadway, on television dramas, and in films, including the classic musical *Gigi* (1958). Her elder sisters, Zsa Zsa and Magda, were also actresses and socialites. And like her sisters, Eva's career was often overshadowed by her string of failed marriages.

Tyler McVey (1912-2003) began his career in radio in 1937 as part of a group of free-lance radio actors whose voices were heard on the various programs originating from Hollywood. He appeared in over 1,000 episodes of radio, ranging from comedies such as *The Great Gildersleeve* to *The Hermit's Cave*, a horror anthology. In addition to his voice work, McVey became an important figure in the American Federation of Radio Artists. When the union allowed TV performers to join, becoming AFTRA, McVey served as president, first of the Los Angeles local, then the national organization. He served on the board of directors for over thirty years. As television began its ascendancy over radio, McVey transitioned into the visual media. His first film role was at Fox with a bit part in *The Day the Earth Stood Still* (1951). At forty years old, McVey launched a new career as a character actor, playing authority figures: police, military, clergy, and lawyers. Included in the list was *Voyage* *to the Bottom of the Sea*, where he appeared twice, playing a general and a Washington official.

Ron Howard (1954-   ) appears briefly as an intrusive child playing in the sand with his bucket. Based on air dates, this was Howard's first (uncredited) TV role with a grand total of one line. Howard had been signed to a contract by Fox to appear in the Deborah Kerr movie *Dark Passage*, which was released in March of 1959. That summer, the five-year-old Ron would appear in four TV shows, including *Johnny Ringo* and *The Twilight Zone*, as part of his contract. The fifth appearance was *The Danny Thomas Show*, in an episode that would launch *The Andy Griffith Show* in 1960. Howard's career included the equally popular *Happy Days* TV series before he switched to the other side of the camera. Ron became a successful movie director with a resume that includes *Splash* (1984), *Apollo 13* (1995), *Beautiful Mind* (2001), *The Da Vinci Code* (2006) and *Rush* (2013). He is considered one of the most successful child actors ever and has completed filming on his third Harry Langdon film with Tom Hanks, based on the books of Dan Brown.

Episode 2: Dossier

Edgar Bergen (1903-1978) was an American ventriloquist, actor and radio performer. Bergen and his alter-ego Charlie McCarthy appeared together with top billing in several films, including the Technicolor extravaganza *The Goldwyn Follies* (1938) opposite the Ritz Brothers. That year they also appeared in *You Can't Cheat an Honest Man* with W. C. Fields. At the height of their popularity in 1938, Bergen was presented an Honorary Oscar (in the form of a wooden Oscar statuette) for his creation of Charlie McCarthy. Although his popular radio series never made the transition to television, Bergen made numerous appearances on the medium during his career. Bergen appeared on the NBC interview program *Here's Hollywood* and on a first season episode of the series

Edgar Bergen with Charlie McCarthy. Copyright Edgar Bergen Estate.

Voyage to the Bottom of the Sea called "The Fear Makers." He was Grandpa Walton in the original *The Waltons* TV-movie, "The Homecoming: A Christmas Story." (1971). Bergen died shortly after completing his scenes in *The Muppet Movie* (1979), making it his final performance. The film was subsequently dedicated to him.

John Williams (1903-1983) was tall, urbane and mustachioed, making him the quintessential British character actor. Williams went from his London stage debut in 1916 as John Darling in a production of *Peter Pan* to a Broadway debut with *The Fake* in 1924. He often returned to Broadway, performing in thirty plays over the next four decades. His first film role was in 1930, debuting in director Mack Sennett's *The Chumps*. In 1953, Williams was awarded a Tony Award for his role as Chief Inspector Hubbard in *Dial M for Murder* on Broadway; he would recreate the role in the film and TV adaptations. Williams became a recognized celebrity as the star of a TV commercial for 120 Music Masterpieces, a four-LP set of classical music excerpts from Columbia Records. This spot became the longest-running national commercial in U.S. television history airing for thirteen years, from 1971 to 1984.

Constantine (John Williams) gets the drop on Victor in the episode "Dossier." Copyright 20th Century Fox Studios.

Kurt Krueger (1916-2006) was born in Germany and raised in Switzerland. He made his screen debut in *Mystery Sea Raider* (1940) and then joined the Broadway cast of Maxwell Anderson's anti-Nazi drama *Candle in the Wind* starring Helen Hayes. Krueger returned to Hollywood, playing a Nazi aviator in *Edge of Darkness* (1943) with Errol Flynn and Ann Sheridan. His first leading role (and his personal favorite) was for RKO in 1944. Produced by Val Lewton and directed by

Robert Wise, *Mademoiselle Fifi* was based on two short stories by Guy de Maupassant about the vital role of the middle-class in war compared to the uselessness of the upper class. After a fight over typecasting with Fox in 1949, he broke his contract and returned to Germany. He continued to make films, including the comedy *Die Blau Stunde* (1953), his only onscreen singing credit, and *La Paura* (1954), the final film in which director Roberto Rossellini worked with his wife Ingrid Bergman. In 1956, he returned to California in time to join the cast in his most memorable role, a German U-boat officer in *The Enemy Below* (1957) against David Hedison, and Robert Mitchum. Krueger continued to act, primarily on television. Shrewd real estate investments had allowed him the luxury of turning down roles while he pursued his other passions; skiing and renovating houses for lease. His last film was *The St Valentine's Day Massacre* (1967).

Anthony Eustrel (1902-1979) was an English actor, equally at home filming in Hollywood or London. His first film role was in the spy drama *Second Bureau* (1936), an English remake of *Deuxième Bureau* (1935). He also had a noted career as a Shakespearean actor with the Stratford Memorial Theatre in the 1940s, before signing with Fox Studios and being cast almost immediately in some of their most famous films of the 1950s such as *The Robe* (1953) and *Titanic* (1953).

Author's Note: David Hedison told me Eustrel directed him in Shakespeare's Much Ado about Nothing *at the Music Box Theatre in New York City in 1952. David's credit was as a page, but he also told me he was the (uncredited) understudy for the role of Claudio.*

Frank Wolff (1928-1971) won the UCLA best actor award twice: once for the title role in *Macbeth in* 1951 and as Satine in *The Lower Depths* (1952). In spite of his collegiate thespian acclaim, he struggled to break into professional films. His break came with increasingly larger roles in five Roger Corman films. A few interspersed television appearances suggested his career was already stalling, so when Corman asked him to fly to Greece and co-star in another low-budget film, the sword & sandal epic *Atlas* (1961), Wolff jumped at the opportunity. Actor Brett Halsey had recently arrived in Rome and had been urging Wolff to join him after *Atlas* wrapped. Wolff agreed and remained in Europe, joining a community of American actors in high demand for gialli films, spaghetti westerns, and Eurospy adventures. Wolff became a well-known character actor in over fifty, mostly Italian, films in the 1960s. He returned to Greece to co-star in the 1963 Best Picture Oscar nominated *America, America* for producer/director/writer Elia Kazan. While filming *Quando le Donne Persero la Coda* (1972), Wolff, who had battled depression his entire life, committed suicide. His unfortunate death affected Brett Halsey, who made the actor's death, thinly disguised, a major theme in his roman à clef novel, *The Magnificent Strangers*, published in 2001.

Ted Otis (1936-) is best remembered for his first film role, one he didn't get a screen credit for. The 1952 biopic of John Philip Sousa, *Stars and Stripes Forever*, ends with a marching band led by Otis as a baton twirling drum major. The part was not a stretch. Under his real name, Ted Smirniotis, he was a nationally famous teacher, performer, and authority on baton twirling who had been teaching twirling for more than seventeen years. Although Otis did move away from batons in his brief film and television career, his real employment was as a lecturer and guest instructor at cheerleading camps.

William Kendis (1916-1980) worked steadily in television through the 1960s. He played characters that were supposed to blend seamlessly into the background, making his career far more extensive than his credits might suggest. When he was given a substantial role, his work was memorable, such as his part as Jack Benny's evil supervisor in the *General Electric Theater* episode "The Fenton Touch," a remake of an episode of the radio show *Suspense* which Benny had previously immortalized. Kendis' first role was in *Come Next Spring* (1956), an Ann Sheridan drama written by Montgomery Pittman. Kendis was directed by Pittman twice more, once for this *Five Fingers* episode and again in a *Twilight Zone* episode.

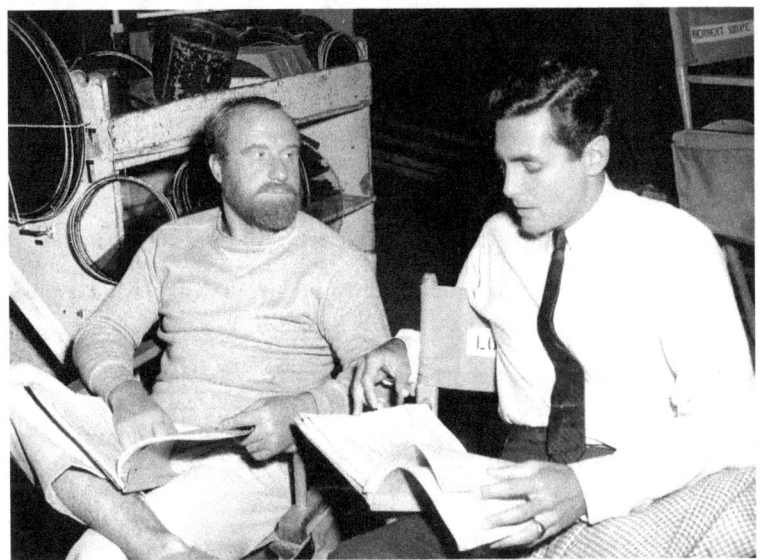

Jack Warden on the set with David Hedison. Since David is sitting in Luciana's set chair, we'll assume Jack was "invited" to "have a seat" in David's set chair. Copyright 20th Century Fox Studios. Photo courtesy of David Hedison.

Episode 3: The Moment of Truth

Jack Warden (1920-2006) had a successful movie career in addition to starring in five television series. Warden's breakthrough film role was his performance as Juror No. 7, a salesman who wants a quick decision in a murder case, in *12 Angry Men* (1957). He received a supporting actor Emmy Award for his performance as Chicago Bears coach George Halas in *Brian's Song* in 1972. Warden was twice nominated for his starring role in the 1980s comedy series *Crazy Like a Fox*. David Hedison also appeared as a guest star on *Crazy Like a Fox*. Warden was also nominated for best supporting actor Academy Awards for his performances in *Shampoo* (1975) and *Heaven Can Wait* (1978). He had notable roles in such films as *All the President's Men* (1976), *And Justice for All* (1979) and *Being There* (1980), *Used Cars* (in which he played a dual role in 1980), *The Verdict* (1982), and *While You Were Sleeping* (1995). Warden appeared in over one hundred movies. His last film was *The Replacements* (2000).

Nehemiah Persoff (1919-   ) was a New York actor discovered by Charles Laughton and cast in his production of *Galileo* in 1947. He made his film debut a year later (uncredited) in *The Naked City* (1948). Persoff became a well-known character actor with credits that crossed over genres in both film and theater. He would work with David Hedison again in the second season *Voyage to the Bottom of the Sea* episode "Deadly Creature Below" and as the Prophet Shemaiah to Hedison's Apostle Philip in *The Greatest Story Ever Told* (1965). His film credits range from *On the Waterfront* (1954) to *Some Like It Hot* (1959) to *An American Tail* (1986). Now retired from acting, he devotes his time to painting, particularly watercolors.

Edward Atienza (1924-   ) was born in London, training for the stage at the London Academy of Music and Dramatic Art. He made his professional stage debut in a 1949 production of *Up in Mabel's Room*, then joined the Shakespeare Memorial Theatre Company from 1950 through 1954. He made his Broadway debut in a 1957 production of Peter Ustinov's *Romanoff and Juliet*. He dabbled in Hollywood, appearing in a handful of TV episodes. He appeared in one film shot in America, the screen version of *Romanoff and Juliet* (1961) as a favor to Peter Ustinov, but returned to Broadway immediately after filming his part to appear in the original cast of David Merrick's *Becket*. He worked extensively in British television and then Canadian television, but he would always return to live theater. His last role was a guest appearance on Canadian

TV crime drama *Taking the Falls*, for which he was nominated for the Academy of Canadian Cinema & Television Gemini Award for Best Performance by an Actor in a Guest Role in a Dramatic Series.

Linda Lawson. Publicity still from *Adventures in Paradise* (season 1). Copyright 20th Century Fox Studios.

Linda Lawson (1936-) was a night club performer at the Sands Motel in Las Vegas. She was recording a track for an LP, one of several jazz vocalists who would be featured on the record *Songs for Your Boyfriend*, arranged by Henry Mancini. She caught the eye of Blake

Edwards, who was collaborating with Mancini on a theme for a new series called *Peter Gunn*. Edwards cast her as a nightclub chanteuse in two episodes of the series, leading to other roles requiring a singer, such as on *Alfred Hitchcock Presents* and *Mike Hammer*. Parlaying her success on TV into a recording contract, in 1959 she released *Introducing Linda Lawson* for Chancellor Records, a Philadelphia label affiliated with Am-Par, the music subsidiary of ABC. This may explain why her next role, on the NBC program *Five Fingers*, was a non-singing role. Lawson was cast the same year as a series regular on the first season of *Adventures in Paradise*, airing on ABC, as a singer and the proprietress of Chez Renee. Soon after the series ended, she married producer John Foreman and gradually concentrated on roles requiring more acting and less singing. Her next major role was as the secretary to a veterinarian recently drafted and assigned to Paris in the 1962 series *Don't Call Me Charlie*. She would appear in season five of *Ben Casey* in a recurring role as Ben's love interest, but would otherwise appear as a guest star for the rest of her career. Her final role before retiring was a season eleven episode of *ER* in 2005.

Lou Krugman (1914-1992) began his career training with the Maude Adams Repertory Shakespeare Company in New York. He made his Broadway debut in 1933 in *Yoshe Kalb*, but found his first love was radio. Starting in 1941, he appeared on every major radio network, performing in over 10,000 episodes of such shows as *Captain Midnight, Dick Tracy, Suspense, The Goldbergs, Yours Truly, Johnny Dollar*, and *Gunsmoke*, working in radio into the 1960s. He debuted in film in *To the Ends of the Earth* (1948) and on television in a 1953 episode of *The Abbott and Costello Show*. In spite of appearances in films such as Robert Wise's *I Want to Live!* (1958) and Billy Wilder's *Irma La Douce* (1963) and over 100 television appearances, he remained a voice man first and foremost, recording over 700 commercials. Even after retiring, Krugman returned to radio, performing with the California Artists Radio Theatre group, completing an award-winning version of *MacBeth* two months before his death.

Charlita Regis (1921-1997) was born Clara de Freitas, a second generation Portuguese from Lowell, Massachusetts, which was a rather anticlimactic origin for a career that specialized in exotic femme fatales. Unable to find acting jobs after a stint with the USO, she changed her name and formed her own dance band: Charlita and her Men of Rhumba. Playing a night club in Mexico City, she was spotted by studio executives in Mexico filming *The Brave Bulls* (1951). She was recruited to play a bar room singer. She would appear in six films in 1951 alone, and admitted to her home town newspaper that she was already concerned with being typecast as a "hip-swinging maraca-shaker." The concerned was justified. She and her band worked the LA nightclubs and she continued to work steadily as a day player, specializing in foreign beauties, usually as a cantina singer or dancer, Polynesian maiden, or Indian princess. Her attempts to break out of this mold were reflected in her stage name. Billed as "Charlita," she tried "Charlita de Freitas" in *Untamed Frontier* (1952), but then went back to her singular name. She married musician William Roeder in 1954. She used her married name in an episode of *Hopalong Cassidy* but "Charlita Roeder" went back to Charlita again immediately. In 1955, William Roeder, under his stage name of Billy Regis, recorded the spectacular trumpet solo that made "Cherry Pink and Apple Blossom White" a hit for the Pérez Prado Orchestra, making him more popular than Perez and therefore fired. He started the Billy Regis Orchestra. Charlita toured with him as a featured vocalist, using Charlita Regis briefly. She would continue to appear in films and television but roles became fewer as she got older. *Billy the Kid Versus Dracula* (1966) was her last film. Music had changed. Her husband was relegated to being the band leader for Beverly Aadland, who was more of a draw because of her underage relationship with Errol Flynn than any music talent. Both would continue to work locally and, thanks to financial decisions made when both were top drawing names, they retired in the 1970s.

Michael Pollard with the cast of *Bonnie and Clyde*. (1967) Copyright Warner Brothers Studio. Photo Courtesy of Michael J. Pollard.

Episode 4: The Unknown Town

Michael J. Pollard (1939-   ) is yet another of this series' guest stars who went on to greater fame. His short stature allowed him to play child roles well into his twenties, including the *Star Trek* episode "Miri" where he played a teen at age twenty-seven. In addition to a recurring role as the diminutive trans-dimensional imp Mister Mxyzptlk in two episodes of *Superboy*, Pollard also appeared in a first season episode of Irwin Allen's *Lost in Space* as a mysterious boy who lives on the other side of a mirror. He received Academy Award and Golden Globe nominations for his work on the film *Bonnie and Clyde* (1967). Pollard originated the role of Hugo Peabody in the Broadway debut of *Bye Bye Birdie*. Adept at comic roles with an odd edge, he was a constant guest on television shows for

20 years ranging from *The Many Loves of Dobie Gillis* and *The Lucy Show* to *The Andy Griffith Show* and *The Girl from U.N.C.L.E.* Pollard also had a memorable part in the Bill Murray Christmas film *Scrooged* (1985).

Salvatore Baccaloni (1900-1969) was an Italian operatic bass. Born in Rome, he made his professional debut as Bartolo in *The Barber of Seville* at Rome's Teatro Adriano in 1922. In 1926, he joined La Scala in Milan under Arturo Toscanini, who urged Baccaloni to focus on comedic character roles. That advice resulted in Baccaloni being considered the greatest basso buffo of 20th century opera. In 1940, he joined the Metropolitan Opera Company where he became renowned. His large repertory included 170 roles in five languages. Baccaloni never refused work, no matter how small the part or obscure the opera. He was under contract to dub the singing voice of actors less vocally gifted. He appeared on four TV episodes, not playing opera singers. His American films were mostly non-singing roles, except the Jerry Lewis film *Rock-a-Bye Baby* (1958) where he sings a lullaby.

David Lewis (1916-2000) was a Broadway actor who became a pioneer of early television, making his first appearance in a 1949 episode of *Captain Video and His Video Rangers*. He worked in theater while appearing on television, eventually choosing the latter as his career. Lewis did character roles, with recurring roles on *The Farmer's Daughter* as Senator Ames and *Batman* as Warden Crichton. In 1978, he joined *General Hospital* as Edward Quartermaine, winning the Daytime Emmy for best supporting actor in 1982. Lewis left the show in 1987 for medical reasons (his character crashed into the Bermuda Triangle and was presumed dead). He returned in 1991. He retired in 1993 and his Quartermaine character was taken over by a new actor.

Jack Albertson (1907-1981) is best known to audiences for starring roles in the TV series *Chico and the Man* and the Gene Wilder version of

Willie Wonka and the Chocolate Factory (1971), but these roles were toward the end of a career that started when he dropped out of high school and headed to New York. His career started in burlesque, first as a soft-shoe man, then as a straight man to Phil Silvers on the Minsky's circuit. He graduated to vaudeville as part of the road troupe of the Dancing Verselle Sisters. He took bit parts in movies and television when possible, but his reputation was made in stage comedy. His first film role was in the Mickey Rooney and Judy Garland vehicle *Strike Up the Band* (1940), but his big break came when he was hired as a regular on Milton Berle's radio show. With the name recognition came his own radio show and progressively better roles on stage, on TV, and in films. In 1968, Albertson won the Oscar for Best Supporting Actor in *The Subject Was Roses*, recreating the character that had already earned him a Tony during its Broadway run. In 1976, he joined the elite club of actors who won the Triple Crown by winning an Emmy for his work on *Chico and the Man*.

Robert Emhardt (1916-1994) left Indiana for the Royal Academy of Dramatic Art in London before joining the BBC's repertory troupe. His TV debut was a BBC production of *Marco's Millions* in 1938. His similarity to Sidney Greenstreet was striking and he was soon serving as Greenstreet's understudy when Greenstreet began an American tour. The tour returned to England, but Emhardt stayed behind. His Broadway debut was in 1942 in *The Pirate*. With the rise of American TV popularity, he became a staple of such New York shows as *Photocrime, Studio One,* and *Suspense*. He made his film debut in *The Iron Mistress* (1952). He remained predominantly a television actor, specializing, in his own words, in "loudmouths, guilt-ridden embezzlers and school principals." He won an Emmy for his performance as one such loudmouth in the "Man in a Hurry" episode of *The Andy Griffith Show* in 1963.

Gavin MacLeod (1931-   ) made his Broadway debut in *A Hatful of Rain* with Shelly Winters and Ben Gazarra. His first film was an uncredited walk through in *The True Story of Lynn Stuart* (1958). It was followed by a credited role in *I Want to Live!* (1958) starring Susan Hayward. This role was noticed by Blake Edwards, who cast him in *Operation Petticoat* (1958). That should have been a breakout role for MacLeod. Instead, it only led to a higher level of character acting roles, mostly of thugs and gunsels. In 1962, he joined the cast of *McHale's Navy*, but left after two seasons to appear in *The Sand Pebbles* (1966) with Steve McQueen. After that film, it appeared he was destined for a career of nondescript costarring roles, such as Moriarty in *Kelly's Heroes*. That changed in 1970 when he was cast as Murray Slaughter on *The Mary Tyler Moore Show*. That show ended in 1977 and MacLeod immediately became Captain Stubing on *The Love Boat* for its ten-year run. His autobiography, *This Is Your Captain Speaking*, was published in 2013.

William Schallert (1922-   ) is still recognized as Captain Kirk's bureaucratic nemesis Nilz Barris in the classic *Star Trek* episode "The Trouble with Tribbles." The son of *Los Angeles Times* drama critic Edwin Schallert, his career choice was preordained. His first film was *The Foxes of Harrow* (1947); his first TV appearance was on *Family Theatre* in 1951. In the 1940s, Schallert acted with The Group Theatre, a Los Angeles equivalent of The Actor's Studio. He did theater, television and stage appearances, ending up with more than 250 episodes of television and 100 plus movie credits, in addition to serving a four year term as president of the Screen Actors Guild. Aside from *Star Trek*, his other role that he is remembered for is as perplexed parent Martin Lane on *The Patty Duke Show*.

Carol Hill (1913-2000) was a longtime West Coast stage actress and stage manager. After the death of a child, she was unable to concentrate on live theater. At the urging of her husband, perennial cowboy character actor Joe Bassett, she began working as a day player. From 1957 to 1964, she appeared in twelve episodes of various shows, the most widely recalled being the *Twilight Zone* episode "Five Characters in Search of an Exit." In 1964, she joined her husband in retirement.

Evan MacNeil enjoyed a brief but promising career in show business. Her first role was an extra in *Bells are Ringing* (1960), just before appearing in *The Hypnotic Eye* (1960). Press for the film suggested her casting was twofold, she resembled Kim Novak and she was easy to hypnotize. Since her self-immolation scene takes place before the opening credits, we'll never know how easily she fell prey to the evil hypnosis of Jacques Bergerac. Starting with *Five Fingers*, she appeared in five episodes of television series and then quietly dropped out of sight.

Earle Hodgins (1893-1964) was a vaudevillian and radio performer, playing the type of comedy roles that would define his career; that of a snake oil salesman with a rapid-fire delivery. By the early 1930s, he was still appearing on radio and stage, but his attention had turned to Hollywood. He left a contract with NBC radio to pursue film work. His first role was a street cop in *Hell's House* (1932), but his next three roles, all in 1934, were as a fast-talking carnival barker, a part he was perfectly suited for. He would subsequently appear in nearly 300 films through 1963, specializing in fast-talking con men of questionable integrity who were comedy relief in westerns. In a ten year span, he would appear in twelve Hopalong Cassidy films and five episodes of Hoppy's TV show in 1952. His television credits were also heavily Western themed. His first role was a 1951 episode of *Red Ryder* and his last was an episode of *Gunsmoke* twelve years and over 101 TV appearances later.

Episode 5: The Men with the Triangle Heads

Monty Woolley (1888-1963) was born into Manhattan high society. He served as an English instructor and drama coach at Yale, where his students included Thornton Wilder and Stephen Vincent Benét. Woolley easily transitioned from teaching into directing plays on Broadway, in collaboration with his long-time friend, composer Cole Porter. In 1936, Woolley left his teaching career for good. He first appeared on Broadway in the musical *On Your Toes* with Ray Bolger. That same year he made his film debut with *Ladies in Love* (1936). Woolley earned a best actor Oscar nomination for his role in the World War II drama *The Pied Piper* (1942) and received a supporting actor nod for *Since You Went Away* (1944). He portrayed himself in a biopic of Cole Porter entitled *Night and Day* (1946) that had been sanitized to the point of fiction. Aside from a 1954 appearance on *The Best of Broadway* recreating his role in the Broadway hit *The Man Who Came to Dinner*, *Five Fingers* was his only other acting appearance on television and his final credited role. The role was a favor to his friend, series producer Martin Manulis, who had also produced Woolley's *Best of Broadway* appearance.

Alfred Ryder (1916-1995) was equally at ease on radio, stage, film and television. His Broadway debut came in 1929 when the 13-year-old portrayed one of the lost boys in *Peter Pan*. He was the voice of Sammy Goldberg in the popular radio comedy *The Goldbergs*. In spite of a long career on Broadway and in such films as *Hamlet* (1964) and *True Grit* (1969), he may be best remembered as a TV character actor, portraying a variety of ethnic bad guys, such as the ghost of Nazi U-boat commander Captain Gerhardt Krueger in two episodes of *Voyage to the Bottom of the Sea*, plus a third as a Norwegian scientist. He played another mad scientist in the "Man Trap" episode of *Star Trek* and was on *Wild, Wild West*. Ryder pared back his onscreen appearances in the mid-1970s to return to his first love, acting and directing on the stage, mostly at the Arena Theatre in Washington, D.C.

Estelle Winwood (1882-1984) was a child actress in London's West End, debuting on Broadway in 1916 in *Hush!* An actress of the old school stage, she avoided television and film as banal and predictable. A brief attempt at films in the 1930s reinforced her distaste and it was not until the early 1950s that she began to warm up to either medium. In her 70s, she made up for lost time. She made sixteen films, the final one being Neil Simon's *Murder by Death* (1976) at age ninety-four, as well as forty-five television appearances. Her final appearance, at age ninety-eight, was on an episode of *Quincy M.E.* dealing with elder abuse.

Robert Brubaker (1916-2010) had a full career as a character actor, but was always on the verge of a break out role. He came to Hollywood from regional theater and took classes at the Ben Bard drama school, eventually becoming a teacher as well. He worked in radio but was unable to break into films. He went to New York and was in rehearsals for a Broadway production when Pearl Harbor was bombed. A stint in the Air Force resulted in being recalled into service twice, once for the Berlin air drop and then again in the Korean War. Both interrupted his career's momentum, but by 1954, he was back in Hollywood. Brubaker worked steadily, and is a rare example of a character actor who had two separate, recurring roles in the same television series. In *Gunsmoke*, he played Jim Buck the stagecoach driver from 1957 to 1962, then returned as Floyd the bartender in 1974-1975. In between, he was a regular on the soap opera *Days of Our Lives* and guested on *Voyage to the Bottom of the Sea*. He retired after an uncredited appearance in *The Sting* (1973), returning once in 1979 for a minor role in a *Live from Lincoln Center* episode "New York City Opera: Street Scene."

Jason Wingreen (1920-) was one of the few actors to have roles in both the *Star Trek* and *Star Wars* universes. He played a Federation scientist in the original *Star Trek* "The Empath" and was the original voice of Boba Fett in *The Empire Strikes Back* (1980), although his voice was overdubbed for the 2004 DVD release. Wingreen also had a recurring role as Judge Arthur Beaumont in eleven episodes of *Matlock*. He is best remembered for his role as Harry Snowden on *All in the Family* and its spin-off series *Archie Bunker's Place*.

Pamela Matthews (1922-2002) has five film credits, mostly in Europe, and *Five Fingers* was her only TV credit. Her real success in show business was behind the scenes. After her first feature, *School for Secrets* (1946), starring Peter Ustinov, she moved to Rome and worked as a dialogue coach for such names as Sophia Loren, Gina Lolobrigida, Anna Magnani, and others. She met her husband Cesare Danova (who also appeared on *Five Fingers* in episode 10) there. She had roles in several Italian films before Cesare's rising career dictated their move to Hollywood. She became a Director of New Talent for 20th Century Fox Studios. She also continued to work as a dialogue coach as needed, most notably on *The Sound of Music* (1965).

Jason Wingreen. *The Twilight Zone* 1960. Copyright CBS Television Network.

Five Fingers: Elegance in Espionage

Bill Couch (1926-1999) was originally a high wire artist in the circus. His brother Chuck left the circus to become a stuntman in Hollywood. When *It's a Mad, Mad, Mad, Mad World* (1963) needed a high wire stunt double for Spencer Tracy, Chuck called Bill to Hollywood. Couch quickly became one of the best "high men" in the stunt business. He also worked as a day actor, undoubtedly a refreshing change from leaping off tall objects. Couch was also the stunt coordinator on many films, including *King Kong* (1976), *The Great Wallendas* (1978), *Star Trek II: The Wrath of Khan* (1982), and *Ghostbusters* (1984).

David Hoffman (1904-1961) was raised in Seattle, Washington, where he began acting in repertory groups. He became a regular at Pasadena Playhouse before moving to New York where his brother Al was a successful composer on Tin Pan Alley. He had some success on Broadway, doing three George Abbott produced plays back to back. He returned to California in 1941 and became a character actor noted for his deadpan delivery. His final role was supposed to be Dr. Plato Zorba in *13 Ghosts* (1960), but his final illness had taken its toll and the role was given to Roy Jenson. Hoffman did make a brief appearance in the film as a messenger.

Episode 6: The Assassin

Don Taylor (1920-1998) gave up a successful career in front of the camera in such highly regarded films as *Father of the Bride* and the 1948 film noir *The Naked City* for an equally successful one behind it. Well known for his roles in war films, in the mid-1960s he switched to directing, helming fifteen films, including *Escape from the Planet of the Apes* (1971) and *The Island of Dr. Moreau* (1977), starring Burt Lancaster and Richard Basehart. Taylor also added over 400 TV episodes to his credits. In his spare time he wrote one-act plays, radio dramas, short stories and screenplays. In 1997, he returned to theater for his final project, writing and directing Mariette Hartley in *Silver Buckles on His Knee* for the University of Las Vegas Theater Group.

John McGiver (1913-1975) left a teaching position in the New York City public school system in 1955 to pursue acting as a profession. This was his second attempt; in 1938 he had worked with New York's Irish Repertory Theatre before enlisting during the war. This time, he found his niche, specializing in straight man roles with an inimitable, precise delivery that worked equally well as an insufferable jewelry salesman in *Breakfast at Tiffany's* (1961) or an unctuous factory owner in the *Voyage to the Bottom of the Sea* episode "The X Factor." His final appearance was an episode of *Ellery Queen* that aired a month after his death.

Nico Minardos (1930-2011) Nico made his film debut as an extra in the 1952 film *Monkey Business*, starring Cary Grant, Ginger Rogers, and Marilyn Monroe, but the majority of Minardos' work was in television, where his swarthy complexion and accent found him playing Mexicans (He was Greek). His film career was often overshadowed by his off-screen life. In 1966, Minardos was filming in location in Peru with actor Eric Fleming. There was a canoe mishap on the Huallaga River. Minardos, a strong swimmer, was unable to rescue Fleming from drowning in the rapids and barely survived himself. Then, in 1986, Minardos found himself embroiled in the Iran-Contra Affair, a result of having business dealings with Saudi arms merchant Adnan Khashoggi. Charged with conspiracy to illegally ship arms to Iran, the indictment was eventually thrown out, but the cost of his legal defense drove him to the brink of bankruptcy and ended his career in show business.

Gregory Morton (1911-1986) was a radio actor turned Broadway thespian turned television character actor. A trained violinist, he was cast in several roles as a musician, including the fiddler in a *Hallmark Hall of*

Fame version of *Johnny Belinda*. An injury ended his violin career, but his music background gave him the edge in roles such as a Russian Maestro who speeds up the ballet on the *Ed Sullivan Show* in the film *Bye Bye Birdie* (1962). His final project was writing and starring in the film *The Adulteress* (1973). In 1980, he published a children's book about coyotes struggling to survive in an urban setting, *Family: A Story*.

Fritz Feld (1900-1993) started his film career in 1916 as an unpaid extra in *William Tell* at the Royal Theater in Berlin. His film debut came a year later in *Der Golem und die Tänzerin*, playing a hotel clerk. He worked in German theater and films, traveling to New York in 1923 as part of a troupe performing Max Reinhardt's stage production of *The Miracle*. The troupe moved on, but Feld stayed. He made his American debut in *A Ship Comes In* (1928) for Cecil B. DeMille Pictures. By the time of his appearance as a Swiss hotel clerk in *I Met Him in Paris* (1937), Feld had developed the character he would come to play for most of his career: insufferably self-important and easily annoyed. Whether he was an aristocrat, a maitre d', or a hotel clerk, he was certain to reach a boiling point. This triggered his trademark move, a popping noise created by slapping his mouth with the palm of his hand. He would first pop in *If You Knew Susie* (1947).

Alan Caillou (1914-2006) was the name that Alan Samuel Lyle-Smythe M.B.E., M.C., adopted for his various careers as an author, actor, screenwriter, and novelist (Caillou is the French word for stone, his code name as an intelligence officer during the war). He wrote about his experiences in the North African campaign in his first book *The World is Six Feet Square* (1954). He started a Shakespeare troupe in Tanganyika (present-day Tanzania) while working as a big game hunter, before moving to Canada as a hunter, then becoming a Canadian radio, television, and theater actor. He wrote his first novel *Rogue's Gambit* in 1955, the first in a series of paperback men's adventures under his own name and as Alex Webb. His skill with writing was noticed and he was hired as a screenwriter in Hollywood, starting with espionage-oriented television, such as four episodes of *Behind Closed Doors*, seven episodes of *The Man from U.N.C.L.E.*, and first season *Voyage to the Bottom of the Sea* episode "The Magnus Beam." He also appeared regularly onscreen, usually as a Brit with ulterior motives. Several of Caillou's novels were filmed: *Rampage* (1963) with Robert Mitchum, *Assault on Agathon* (1977) with Nico Minardos, and *Cheetah* (1989) for Walt Disney.

Avis Scott (1918-2010) is best remembered for an event that happened early in British television. After a career as a child actor in England, she transitioned successfully into adult roles. She appeared in the film *Brief Encounter* (1945) based on the Noel Coward play *Still Life*. She worked with Noel Coward again, appearing in the West End production of *Present Laughter* in 1947-1948. Until this point, she had been using her birth name of Avis Scutt. Resisting suggestions to change her name for years, she finally acquiesced after Noel Coward said, "Scutt sounds like a great piece of rabbit!" Scott was hired as an onscreen continuity announcer for BBC television. Ten weeks later, in January of 1955, she was fired for being "too sexy." The press had a field day with the story and she was unable to shake the notoriety. Her twelve year career as a serious actress was reduced to offers for cheesecake roles. She struggled for two years before giving up and heading to Broadway, but Equity rules kept her from the stage. With no other options, she went to Hollywood to work in television. Her first role was in *Five Fingers*, followed by an episode of *Thriller* that required heavy make-up, just to prove she was an actress first and foremost. She returned to the London stage briefly before retiring in California.

Maya Medwar (no dates) aka Maria Medwar was an Egyptian movie actress and a belly dancer who trained under Ali Reda, a legendary dancer and choreographer of Egypt's golden age of film. Medwar became a heroine during the 1952 Cairo riots by leading American news correspondents out of a burning hotel and through the mobs to safety. Her arrival in Los Angeles in late 1957 was fortuitous. Although she would never ignite a career in film, she arrived there as the Arabic themed night-club trend began. She found work at *The Fez*, the first nightclub on the West Coast, and became a star. Her signature move, a difficult vertical reverse figure eight hip movement, is still known as "The Maya."

Episode 7: The Man Who Got Away

Arlene Francis (1907-2001) was a regular panelist on the television game show *What's My Line?* for twenty-five years. She regularly appeared on the original network run from 1950 to 1967, and then on the syndication revival from 1968 to 1975. The heart-shaped pendant that Francis always wore on *What's My Line* was made by Hedison Manufacturing Co. of Providence, Rhode Island. The jewelry firm was owned by Harry Hedison, an uncle of David Hedison. Francis was a well-known New York City personality, appearing on Broadway and radio where she hosted several programs, including a midday chat show on WOR-AM that ran from 1960 to 1984. She wrote an autobiography in 1978. Francis previously had written a self-help book, *That Certain Something: The Magic of Charm* in 1960, and a cookbook, *No Time for Cooking* in 1961.

Leo Gordon (1922-2000) was a professional bad guy for more than forty years in film and television, having previously served to four years in Folsom State Prison for armed robbery. One of his first films was *Riot in Cell Block 11* (1954), filmed at Gordon's former home, Folsom Prison. He was still remembered by the guards there, who remained wary of him as one of their toughest inmates. He appeared in over 100 episodes of television, mostly as western outlaws, and in seventy films. Gordon was also a screenwriter with film credits such as *Attack of the Giant Leeches*

(1959) and *Tobruk* (1966). His television writing credits include thirty-eight episodes of *The Case of the Dangerous Robin* and twelve episodes of *Adam-12*.

John Hubbard (1914-1988) started his career in Chicago theater where he was spotted by talent scouts and sent to Hollywood. The studios weren't quite sure what to do with him, as reflected by his name changes. He started in musicals and Hal Roach comedies as "Jack Hubbard" at Paramount before becoming leading man "Anthony Allan" in several MGM films during the war years. After he returned from his military service, he became "John Hubbard," but found himself in smaller and smaller roles. By 1950, he was essentially a television actor, including costarring as Colonel U. Charles Barker in the military comedy *Don't Call Me Charlie*, appearing in all eighteen episodes, alongside *Five Fingers* co-star Alan Napier.

Dolores Donlon (1926-   ) became a model in 1945 in New York under the name Pat Van Iver, quickly becoming a staple of the New York photography scene. More than 300,000 GIs voted her pin-up pose as "picture of the year" in 1945, leading to an invitation to take a screen test from Samuel Goldwyn's office. She began a cross-country career, flying to Hollywood to do uncredited bit parts in films while continuing her successful modeling career in New York. She married Hollywood agent and producer Vic Orsatti in 1949. By 1954, she was living in Hollywood and, with a little help from her husband, became Dolores Donlon in her first substantial film role, a costar in *The Long Wait* (1954). She still modeled, most notably being named *Playboy's* August Playmate of the Month in 1957. Her marriage collapsed in 1959 and her career plateaued after the divorce in 1960. She starred in Franco Rossi's 1961 film *Odissea nuda*. She met violinist Robert de Pasquale on a trip home and married him the next year. She then retired from acting to raise her family.

William Phipps (1922-   ) hitchhiked to Hollywood from Indiana after World War II. He enrolled in the Actors' Lab in Hollywood, alongside fellow actor Russell Johnson. Phipps and Johnson alternated in a role in a play at the Actors' Lab. Phipps was in the evening performance one night when Charles Laughton was in the audience. Impressed by the performance, Laughton came backstage afterwards to ask Phipps if he'd consider a role in a small project. Phipps agreed, and found himself in *Galileo* (1947), a short film version of Laughton's translation of Bertolt Brecht's play. He was a charter enrollee of Charles Laughton's new acting school alongside other budding actors that Laughton thought had potential, such as Shelley Winters and Jane Wyatt. Phipps worked steadily into the 1960s in a variety of film and television projects, primarily sci-fi and westerns. He moved to Hawaii and lived for five years as a beachcomber before returning to Hollywood to portray Teddy Roosevelt in the 1976 television movie *Eleanor and Franklin*. Phipps considered his career highlight to be the speaking voice of Prince Charming in Disney's animated *Cinderella* (1950).

Arthur Hanson (1915-1991) began his career in 1951, returning from military service in Japan and using the GI Bill to study acting. With an eye on becoming a New York stage actor, he almost immediately found New York television had a higher demand for actors. His first significant role was filmed in Morocco, a 1955 episode of *Captain Gallant of the Foreign Legion*, a Buster Crabbe series that was filming outside of New York or Hollywood. He moved to Los Angeles later that year and quickly became a character actor in television, specializing in clergy and doctors. His first two films *Outside the Law* (1956) and *Zero Hour!* (1957) were shot in Hollywood, but he worked primarily in television, possibly because every other film he appeared in required air travel: Connecticut, Utah and Mexico in 1959 for *They Came to Cordura* and *It Happened to Jane*. And he had to travel again in 1968 for *The Boston Strangler*. His final film role was an uncredited walk-through in *The Hindenburg* (1975) and that nearly required a flight to Germany. He continued to work in Hollywood until his retirement in 1985.

Other cast identified from "Man Who Got Away" episode (UCLA Library Catalog).

Pete Jolly (1932-2004) appeared on the CBS nationwide radio program *Hobby Lobby* in 1939, billed as the "Boy Wonder Accordionist." The nickname didn't last long. In addition to his accordion, Jolly became one of the top jazz pianists on the West Coast. He was known for his disciplined work as a studio musician as well as his improvisation in live performances. He moved to Los Angeles in 1953. Within a year, he had his first album and his first soundtrack credit, performing jazz with *Shorty Rogers and His Giants* in Sinatra's *The Man with the Golden Arm* (1955). Although his *Five Fingers* appearance was light-hearted, he was taken very seriously at the studios. His versatility was constantly in demand, though rarely credited. He would perform on the soundtrack of over 200 films, plus television, ranging from *Mannix* to *The Love Boat*. After working at the studio all day, he would perform at jazz clubs all night. His first love was the jazz trio. He formed the *Pete Jolly Trio* in 1964; this trio would perform until Jolly's health began to fail in 2004.

Rachel Stephens (1932-   ) received her MA from Indiana University and went to New York with a plan. She had no connections to break into the business, so she would break into the production side of the industry and learn the ins and outs of getting into the performance side. She took a job as a secretary for CBS before moving up to research assistant, all the time auditioning. In 1956, Twentieth Century Fox saw her on an episode of *Lamp Unto My Feet* and asked her to do come to Hollywood for a screen test. The test was delayed and finally they signed her to a three month option. She was never offered a long-term contract, merely additional three month options. In 1962, frustrated by six years of uncredited and minor roles, she decided to leave the studio and tour with the Gypsy Rose Lee production of *Auntie Mame*. She continues to perform, still touring the country after forty-five years.

Nick Dennis (1904-1980) was a character actor who debuted on Broadway in 1936. His break came as a member of the original Broadway cast of *A Streetcar Named Desire*. By the end of the show's run in 1949, a film version was already in the plans and Dennis joined Brando and other cast members on a permanent move west. The 1951 film version of *Streetcar* launched his career as a supporting actor, with the Thessalian born Dennis usually playing ethnic characters with flamboyant personalities. In 1962, he became a recurring character as hospital orderly Nick Kanavaras on *Ben Casey*, offering a whimsical counterpoint to Vince Edward's grimness. He ended his career in the mid-1970s playing a similarly lighthearted foil as Telly Savalas' Uncle Constantine on *Kojak*.

Albert Carrier (1919-2002) was born in northern Italy, but immigrated to Mexico as a war refugee. His appeared in five Mexican films, but was better known for his off-screen romance with such Mexican film stars as Beatriz Ramos. He arrived in Hollywood in 1955. When it was discovered Carrier was fluent in French from being raised on the Italian-French border, he was suddenly in demand for character roles and guest shots. His films ranged from a gendarme in Hitchcock's *The Man Who Knew Too Much* (1956) to a French diplomat in *Batman: The Movie* (1966). He was even higher in demand on television, playing French crooks, waiters and hotel concierges, including an appearance as Lafayette on *Daniel Boone*. Ironically, Carrier, the go-to actor for French accents, found himself playing a Bolivian in his last, and most significant, film role as a sugar company mogul in *Scarface* (1983).

John Morley (1912-1991) was born in Canada, heading to New York after graduation from the University of Toronto in 1934. He was on Broadway by 1936, debuting in *Idiot's Delight* with the Lunts. After a stint in the US Navy, he worked in radio, where he caught the attention of Helen Hayes, who cast him in several episodes of her 1947 television series *Helen Hayes Electric Theatre*. In 1950, Morley came to Hollywood after his last Broadway show *Lost in the Stars* closed. He had a bit part in *Born Yesterday*, decided it wasn't for him and joined a touring company. It would take another seven years before he tried again. In 1957, he appeared in two television episodes and two films. It would be his most successful year in Hollywood. He would continue to work in West Coast theater, but he never regained the success of his early career.

Michael Keith made his New York stage debut in the original production of *Mister Roberts*, but not under his name. The cast included Robert Keith as a star, and his son Brian Keith was also in the ensemble, and the producers thought three was one too many Keiths. He subsequently joined a national touring company of *John Loves Mary* for two years. When the tour ended in California, he began working as a day actor while auditioning for local theater. In 1956, he joined a long-running production of *Under the Yum Yum Tree* at the lvar Theater, opposite Bill Bixby. He was cast as the next door neighbor in the pilot episode of *The Dick Van Dyke Show*, but producer Carl Reiner wanted comedians not actors, and the role was recast with Jerry Paris as Jerry Helper. His biggest movie role was in the 1963 American version of *King Kong vs. Godzilla*. In addition to the film being dubbed in English, Keith and two other actors filmed footage that was inserted into the film. The Japanese version was a major hit in Asia; the badly edited American version with Keith as UN newscaster Eric Carter did not fare as well, but has become a staple in syndication on late night local TV.

J. M. Kerrigan. Copyright J. M. Kerrigan Estate.

Episode 8: The Emerald Curtain

Michael David (1930-1999) was an up and coming UK stage actor who had just returned from Moscow where his theater company had performed *Hamlet*. Fox was casting local actors to fill in the cast of *The Inn of the Sixth Happiness* (1958), then filming in Wales, and David used the opportunity to return to his native land. In spite of having no film experience and minimal television exposure, he was cast in a co-star role and offered a studio contract. His first appearance in America was *Five Fingers*, followed by the Marilyn Monroe film *Let's Make Love* (1960). The studio wasn't quite sure what to do with David, and his career suffered accordingly. When he found himself co-starring in *Snow White and the Three Stooges* (1961), he returned to England. He would continue to appear in British television and on the London stage for the rest of his career.

J. M. Kerrigan (1884-1964) was an Irish newspaper reporter who joined Dublin's Abbey Players in 1907 and appeared in stage productions, including several that toured Europe and appeared on Broadway. He was directing and headlining silent films in Ireland, as well, when Irish nationalism violence began to increase and he decided to move to New York in 1917. Having already appeared on Broadway, he easily returned to the New York stage. He began alternating between Broadway and Hollywood, building an impressive body of work on both coasts. In 1935, he went to Hollywood at the request of John Ford, who was reuniting a number of the Abbey Players to appear in his film about Irish nationalism, *The Informer*. This time, Kerrigan stayed, and by his death in 1964, he had added another seventy-eight films, but only a handful of TV appearances, to his résumé.

Cyril Delevanti (1889-1975) came to the United States a seasoned third generation show business performer. His grandfather was a popular Harlequinade performer and his father was an orchestra leader. He arrived in New York in 1920, just as Ethel Barrymore was finishing her Broadway run in *Declassee*. He joined the touring company and crossed the country with Barrymore. He never made it back to New York, finding steady work in the Los Angeles theater scene. His first film appearance was in *Devotion* (1931). In 1938, he appeared in the Buster Crabbe cliffhanger *Red Barry* for director Ford Beebe, who would become his son-in-law.

Not surprisingly, the 1940s were very busy for Delevanti as Beebe steered work his way in additional serials such as *Adventures of Smilin' Jack* (1943) and *Jungle Queen* (1945). Delevanti, who was now in his late fifties, was exhausted by the physical demands of serial work.

He decided to accept a position in Texas to resurrect the disbanded Little Theatre Corpus Christi. In 1947, he arrived there to raise public interest and funds for the theater, serving as director for their first season in 1948. He returned to Hollywood after that and split his time between theater and character roles.

He worked with David Hedison again in the *Voyage to the Bottom of the Sea* second season episode "The Left Handed Man" and in *The Greatest Story Ever Told* (1965). Delevanti continued to work until his death. His final role was in the Blaxploitation film *Black Eye* (1974). The high mark of his film career is *The Night of the Iguana* (1964), as Deborah Kerr's elderly grandfather poet Nonno.

Jimmy Murphy (1935-   ) played one of the Bowery Boys in some of the last films in the series. His first appearance as Myron in *Crashing Las Vegas* (1956), replacing Bennie Bartlett, was also the last appearance of Leo Gorcey. He appeared in five films; the series limped along for two additional films. His career did not recover, and he was relegated to minor roles, usually as a tough guy. He was an uncredited extra in the David Hedison narrated *Rally 'Round the Flag, Boys!* (1958).

Linda Hutchings (1938-2013) was a local girl, a divorced mother of two boys, working as a secretary and modeling on the side, looking to make ends meet. She was discovered by a talent agent, who signed her to a contract. She was immediately cast in a supporting role in *The Best of Everything* (1959), the publicity for which included a contest to find her a new stage name. The winning entry was the uninspired "Linda

Hutchins," which she used interchangeably with her real surname. She had mixed success under both names and was not enamored of working in film or television. She married actor/publicist Bob Palmer (aka actor Boyd Holister) in 1964 and retired from show business. She became an ardent supporter of open space and equestrian trails in the Santa Monica Mountains.

Bern Hoffman (1913-1979) was a burly college athlete who studied to be a doctor, only to become an explosives expert during World War II. He made his Broadway debut in 1944 in a revival of *The Merry Widow*. After an unsuccessful attempt to break into movies, he returned to Broadway where he originated the roles of Joey Biltmore in *Guys and Dolls* and Earthquake McGoon in *Lil' Abner*. After two years in *Lil' Abner*, he returned to Hollywood to reprise his role as McGoon in the 1959 film version. This time, he stayed. Hollywood found ample roles for the 6-foot 2-inch, 285 pounds actor and not always as the heavy. He appeared in twelve episodes of *Bonanza* as Sam the Bartender. In real life, Hoffman was a highly respected civic leader in his adopted home of North Hollywood.

Francis Bethencourt (1923-2001) made his acting debut at the Arts Theatre in London after serving as a pilot during World War II. His break out role was in John Gielgud's West End production of *Lady Windermere's Fan*. His first US role was in 1948 in the touring company of the Maurice Evans production of *The Happy Time*. It was also nearly his last US role. Bethencourt, who later admitted he took the job for the paid trip to Hollywood in hopes studio scouts would see him, found himself in a critically acclaimed show with no audiences. The show lost so much money in San Francisco, Los Angeles canceled the booking before they got there.

He was originally credited as Baron Francis de Bethencourt, claiming peerage as a descendant of Jean de Béthencourt, who conquered the

Canary Islands in 1402. He dropped the title and nobiliary particle as the newly renamed Francis Bethencourt prepared to become a US citizen. He was well-known as a socialite. When *Time* magazine mentioned his marriage to Nancy, daughter of Broadway playwright-producer Elliott Nugent, they dryly listed her as an "actress" and him as a "sometime cinemactor." He worked primarily in theater, but was perfectly content to fly out to Los Angeles for the occasional television role. During his lifetime, he was best known as the derby-topped Englishman spokesperson going door to door in television ads, touting "New Secret antiperspirant spray deodorant." He returned to the New York Theater. His last Broadway appearance was in *Dirty Linen & New-Found-Land*, a 1977 farce.

Bethencourt was also featured in Episode 14: "The Search for Edvard Stoyan."

CHAPTER 15

GUEST STARS EPISODES 9–16

Episode 9: The Temple of the Swinging Doll

Viveca Lindfors (1920-1995) was a Swedish actress, equally at home on stage and screen. Born in Uppsala, she trained with the Royal Dramatic Theatre School in Stockholm, quickly becoming a major presence in Swedish theater and film. She moved to the United States in 1946, dividing her time between Broadway and Hollywood. Lindfors played Cordelia to Orson Welles' King Lear on Broadway in 1956, and would appear in more than 100 films including *Dark City* (1950), *King of Kings* (1961), and *Creepshow* (1982).

In addition to this *Five Fingers* role, she also appeared on *Voyage to the Bottom of the Sea* in the episode "Hot Line," which also reunited her with Richard Basehart, with whom she starred in a 1962 television version of *The Paradine Case*. One of her last performances was in the original *Stargate* (1994) film. Viveca Lindfors was a founding member of the Actors' Studio West.

Viveca Lindfors. Copyright Estate of Viveca Lindfors.

Clu Gulager (1928-) was signed by Universal in 1960 as a contract player after years in New York theater. Almost immediately he began playing cowboys, an easy task for the Oklahoma-raised actor, especially at a time when Westerns were dominating the television networks. His casting on the top rated NBC series *The Virginian* from 1964 to 1968 cemented his image as a cowboy. Even when TV tastes turned to mysteries, Gulager's guest appearances were invariably cowboys or sheriffs. Gulager is the father of director John Gulager, and appeared in the younger Gulager's film *Feast* as a shotgun-toting bartender, reprising the role in *Feast 2* in 2008 and *Feast III* in 2009. He has two films coming out in 2015.

John Emery (1920-1964) was a second generation Broadway actor who rose to prominence as Captain O'Shea in the original Broadway production of *Parnell*. Alternating between theater, television, and movies, Emery was equally at ease with Shakespeare on Broadway as he was with battling Martians in *Rocketship X-M* (1950). *Rocketship X-M* was directed, co-written and produced by Kurt Neumann, who would direct David Hedison eight years later in *The Fly* (1958).

Sterling Holloway (1905-1992) was a popular American character actor, best remembered as the voice of Winnie the Pooh in the Walt Disney animated films. He spent his early years playing teen comic sidekicks in movies, starting with *The Battling Kangaroo* (1926). His big break had come the year before when he introduced the first hit song of Rodgers and Hart, "Manhattan," in the Broadway play *Garrick Gaieties*. His first love was live theater, but his acclaim would be for his voice work. His first animated film was as the Stork in *Dumbo* (1941), the start of a forty year relationship with Disney that culminated in being named a Disney Legend in 1991.

Rodolfo Hoyos, Jr. (1916-1984) was born in Mexico City, the son of actor, opera singer and vocal coach Rodolfo Hoyos. Rodolfo, Jr. started as an uncredited Mexican extra in films such as *Gilda* (1946) but quickly became a staple in the TV western genre. From *The Cisco Kid* in 1952 to *The High Chaparral* in 1970, if the show had a Mexican role, Hoyos was cast. Hoyos was first choice for any role that required a vaguely Latino ethnicity, be it a Tijuana prison guard on *CPO Sharkey*, a Puerto Rican mayor on *The Flying Nun*, or a Polynesian chief on *Adventures in Paradise*. His final role, filmed a few months before his death, was as a Central American general in the film *Love & Money* (1982).

Joan Tabor (1932-1968) was a Chicago model who first appeared on television in 1957. Her career was just starting to build momentum when it was overshadowed by her marriage to Broderick Crawford from 1962 to 1965. Her TV roles dwindled, first as she and her new husband embarked on a stage production of *Born Yesterday*, then as part of a battle with her previous husband, David Gold, over custody of their daughter. By the time she was able to return to her career, she and Crawford had started tabloid-worthy divorce proceedings. Her last appearance was a 1964 episode of *Mister Ed*. Tabor died in December 1968 from an accidental overdose of flu medication.

Casey Adams (1917-2000) was the stage name of Max Showalter. He used his real name on stage on both coasts before 20th Century Fox offered a contract and a name change. A 1962 episode of *Hawaiian Eye* was the last time he was billed as Adams. Max continued to work in television and film, but he was far more interested in live theater. He appeared as Horace Vandergelder in a Vegas casino production of *Hello, Dolly!* opposite Betty Grable. When Grable took over the role on Broadway in 1967, she brought Showalter with her. He would be the preferred Horace Vandergelder in subsequent touring companies. By his estimation, Max performed the role over 3000 times with leading ladies such as Carol Channing, Ginger Rogers, and Betsy Palmer.

Johnny Seven (1926-2010) began singing and acting as a teenager. During the Philippines campaign in World War II, he also performed in USO shows, where he picked up the nickname that would become his stage name. Seven began his career performing in New York theater and television before being brought to Hollywood. In a career that spanned fifty years as a character actor, he appeared in over a dozen films and over 100 TV episodes, including a recurring role as Lt. Carl Reese on the television series *Ironside*.

Arline Hunter (1930-   ) may best be known for who she wasn't. Her career started with doing nudie cutie shorts. In one, *The Apple-Knockers and the Coke* (1948), she looked so much like Marilyn Monroe that rumors still persist that it was actually Monroe. Hunter built on this notoriety by being named Playboy Playmate of the Month for August 1954, which in turn allowed her to appear in low budget exploitation films as harem girls and strippers. It would take another four years to get roles in more mainstream film and even then she was primarily eye candy. She did better in television, landing roles that actually required wardrobe. By 1965, her career had run its course. Her final film was *White Lightnin' Road* (1967).

Episode 10: The Final Dream

Cesare Danova (1926-1992), was born Cesare Deitinger in Bergamo, Italy. He adopted the stage name Danova as he launched his career in postwar Italy. His debut film was *La Figlia del Capitano* (1947). He signed with MGM in 1956 after a variety of films across Europe. His first major role was in *Tarzan, the Ape Man* (1959), a fiasco due to

Alain Fabre (Cesare Danova) shares a toast with Victor. Copyright 20th Century Fox Studios.

MGM's unsuccessful attempt to reuse colorized footage from the Johnny Weissmuller films.

His big break was supposed to be the role of Apollodorus in Cleopatra (1963). The bulk of his role was edited out in favor of more screen time for Elizabeth Taylor and Richard Burton after their affair was made public. He became a supporting player, usually as a suave rival to the leading man, such as Count Mancini in the Elvis film *Viva Las Vegas* (1964). Other films he is known for are *Mean Streets* (1973) and *National Lampoon's Animal House* (1978).

In 1967, Danova had another shot with the TV series *Garrison's Gorillas*. He played the role of Actor, but the series only ran for twenty-six episodes. He was guest star on numerous television series, including *Murder, She Wrote, Maude, Falcon Crest,* and the revival of *Mission: Impossible* (1988-1990).

Danova died of a heart attack at the Academy of Motion Picture Arts and Sciences headquarters in Los Angeles while attending a meeting of the Foreign Language Film committee.

John Hoyt (1905-1991) was John Hoysradt, a history teacher with a knack for comedy and impressions. After a stint with Orson Welles' Mercury Theatre, he shortened his name to Hoyt. Known primarily for playing villains and unyielding authority figures including a general on *Voyage to the Bottom of the Sea*, he also portrayed Dr. Philip Boyce on *Star Trek's* first pilot episode "The Cage." Hoyt's final role was a recurring role as the grandfather on *Gimme a Break*!

Milton Seltzer (1918-2005) possibly holds the record for most prolific actor ever as he apparently guest starred on more TV series than anyone else, according to the book *Television Guest Stars: An Illustrated Chronicle for Performers of the Sixties and Seventies*. Seltzer started his career with supporting roles on Broadway and moved into New York TV productions, playing a variety of ethnicities. He moved to California and, although Seltzer occasionally did extra work in films, most notably Hitchcock's *Marnie* (1964), he worked constantly on the small screen, including an appearance on *Voyage to the Bottom of the Sea*, in the episode "The Blizzard-Makers."

John Banner (1910-1973) will forever be remembered as the bumbling Sergeant Schultz on *Hogan's Heroes*. Banner was an Austrian Jew whose theater troupe was stranded in Switzerland when the Nazis annexed Austria. So Banner immigrated to the United States, served in the Air Force during World War II and then launched his career playing Nazis, painfully ironic considering his family died in the concentration camps. These roles included Gregor Strasser in *Hitler* (1962), which starred Richard Basehart in the title role. He also appeared on *Voyage*

Five Fingers: Elegance in Espionage

to the Bottom of the Sea as a Russian leader in the episode "Hot Line." Banner retired to his hometown of Vienna, Austria, where he is buried.

Mark Bailey (1934-) was an actor whose athletic build gave him an edge playing parts that suggested of degree of physicality, as epitomized by his role on Batman as Zsa Zsa Gabor's musclebound henchman. His career was dominated by appearances as guards, police and army officers. During the one season of *Garrison's Gorillas*, he appeared five times, playing four German officers and a prison guard.

Peter Lorre with the cast of *Silk Stockings* (1957).
Copyright MGM Studios.

Episode 11: Thin Ice

Peter Lorre (1904-1964) became an international sensation in 1931 as a serial killer who preys on little girls in the Fritz Lang film *M*. The rise of Nazism forced Lorre from Germany, fleeing first to Paris, then London. He was noticed by Ivor Mantagu, Alfred Hitchcock's associate producer and cast in *The Man Who Knew Too Much* (1934), in spite of his limited English. Lorre learned his part phonetically and never looked back. He starred as the Japanese detective/spy Kentaro Moto in *Think Fast, Mr. Moto* (1937). It proved so successful that Lorre would make eight Mr. Moto films in two years. Growing anti-Japanese sentiment in the buildup toward World War II ended this series.

Lorre became a featured player at Warner Brothers, where he created some of his most memorable characters: Joel Cairo in *The Maltese Falcon* (1941), Ugarte in the film classic *Casablanca* (1942), and Dr. Einstein in *Arsenic and Old Lace* (1944). When the war ended, Lorre concentrated on radio and stage work and returned to Germany in 1951 to co-write, direct and star in *Der Verlorene (The Lost One)* (1951), a critically acclaimed art film. Returning to the United States, he refused to go back to this grueling work load, instead focusing on character roles, often spoofing his former "creepy" image. In 1956, both Lorre and Vincent Price attended Bela Lugosi's funeral. According to Price, Lorre asked him, "Do you think we should drive a stake through his heart . . . just in case?"

Brett Halsey (1933-   ) was working as a page at the CBS studios in Hollywood when he was noticed by Jack Benny and Mary Livingston. They arranged an audition with Universal Studios. Halsey was given a contract and put to work as an extra on such films as *The Glass Web* (1953). By the next year, he had already reached co-star billing in *Ma and Pa Kettle at Home* (1954). He played David Hedison's adult son in the sequel *Return of the Fly* (1959) with Vincent Price, but chafed at a career seemingly locked into supporting and co-starring roles.

From 1960 to 1962 he was married to Luciana Paluzzi, and co-starred with her in the 1961 film *Return to Peyton Place*. From 1961 to1962, Halsey starred with Barry Coe and Gary Lockwood in the ABC television series *Follow the Sun*, about three freelance magazine writers living in Hawaii.

Learning the series would not be renewed, the newly divorced Halsey relocated to Italy where he found himself among a coterie of expatriate actors highly sought after for sword and sandal epics, spaghetti westerns, and Eurospy films. Except for occasional trips to Hollywood for guest appearances, he lived and worked in Italy. His experiences there are chronicled in his roman à clef novel, *The Magnificent Strangers*, published in 2001.

Brett permanently returned to the United States in the early 1970s with his third wife, German actress and singer Heidi Brühl, immediately finding work in daytime serials *General Hospital* and *Love is a Many Splendored Thing*. He originated the role of John Abbott on *The Young and the Restless*. Those roles inspired his first book, *Yesterday's Children* (1990), another roman à clef about life among the soap opera crowd. Halsey currently resides in California with his fifth wife, Victoria. He has recently published another book, a suspense novel called *A Grave Misunderstanding* (2014).

Alan Young (1919-) is an Emmy Award-winning English-born character actor, best known, depending on your age, as either the hapless owner of the talking horse named Mister Ed or as the voice of Scrooge McDuck. Young was a broadcaster for the Canadian Broadcasting Corporation, moving in 1944 to American radio with *The Alan Young Show*, NBC's summer replacement for Eddie Cantor's radio show. The television version of *The Alan Young Show* began in 1950. After its cancellation, Young appeared in films, including the non-leonine lead in *Androcles and the Lion* (1952) and the non-time traveling lead in *The Time Machine* (1960).

Peter Brocco (1903-1992) was a character actor who transitioned from small time hoods to elderly eccentrics over a sixty year career. He appeared in several episodes of *The Adventures of Superman*. In a series that minimized violence, Brocco managed to play characters who died in two episodes. His most reliable source of work was science-fiction television series; he appeared in everything from *The Twilight Zone* and *The Outer Limits* to *Lost in Space*. He appeared as an Organian council member in the *Star Trek* episode "Errand of Mercy." He played a Greek fisherman in the *Voyage to the Bottom of the Sea* episode "City Beneath the Sea." He later played a dementia patient in the Academy Award-winning film *One Flew Over the Cuckoo's Nest* (1975).

Marc Platt (1913-2014) was a ballet dancer and musical theater performer who began his career as an original member of the Ballet Russe de Monte Carlo. His most notable musical theater role was Dream Curly in the original Broadway production of *Oklahoma!* On film, Platt's best-known role was Daniel Pontipee, the fourth-oldest brother in the movie *Seven Brides for Seven Brothers* (1954). After he stopped dancing, Platt ran the Radio City Music Hall Ballet for several years before transitioning into full-time teaching.

James Fairfax (1897-1961) was a regular on *The Gale Storm Show*, playing an impish steward for three seasons. When the character was written out of season four, his next job was as the bootblack on *Five Fingers*. As an experiment, he used "Jimmy Fairfax" instead of the James Fairfax which he had been using since his first role in 1947. It was a short lived experiment. He used the name one more time on an episode of *Peter Gunn*, and then switched back. He retired in 1960 and moved to Tahiti.

Joe Abdullah (1926-1999) was a first generation American, born of Syrian immigrants in a section of Lawrence, Massachusetts, that remains a proud bastion of their heritage. Finding no success on Broadway, he headed west. His swarthy complexion usually limited him to play a variety of ethnicities. However, in the classic *Playhouse 90* episode "Requiem for a Heavyweight," where he played the fight announcer, Abdullah showed he was more than capable of a dramatic performance without the use of stereotypical accents.

The Featured skaters in this episode were:

Frank Lucas (1926-2002). Lucas was professional ice skater who spent eleven years touring in "Hollywood on Ice," Sonja Henie's traveling ice show. Starting as a member of the skating equivalent of a chorus line, the six-foot four-inch skater would eventually be featured in duets with the five-foot two-inch Henie. He retired from skating as the novelty of ice shows diminished, moved to his adopted home of Las Vegas and opened a hair salon.

Dennis Parr (1936-1992) was also a professional ice skating alumnus of Sonja Henie's shows. Soon after his appearance on *Five Fingers*, he suffered a career ending knee injury. Parr then went into choreography until 1968, when he opened a costume shop catering to Vegas acts.

Essi Davis began her career in 1947 as a member of Sonja Henie's Revue, which then split into multiple tour companies such as the "Hollywood on Ice" revue. She also appeared in several of Henie's skate-centric films. Increasingly popular with her acrobatic skating, in 1953 she joined the "Stars Over Ice," headlining as the "ballerina of the blades." Long after the craze for the elaborate costumed extravaganzas faded, Davis' athleticism continued to attract an audience; as late as 1971 she continued to perform her acrobatic ballets on ice for adoring fans.

Episode 12: Operation Ramrod

Oscar Homolka (1898-1978) studied at the Royal Dramatic Academy in Vienna, launching a promising career in Austrian theater and then German films. Following Hitler's rise to power, he fled to England, where he made a handful of films, notably Hitchcock's *Sabotage* (1936). Joining the flood of Jewish actors immigrating to the US as World War II worsened, Homolka quickly became a staple on Broadway. He was nominated for an Oscar for *I Remember Mama* (1948), re-creating his role from the Rodgers and Hammerstein Broadway show of the same name. Television never explored his versatility, and he was predominantly cast as Russians and German heavies. This typecasting then spilled over into his movie roles as well. He returned to England in the mid-1960s to play the Soviet KGB Colonel Stok in two Harry Palmer films, *Funeral in Berlin* (1966) and *Billion Dollar Brain* (1967), opposite Michael Caine. His last film was Blake Edwards' romantic drama *The Tamarind Seed* in 1974. He continued to work into his mid-70s and then retired.

Ray Anthony (1922-) was bandleader, trumpeter, songwriter, and actor. He played in Glenn Miller's band from 1940 to 1941, appearing in the Glenn Miller vehicle *Sun Valley Serenade* (1941) before joining the Navy during World War II. After the war and Glenn Miller's death, Anthony toured with the Jimmy Dorsey and Al Donahue bands before forming the Ray Anthony Orchestra. It became a very popular dance band, with hit records such as "The Bunny Hop," "The Hokey Pokey," and a swinging take on the theme music from *Dragnet*. Anthony was the musical director on the series *TV's Top Tunes*. He only appeared as himself with his band on these various films and show.

That changed with his 1955 marriage to Mamie Van Doren. He appeared in four of his wife's movies, including *High School Confidential* (1958). His role on *Five Fingers* was his last dramatic role; he and Mamie divorced soon after. His music career continued where his film career faltered, with the theme from *Peter Gunn*. Anthony remains active as a bandleader. His friendship with Hugh Hefner resulted in his appearance in numerous episodes of Hef's reality show *The Girls Next Door* (2005-2010).

Ray Anthony. Copyright Ray Anthony.

Erin O'Brien (1934-   ) is a native Angelino who won on *Arthur Godfrey's Talent Scouts* in 1955. She appeared regularly as a guest vocalist on the *Steve Allen Plymouth Show* and *The George Gobel Show*. In 1957, she was brought in by Warner Brothers to screen test for the lead in *Marjorie Morningstar* with Gene Kelly, but the five-foot seven-inch Kelly felt she was too tall. Warner signed her anyway, but gave the role to Natalie Wood.

Instead, O'Brien was cast in *Onionhead* (1958), an Andy Griffith drama, and then *Girl on the Run* (1958), which is considered the first made-for-TV movie and was the pilot for the TV series *77 Sunset Strip*. She was also in the 1959 film, *John Paul Jones*. Erin made numerous guest appearances, mostly on western television series, usually playing a singer or ingénue. She retired after her second marriage and the subsequent birth of twins in 1965, but not before appearing as Amazon Number One in *In Like Flint*.

Leonard Bell (1924-1995) had a 15-year career of steady but unremarkable minor parts: salesmen, thugs, and townsfolk. His final film, *Four Rode Out* (1970) with Sue Lyon and Pernell Roberts, would be the one he would be remembered for, at least among Euro western fans.

Carl Esmond (1902-2004) was an established leading man in Berlin when, in 1933, he joined the exodus to England to avoid the Nazi takeover. In London, he quickly regained his leading man status and branched out into big screen operettas. He was the hated German fighter pilot ace against Errol Flynn in *The Dawn Patrol* (1938). Although the post-war years made playing the Nazi bad guy almost obligatory for him, the suave actor with his trademark pencil moustache was still cast as a romantic lead, but as the cad with ulterior motives.

Walter Flanagan (1928-2007) graduated from the University of Houston and then moved to New York to pursue an acting career.

He remained primarily a stage performer throughout his career; by his retirement in 2002, he had performed in forty-eight states in a variety of touring companies. Rarely in one place long enough to even audition, his 1959 appearance on *Five Fingers* was his only Hollywood credit until *The Gang That Couldn't Shoot Straight* in 1971. After that, he did three movies: *Shakedown* (1988), *Ghostbusters II* (1989), *The Bonfire of the Vanities* (1990), and an *ABC Afterschool Special* in 1989, before ending his career on tour.

Roy Jenson (1927-2007) was a professional Canadian football player for the Calgary Stampeders and the BC Lions from 1951to1957, working as a stunt man in the off-season. After his football career, he split his time between stunt work and an array of minor roles. His stunt work tapered off in the late 1960s, but he did occasionally return to the field. His last credited stunt work was for *Cherry 2000* (1987).

He appeared in *How the West Was Won*, *Our Man Flint*, *Big Jake*, *Harper*, *Soylent Green*, *The Getaway*, *The Way We Were*, and *Chinatown*. Jenson worked frequently with the directors John Milius (*Dillinger*, *The Wind and the Lion*, *Red Dawn*) and Clint Eastwood (*Thunderbolt and Lightfoot*, *The Gauntlet*, *Every Which Way but Loose*, *Any Which Way You Can*, *Honkytonk Man*).

As a character actor, Jenson had the dubious honor of being beaten up or killed with/by David Hedison in a surprising number of appearances. In addition to being knocked out by Hedison in *Five Fingers*, Jenson was a sailor in a brawl with Hedison's Marine unit in *Marines Let's Go*, and was killed by the titular creature in the *Voyage to the Bottom of the Sea* episode "The Menfish." Finally they were both members of a gang of kidnappers who were killed in *The Gambler: The Adventure Continues* (1983).

George Trevino was the anglicized name of Jorge Treviño, a longtime fixture in the Mexican entertainment industry. A founding member of Asociación Nacional de Actores, the Mexican Actors' Guild, in 1934, he was already national figure as part of radio comedy team "Panseco and Panque" with Arturo Manrique. The two appeared in over a dozen movies, often as the comedy relief in dramas through the 1930s. In the 1940s the team broke up, and Treviño began working in more dramatic roles.

In 1952, two US television shows filmed in Mexico City, and Treviño, who was fluent in English, found himself with US TV credits. He began appearing in any US film shooting in Mexico until 1955. After filming *The Beast of Hollow Mountain* he was cast in *The Bottom of the Bottle*, a film starring Joseph Cotton shot in Arizona. He remained in Hollywood for five years, where, as an unknown in Hollywood in his 60s, he found himself limited to border guards, barkeeps and policía. Aside from an episode of *I Love Lucy* playing Desi Arnaz's Cuban uncle, his career faltered. With his health also failing, he returned to Mexico. His last film appearance was in *The Last Sunset* (1961), filmed in Aguascalientes, Mexico.

Episode 13: The Judas Goat

Margaret Lindsay (1910-1981) was born in Iowa, but an early theater career in England allowed her to develop a British accent so flawless it was one of the reasons Universal signed her in 1932. Arriving in Hollywood, she discovered the role Universal wanted her for, in *The Old Dark House* (1932) starring Boris Karloff, had already been given to another actress. Some publicist chicanery ensued; Lindsay's new biography noted she was a London suburbanite's daughter. Her performance in the film was noticed and Warner Brothers bought out her contract. There, she was cast four times as the love interest of James Cagney and co-starred with Bette Davis in four films, two of which won Oscars for Davis. Following a highly lauded role as Hephzibah in *The*

House of the Seven Gables (1940) opposite Vincent Price, Lindsay signed with Columbia and had the recurring role of budding mystery writer Nikki Porter in all seven *Ellery Queen* films.

The Countess (Kitty Mattern) and Bruno (Albert Szabo) being hauled away by the local [unnamed and uncredited] constabulary. Copyright 20th Century Fox Studios.

Kitty Mattern (1912-1998) was a Viennese cabaret performer who moved to New York in 1938 where she worked both on and off Broadway. Moving to the West Coast in 1951, she worked primarily in theater and in minor, uncredited roles. Her appearance on *Five Fingers* was her only credited American role. She resumed a career on the German and Austrian stages, often working with her husband, actor/director (and also a former cabaret star) Sig Arno. He would shuttle back and forth for another two years before relocating to Germany. There, she appeared in a few films, including a co-star credit in the hit Eurowestern *Shatterhand* (1964).

Frank DeKova (1910-1981) left a teaching position in New York to play Shakespeare off Broadway. It was the start of a long career in a variety of roles on stage and screen, ranging from hired thugs to Mexican colonels, but playing Indians was almost a steady occupation for him in the 1960s. It was as an Indian that he achieved his greatest recognition and where he was discovered to have a flair for deadpan humor delivery. DeKova spent two seasons on the cult western comedy series *F Troop* as the scheming Hekawi Chief Wild Eagle. DeKova continued to work for the rest of his life, but never achieved the same level of success. His final project was voice work in Ralph Bakshi's animated film *Hey Good Lookin'* (1982), released after his death.

Vladimir Sokoloff (1889-1962) was born in Moscow, dropping out of the University of Moscow for the Moscow Academy of Dramatic Art. He joined the Moscow Art Theatre, where he worked his way up from actor to assistant director to director. He moved to the United States in 1937, after acting stints in Berlin and Paris. He immediately found himself in demand by both film and television for an uncanny ability to mimic any nationality, ranging from Filipino in *Back to Bataan* (1945) to Romanian in *I was a Teenage Werewolf* (1957). His final film was the historical war epic *Taras Bulba* (1962), released ten months after his death.

Albert Szabo (1919-1994) was a character actor known for playing menacing henchmen, usually German or Russian, in 1960s TV and films. The same threatening glare that spelled trouble on *Mission: Impossible* was equally effective when played for laughs on such shows as *Green Acres*.

John Graham (no dates) was a British stage actor who moved to New York City. He went from Broadway to live television with an appearance on *Lights Out* in 1948. After a 1958 appearance on *The Phil*

Silvers Show, that particular show moved from New York to Hollywood. Graham saw the industry consolidating there and joined the trek west. A character actor whose onstage presence suggested sophistication, he was regularly called upon to play doctors, lawyers, and school administrators. He worked with Hedison again after *Five Fingers* as the newspaper syndicate underwriter of the expedition and employer of David Hedison in *The Lost World* (1960). In 1980, Graham returned to England, where he continued to work as a character actor until his retirement in 1986.

Violet Rensing (1927-2011) arrived in California in 1953 with her husband and 5-year old son. Rensing was the daughter of noted German soprano Violetta Schadow, a woman who once sued the Nazis because they were letting less loyal party members perform the better roles (she lost). As a result of her early exposure to the arts, Rensing was already a seasoned actress who had been on stage since she was 14. She worked steadily in television with occasional films, most notably starring in *When Hell Broke Loose* (1958) with Charles Bronson. She also appeared in two episodes of the Wally Cox series *The Adventures of Hiram Holliday* with child actor Rene Kroper, her son. She retired in 1966, as roles allowing for her German accent fell out of favor.

Willy Kaufman (1891-1966) was a German character actor who was forced to flee to the United States in 1937. He dabbled briefly on stage in New York before arriving California in 1939. In Hollywood in the pre-war years, he worked steadily in minor roles requiring a German accent. When the war broke out, his career suffered and never recovered. He continued to work, but was relegated to uncredited background characters. He would finally be cast in another role with a screen credit in an episode of *The Man Called X* in 1956 (alongside fellow expatriate Violet Rensing), but his career never recovered.

Deborah Sydes (1951-) was the youngest of three siblings who worked as child actors. Her first role was in *The Glenn Miller Story* (1954); she played the daughter of Glenn Miller with her real-life brother Anthony Sydes playing her brother. The next year, she and her sister Carol played the same character at different ages in *The McConnell Story (*1955). Her sister Carol continued acting after both of her siblings had left the business, culminating in the title role in *Gidget Goes to Rome* (1963). In interviews, Carol would explain her parents didn't want any of the Sydes children acting, only permitting their careers for financial reasons. This is why, at age nine, Deborah retired from show business after her *Five Fingers* appearance.

Greg Dunn (1918-1964) was a radio and TV announcer in Omaha who decided to forgo a career as a horror movie host and community theater stalwart and try his luck in Hollywood. Upon arriving in June 1959, he immediately found work starting with a part in *Have Gun-Will Travel*. His career was cut short by a fatal heart attack soon after shooting an episode of *Hazel*.

Bobby Slade (1949-) worked briefly as a child actor. His first credited role was on *Five Fingers*, followed by minor roles on episodes of *The Loretta Young Show* and *Checkmate*. His fourth and final role was as Laurence Harvey's character as a boy in the film version of Arthur Miller's *Summer and Smoke* (1961). His career ended with the onset of puberty.

Peg Fellows (1917-) worked as an extra in films and television often enough to maintain a Screen Actors Guild membership for a number of years, but did not pursue a professional career. Small roles on episodes of *Five Fingers* and *Lock Up* were her only credited roles onscreen. Fellows was active as both cast and crew in a San Marino community theater and as a top amateur golfer in Los Angeles.

Episode 14: The Search for Edvard Stoyan

Hugo Haas (1901-1968) was the undisputed king of Czech comedy films when he was forced to flee the Nazi invasion in 1939 with his wife, Maria Bibikov. His losses were immeasurable. His brother would die in a concentration camp, and his newborn son, too sickly to travel, was left with his brother's wife, who had forged papers protecting her. The toast of Czechoslovakia and his wife arrived in New York penniless, total unknowns who knew no English. He was recruited by the government to read shortwave radio reports to the Czech underground and narrate propaganda films while learning English. By 1942, his English was sufficient to resume acting. He appeared on Broadway in minor roles but his accent was too thick for the theater. Instead, he headed west and became a character actor of the "threatening foreigner" type such as his role as Van Brun in *King Solomon's Mine* (1950). In between roles, he became an acting teacher, where his students included Gregory Peck. His financial footing secure again, he began writing, producing, starring, and directing his own series of films. The films were shot at the old Chaplin studios, now the Jim Henson Studios, which Haas purchased. The films were not received well; his limited budgets and pervasive theme of loss were misunderstood and dismissed as low-budget melodramas. Unable to recapture his glory days in Czechoslovakia and his savings depleted, he did one last series of television episodes (including *Five Fingers*) to pay for his return to Europe. He arrived in Vienna to a hero's welcome and made sporadic television appearances. His ultimate dream of returning home was ruined by the Soviet occupation of Czechoslovakia in 1968. Haas died a few months later. Biographers noted that although his career was built on his comedic timing, after his brother's death and his exile, he never performed another comedy.

Martin Balsam (1919-1996) was barely out of the Army Air Corps after World War II when Elia Kazan and Lee Strasberg recruited him for the Actors' Studio. He worked in New York in a grueling schedule often performing on live television dramas then rushing to do an evening performance on Broadway. He filmed his breakout film, *12 Angry Men* (1957), at the same time as he was performing in Paddy Chayefsky's *Middle of the Night*. In 1958, he moved to Hollywood and continued an unparalleled career in supporting roles that would see him win the Best Supporting Actor Oscar for *A Thousand Clowns* (1965). He returned to Broadway in 1968, winning the Tony for *You Know I Can't Hear You When the Water's Running*. Balsam, looking for new challenges, began appearing in European films. Enamored of Italy, he moved there and began alternating between European and American roles. After fifty years and hundreds of appearances, he died of a heart attack while vacationing in Italy.

David J. Stewart (1915-1966) was a permanent member of the repertory company of Lincoln Center and a fixture on Broadway. As with any seasoned stage actor, this opened the door for the live television shows. He worked in Hollywood but with minor character roles, including one on *Voyage to the Bottom of the Sea*, "The Sky's on Fire" and such forgettable films as the 1957 rockabilly-themed *Carnival Rock*. It was no surprise Stewart chose to focus on his Broadway roles such as the Tennessee Williams play *Camino Real*, directed by Elia Kazan. Stewart died of complications following heart surgery. His *Voyage* episode was directed by a *Five Fingers* director, Gerald Mayer.

Margaret Phillips (1923-1984) left her native Wales as a sixteen-year-old, in search of the footlights. She enrolled at the Woodstock Theater in New York. At age 19, she debuted on Broadway in the Carol Channing vehicle *Proof Thro' the Night*, launching a distinguished stage career that would span the 1940s and 1950s. Phillips also appeared on a variety of the live television series out of New York. With a solid résumé of stage and television, she decided to test the waters in Hollywood.

She was immediately was cast in *The Nun's Story* (1959) and sent to film in Europe. Her next appearance, on *Five Fingers*, was actually her first role filmed in California, and Phillips soon decided she did not care for Tinseltown. She remained for two years and then returned to her beloved New York theater performing both on and off Broadway and touring with various repertory companies for rest of her career.

William Roerick (1911-1995) was another actor who transitioned from theater to live television to Hollywood. During World War II, he toured with *This Is the Army*, an Irving Berlin show that raised money for emergency relief. Warner Brothers quickly made a film version to support morale and Roerick, already known for his role in *Hamlet*, starring Sir John Gielgud, Lillian Gish, and Dame Judith Anderson, and as an original cast member of *Our Town*, had his first film credit. It would be another nine years and the rise of the New York television industry before he saw another one. He moved to Hollywood in 1956 and appeared regularly in roles requiring an urbane presence. His appearance on *Five Fingers* gave him an edge on his next role on the *Westinghouse Desilu Playhouse* episode "The Man in the Funny Suit," a behind-the-scenes drama about Ed Wynn's appearance in "Requiem for a Heavyweight" on *Playhouse 90*. Roerick played *Playhouse 90* producer Martin Manulis, who was also a producer of *Five Fingers*. For the last fifteen years of his life, he played Henry Chamberlain on the daytime soap opera *The Guiding Light*.

Alvaro Guillot (1931-2010) was born in Uruguay and raised in Paris. A noted artist and early proponent of natural surrealism, tried his hand at acting before he became a professional artist. His first role was in a 1957 low-budget film called *Pharaoh's Curse*, followed by a minor role in *Thunder in the Sun* (1959). Although his only other credits are episodes of *Five Fingers* and *Sea Hunt*, he worked steadily, first as an extra and then with a fellow Frenchman with a Hollywood Press Agency. He fell in love with a Broadway actress in 1960 and followed her back to New

York. The romance wore off quickly and Guillot turned to vending his paintings on the streets. His art found a gallery, and he soon became a leading modern artist.

Alex de Naszody (1914-1996) was a Hungarian film actor and member of the National Theatre who fled to Canada in 1944 when German forces occupied their former ally. His timing and location were fortuitous. After World War II, Canadian theater figures decided the country needed its own professional theater troupes. Alex de Naszody became stage manager for the Canadian Repertory Theater in Ottawa. When the world-renowned Stratford Shakespeare Festival was founded in 1953, he joined the new organization as a manager, who also performed. He also began also appearing on Canadian television. He immigrated to California in 1960. His first role was on *Zane Grey Theater*, followed by an uncredited part in the early scenes of *The Lost World* (1960) starring Claude Rains and David Hedison. When his naturalization papers were approved, he changed his name back to Sándor Naszódy, an approximation of his original name in Hungarian, which had been anglicized upon arrival in Canada. He appeared in several more films and on television, but his first love remained live theater.

Werner Reichow (1922-1973) was born in Tempelburg, Germany (now Czaplinek, Poland). He was the younger brother of Berlin stage and film actor Otto Reichow. Reichow and his family were vocal opponents of Nazism. When Hitler took over, the Reichows were blacklisted. When an older brother was killed by Nazi thugs, the family immigrated to France in 1936 and Otto went on to Los Angeles in 1937. In 1951, Werner joined his brother in Los Angeles. Werner also joined his brother Otto as an actor, working together in four movies and a 1955 *Schlitz Playhouse* episode. Werner, being younger, started acting later than his brother and had fewer roles, most of which were uncredited. Among his appearances, he played a crewman aboard the U-boat captained by

Curt Jurgens that battled David Hedison's destroyer in *The Enemy Below* (1957). The next year, Reichow and his brother played Nazis menacing Curt Jurgens and Danny Kaye in *Me and the Colonel* (1958).

Francis Bethencourt: In 1977, Bethencourt toured the country with an ensemble cast performing several George Bernard Shaw plays. Bethencourt played the lead in Shaw's *Heartbreak House,* and *Don Juan in Hell*, which also starred William Roerick, his co-conspirator in "The Search for Edvard Stoyan."

See Bethencourt's more complete entry in Episode 8.

Episode 15: A Shot in the Dark

Ronald Howard (1918-1996) was the son of the actor Leslie Howard. He pursued a career in journalism until the acting bug struck. His first role, a bit part in *"Pimpernel" Smith* (1941), directed by and starring his father, never made it out of the cutting room, so his official debut was in the movie *While the Sun Shines* (1947). He is best remembered as Sherlock Holmes in the 1954 series that ran in the US, Canada and Britain, and for the short-lived *Cowboy in Africa* series. He continued to work in both Britain and America into the 1970s, growing increasingly unhappy with the quality of roles offered. He retired to England and operated an art gallery while composing a biography of his father.

Neile Adams (1932-   ) started her career as a dancer, joining the cast of the original production of *Kismet* on Broadway, rising from dancer to understudy for one of the princesses of Ababu. She was noticed by Bob Fosse, who brought her to national attention in the original production of *The Pajama Game*. She left Broadway in 1956, having married an up and coming unknown actor named Steve McQueen. Adams appeared on *Five Fingers* in between the birth of her children (Terry McQueen in June 1959, and Chad McQueen in December 1960), one of three appearances before temporarily retiring to play housewife. Adams and Hedison reunited for a 1967 episode of *The Hollywood Palace* variety show, hosted by Milton Berle. She danced and appeared with Hedison in a *Voyage* spoof, with Berle as the most expendable member of the *Seaview* crew. In addition to numerous appearances in documentaries about her late husband, Steve McQueen, Adams continues to perform with a highly lauded one-woman cabaret act.

Alf Kjellin (1920-1988) was a Swedish actor who made his mark in show business after appearing in the Alf Sjoberg-directed *Hets* (1944). The film, written by Ingmar Bergman, was released in the US as *Torment*. David O. Selznick saw the film and brought Kjellin to California to appear in *Madame Bovary* (1949), a period piece starring Selznick's wife, actress Jennifer Jones. Disliking both his new stage name Christopher Kent and the poor quality of the roles offered, Kjellin returned to Sweden and studied directing. When he came back to Hollywood in 1959, he was a seasoned director. Although it took several years to ease into the director's chair, he began acting again upon arrival. *Five Fingers* was his first appearance this second trip. After directing a 1961 episode of *Alfred Hitchcock Presents*, he became highly sought after as a director, helming eleven episodes of *The Alfred Hitchcock Hour*, more than any other director on the series. He would occasionally take a small role in a film or TV series. One of his more interesting credits was 1978's *Project UFO* where Kjellin appeared in an episode with both David Hedison and Marta Kristen called "Sighting 4011: The Dollhouse Incident." The spacecraft interior was designed by Robert Kinoshita, who designed the sets for Irwin Allen, and elements of *Lost in Space, Voyage to the Bottom of the Sea,* and *Time Tunnel* all appear as alien technology. In 1974, Kjellin was awarded the Royal Order of Vasa with the rank of Knight First Class by King Carl XVI of Sweden for his "most excellent contribution to the arts of the theater and film as actor, writer, director and producer."

FIVE FINGERS: ELEGANCE IN ESPIONAGE

Robert Carricart (1917-1993) left the army after World War II and studied drama on the GI bill. He began his career doing Shakespeare on Broadway and, as with so many stage actors, dabbled in live television. Born in France of Monégasque parents, his heritage gave him a familiarity with both French and Italian, which he parlayed into more than 100 appearances in television and film as a character actor, only slowing down in the 1980s due to age. He was best known for being a regular in the series *T.H.E. Cat*. He was also in a 1961 episode of the series *Hong Kong*, "Lesson in Fear," that guest starred David Hedison as the villain.

Joanna Moore (1934-1997) was spotted at a cocktail party by a producer at Universal, and made her television debut in a 1956 episode of *Lux Video Theatre*. Success came quickly and, by 1962, she had a recurring role as Sheriff Andy Taylor's girlfriend in the third season of *The Andy Griffith Show*. This would turn out to be the peak of her career; later that year she married actor Ryan O'Neal and had two children, Tatum and Griffin O'Neal. Her bitter 1967 divorce from O'Neal triggered a downward spiral of depression and substance abuse that also took a toll on her career. Moore lost custody of her children in 1970 due to the severity of her addiction problem. By 1977, her career had evaporated and 13-year old Tatum became her sole financial support, going so far as to buy a condo for her. Her career never recovered. She appeared in two more projects in the 1980s. She died in 1997 of lung cancer with Tatum at her side.

Harold Ayer (1916-2003) was born in London, the son of American composer, lyricist, and performer Nat D. Ayer. A "backstage baby," Ayer was raised in the wings as his father composed and performed in Edwardian musical comedy. Trained at London's Royal Academy of Dramatic Art, his first screen role was as a soldier in *The Third Man* (1949) starring Orson Welles. A headliner on the London stage and a staple of British film for over a decade, he moved to California in 1959.

His first American role was on *Five Fingers* and, although he would work steadily for the next forty years in such roles as the bartender in the Oscar winning movie *The Sting* (1973), he was never able to make the jump to headliner in the United States.

Jay Adler (1896-1978) was born into a theatrical dynasty, the eldest son of Jacob Adler, the biggest star of the Yiddish-language theater. All the Adlers started in Yiddish theater and moved to Broadway. Although his career was overshadowed by his more famous siblings, director Luther and Stella of acting school fame, his woebegone countenance could be threatening or sympathy evoking. Adler used it both ways in a career that spanned from 1937 to 1976 and included multiple appearances on *The Untouchables*, *Twilight Zone* and *77 Sunset Strip*, in addition to over forty-five films.

Mario Gallo (1923-1984) was a Brooklyn-born character actor who found work in New York in the early days of TV, before heading to California in the late 1950s. Not surprisingly, his specialty was Italian New Yorkers, as evidenced in films such as *Raging Bull* (1980). His best known role was as Tomas Delvecchio, Judd Hirsch's father in the series *Delvecchio*.

Episode 16: Counterfeit

Cesar Romero (1907-1994) is most fondly remembered as The Joker in the 1960s television series *Batman*. That role overshadowed a long and colorful career as a cowboy (he starred as *The Cisco Kid* in six films) and a "Latin Lover." In 1953, he was the lead in the espionage TV series *Passport to Danger*, a series very reminiscent of the *Five Fingers* concept. Romero is a US diplomatic courier who travels to exotic locations, encounters political intrigues and escapes using his continental sophistication and American resourcefulness. Romero had negotiated an extraordinarily generous contract that included profit sharing. When the series ended after four years, Romero was wealthy enough to never work again. But his love for the work was great enough that he continued to accept roles, although with much more selectivity.

Among his many television credits, Romero played Don Diego de la Vega's uncle in four episodes of Disney's *Zorro*, was a regular guest on *The Red Skelton Hour*, and even appeared as Count Dracula on Rod Serling's *Night Gallery*. With his career reenergized by *Batman*, he took the role of A. J. Arno, the crooked business leader who is the foil to Kurt Russell's Dexter Riley in three Disney films, starting with *The Computer Wore Tennis Shoes* (1969). He would return to his "Latin Lover" roots as Peter Stavros in *Falcon Crest* (1985–1987), filming fifty-one episodes as Jane Wyman's love interest.

Joseph Ruskin (1924-2014) was a character actor whose pockmarked cheeks gave him an ominous appearance that belied his deep concern for his fellow actors. He was a driving force behind the scenes of the merger of the two actors' unions, SAG and AFTRA, serving on the SAG board before and after the merger as the First National Vice President. In 1979, he became the first Western Region Vice President of Actors Equity. His career started in summer stock, which led to off-Broadway and the New York television industry. A leading role in an episode of the *Naked City* TV series convinced Ruskin to head to Hollywood, where he appeared in twenty-five films and hundreds of television shows. His notable film appearances include *Prizzi's Honor* (1985). He was the only actor to appear onscreen in four of the five Star Trek series. Ruskin would return to threaten David Hedison again in "The Magnus Beam," a first season episode of *Voyage to the Bottom of the Sea*.

Yale Wexler (1930-1996) left show business to become a major hotel and real estate developer in the Chicago area. The youngest child of RadioShack founder Simon Wexler, he trained in drama at Carnegie Tech while spending his summers working the summer theater circuit in New England before being cast on Broadway in *Tea & Sympathy*, starring Deborah Kerr and directed by Elia Kazan. He did a number of uncredited roles on live soap operas and TV series, taking late-night classes from director Harold Clurman with other actors willing to train after their nightly performances. His first film was *Time Limit* (1957) starring Richard Widmark and Richard Basehart, followed by his first starring role in *Stakeout on Dope Street* (1958). Not satisfied with the roles being offered, he passed the real estate exam, bought a parcel of land and built a hotel in Beverly Hills. The decision proved prudent, so much so that Wexler was then referred to by columnist Walter Winchell as a "part time actor and full time millionaire." In a later interview Wexler noted that he found the nuances of real estate development were similar to producing a film. He returned to Chicago in 1974, and launched a new career in hotel development and management. He continued to produce films as a hobby and chaired the Chicago International Film Festival.

Eric Feldary (1912-1968) was a Hungarian athlete turned actor. In 1930, he was Juniors foils champion and represented Hungary on their 1936 Olympic fencing team. He immigrated to the US, and by 1941 he was appearing as a costar in such films as *Hold Back the Dawn* (1941) and *For Whom the Bell Tolls* (1943). On television, he was able to use his fencing skills a number of times, including episodes of *The Adventures of Jim Bowie* and the Canadian show *The Adventures of Hiram Holliday*. He appeared in a first season episode of *Voyage to the Bottom of the Sea*, "The Last Battle," playing a surviving Nazi trying to establish the Fourth Reich. He died of burns suffered in a gas explosion that destroyed his West Hollywood home.

Michael Granger (1923-1981) worked steadily as a character actor from 1952 until 1961. He had greater success in television, his films tending toward the lower end of the budgetary spectrum, such as *Creature with The Atom Brain* (1953) and *Jungle Moon Men* (1955). Leaving Hollywood with such career highlights, he spent a year off-Broadway before landing the defining role of his career in 1964. He played Lazar Wolf, the butcher, in the original cast of *Fiddler on the Roof*.

Richard Morris (1924-1996) studied acting under Sanford Meisner at the Neighborhood Playhouse in Manhattan. He also wrote sketch comedy routines, one of which caught the eye of a talent scout from Universal Studios. Morris was soon under contact in California and he moved to Los Angeles, where he wrote screenplays, starting with *Finders Keepers* (1951) and *Ma and Pa Kettle at the Fair* (1952). After writing three episodes of *Private Secretary* for Ann Southern, he was hired as head writer of *The Loretta Young Show*, where he would also direct fifty episodes. Morris left *The Loretta Young Show* to write the book for the Broadway musical *The Unsinkable Molly Brown*. He returned to Hollywood with the screenplay for *Thoroughly Modern Millie* (1967) starring Julie Andrews and Carol Channing. He appeared onscreen four times in his career. His first was an uncredited film appearance in *The Prince Who Was a Thief* (1951), followed by three television appearances in episodes of *Five Fingers*, *The United States Steel Hour*, and *Gazette*.

Joseph Waring (1925-1997) served in the Navy during World War II, then performing with the USO. After the war, a plan by former USO performers was formulated to create a traveling repertory company of veterans that would travel by covered wagon and tour sixty-eight towns from Montana to Los Angeles, performing live theater for the locals. Waring was first to sign on to the project. The publicity generated by the troupe's arrival in Los Angeles, opened doors for many of the fledgling actors. Over the next four decades, he worked as a character actor and was often better known for who he was dating at the time than his roles. At age seventy, Waring volunteered as an usher at the Civic Arts Plaza in Thousand Oaks. He remained so devoted to his craft that he was promoted to the paid part-time position of staff usher. When he died, two antique theater chairs were installed in the lobby of the theater in his memory.

Peter Brocco See entry for previous appearance in Episode 10.

Montgomery Pittman See entry as crew member in Chapter 16.

Chapter 16

The Crew of Five Fingers

The Creator:

Dick Berg (1922-2009) was a prolific producer and screen writer who also wrote the pilot episode of *Five Fingers*. Born in New York, he went to Hollywood to find work as a writer, but instead became a dialogue coach for Roy Rogers and the other Western stars at Republic Pictures. Still wishing to be a writer, he went back to New York where the burgeoning television industry offered more opportunities. Managing an art gallery in Connecticut by day, he wrote scripts on speculation, selling over a dozen to *Robert Montgomery Presents* and *Playhouse 90*. His script for the *Studio One* episode "The Drop of a Hat" was adapted for the stage and caught the attention of Hecht Hill

Lancaster, the production company formed by Burt Lancaster with his agent Harold Hecht. Berg came back to Hollywood, this time as a screenwriter.

He was hired by Fox as part of a team to develop new series. At the same time Berg was creating *Five Fingers* for Fox, he created the series *Johnny Staccato* for Revue Studios at Universal (both would air on NBC). There are similarities in how music and intrigue share equal billing, allowing spy Victor Sebastian's cover as a talent agent and Johnny Staccato's crime solving jazz pianist to also feature performers and musicians not normally tapped for television. Berg is also credited with creating the series *Checkmate*. After leaving Fox, Berg became a producer at Universal via his Stonehenge Productions. Although he would make a handful of movies, Berg was a television producer first and foremost. Stonehenge Productions would create the concept of a "made-for-TV movie" and then produce a dozen of these "movies of the week." They were also an early developer of the concept of "miniseries." Berg's preference for miniseries was scripts based on historical events or with strong social undertones. Among the works he adapted for cable and network television were works by James Michener, Ray Bradbury, Irving Wallace, and Elmore Leonard. Berg is also credited with launching the careers of directors Sydney Pollack, Mark Rydell, and Stuart Rosenberg.

The Producers:

Martin Manulis (1915-2007) joined CBS as a staff producer in 1951. He had been hired as managing director of the Westport Country Playhouse in Connecticut in 1945, after serving as a Navy press liaison officer in Europe during the war. In the era of live television which relied heavily on stage actors, he should have had a seamless transition to television producer. Manulis however, not only had no hands-on experience in television, he didn't even own a television. He took a crash course in television production and was assigned to take over *Casey,*

Crime Photographer, the prime time crime drama that, two months into its first season, was floundering in the ratings. Manulis, in a gutsy move for a novice producer, replaced Richard Carlyle as Casey, hiring Darren McGavin for the role. It paid off and the ratings became respectable enough to warrant a second season. After six months, Manulis took over as producer of the series *Suspense*. After a year, he was handed his first major project, *Playhouse 90*. He produced over sixty episodes, including all episodes in the first two seasons, resulting in his winning eleven Emmys in those two seasons alone. His reputation firmly established, Manulis was made head of production for 20th Century Fox Television, where he oversaw the creation and production of such series as *Five Fingers*, *The Many Loves of Dobie Gillis*, and *Adventures in Paradise*. He remained there until 1961, when he began producing films, which included his best known work to date, *Days of Wine and Roses* (1962). The call of television remained strong and after a brief sojourn back to his theatrical roots, he served as director of the American Film Institute. He returned to television with a PBS adaptation of Robert Anderson's play *Double Solitaire* (1974), and then served as executive producer of the series *James at 16*. The three part mini-series *Chiefs* (1983) proved so successful that he pushed the miniseries boundary with his next project. *Space* (1985) was a thirteen-hour mini-series based on James A. Michener's novel on NASA and the American space program. Manulis ended his career as artistic director of the Ahmanson Theatre from 1987 to 1989.

Herbert Swope, Jr. (1915-2008) was born and raised in New York. He was the son of Herbert Bayard Swope Sr. Swope Senior was the winner of the first Pulitzer Prize for reporting, a founder of the Algonquin round table, and a possible inspiration for the literary character Jay Gatsby. Having grown up among his father's poker buddies and house guests such as F. Scott Fitzgerald, Dorothy Parker, Somerset Maugham, and Noel Coward, Swope Junior was a staple in New York society circles. One of the Swope family pastimes was croquet; many of the current rules were developed by Swope's father and his guests. Both father and son are in the United States Croquet Hall of Fame. Swope served aboard a US Naval minesweeper during World War II before joining CBS Television as a remote unit director. Because remote units handled sporting events, he quickly became head of a new department at CBS: Sportscasting. Joining NBC at the birth of live television, he produced and directed such series as *The Black Robe*, *The Clock*, and *Lights Out*. After producing thirty-eight episodes of *Lights Out* in two years, he decided to take a break by producing the drama *Fragile Fox* on Broadway. By the time he decided to return to producing television and film, the industry had moved west. He went to Hollywood and before he even looked for work, he was part of Samuel Goldwyn's group of croquet players with fellow enthusiasts George Sanders, Louis Jourdan, and Michael Romanoff.

Swope served as producer for a handful of unremarkable film dramas for 20th Century Fox before switching to their television unit. There he served as executive producer of *The Many Loves of Dobie Gillis* and produced *Five Fingers*. *Five Fingers* in particular benefited from Swope's networking over the croquet wickets as many of the guest stars swung the croquet mallet. Series regular Michael Romanoff was also in the United States Croquet Hall of Fame.

With *Five Fingers* canceled and *The Many Loves of Dobie Gillis* doing well, Swope decided to return home to New York. He produced two additional shows that reached Broadway. Neither was successful. *Step on a Crack* closed on opening night in 1962 and *Fair Game for Lovers* only lasted five days in 1964.

In 1974, Swope relocated to that last bastion of old society, Palm Beach, Florida. In addition to his society events, he began hosting a radio show, "Swope's Scope," on WSBR in Boca Raton, interviewing the actors and actresses passing through Florida. He also worked as a TV and movie critic for the *Palm Beach Daily News*. At the time of his death,

Swope was writing an autobiography of his youth among writers, literati, and croquet games titled *A Perfectly Normal Childhood*.

Series Directors:

Robert Stevens (1920-1989) directed "Station Break," the original pilot. He was contracted to direct a total of four episodes of *Five Fingers*, but was hired away to direct the pilot for another new show: *The Twilight Zone*. He did a second episode of *Twilight Zone* before Alfred Hitchcock hired him away from Rod Serling. Stevens directed nearly fifty episodes of *Alfred Hitchcock Presents* and *The Alfred Hitchcock Hour*, winning an Emmy in the process. Hitchcock had noticed Stevens' ability to frame shots with odd angles to create atmosphere, a talent developed during his three years directing 105 episodes of *Suspense* for Martin Manulis.

After his stint on the *Hitchcock* show, Stevens worked less, but was the first one called to direct any episode with a supernatural or surreal element, one that required his uncanny knack for mirror shots or skewed camera angles. Stevens, unfortunately, suffered a fatal heart attack at his Westport, Connecticut, summer home when he was assaulted in a home invasion. In true *Twilight Zone* fashion, the two episodes of the series he had directed had been written by Rod Serling, while Serling was living in Westport, Connecticut.

Andrew McCullough (1924-) directed two *Five Fingers* episodes: "Station Break" (the fifty minute aired episode), and "Men With Triangle Heads," which he also wrote. McCullough started his career directing the TV show *Out There* in 1951, but made his reputation on the CBS series *Omnibus*, directing the first season and then alternating with other directors for the rest of the series, continuing when it moved to ABC. As part of the *Omnibus* series, he co-directed *King Lear* with noted Shakespearian director Peter Brook, using Brook's ninety minute stage version of the play which starred Orson Welles in his television debut.

His anti-war script "The General's Other Son" was performed on *Playhouse 90* in 1958. It was popular enough that McCullough expanded it into a full length drama which Robert Montgomery then attempted to bring to Broadway. McCullough directed television into the mid-1960s, but his style of directing, long, carefully framed scenes, was falling out of vogue. He had been directing West Coast theater since his arrival in 1957 and, as television offers dried up, he returned to the theater. He was not necessarily happy about his diminished role in television (he worked as a second unit director and as a second assistant director on a season of *Happy Days* in 1978-79) and penned a novel to vented his frustrations. *Rough Cut* (1976) was a fictionalized story of an actor who gives up love for renewed fame and fortune, only to realize that in Hollywood, power trumps everything, even life.

He would return to television as the stage manager for seventy-two episodes of *Family Ties*, directing fourteen more episodes. As stage manager on the 1987 *Family Ties* hour-long episode "A, My Name is Alex," he was part of the team that won the Outstanding Directorial Achievement Award from the Directors Guild of America.

Montgomery Pittman (1917-1962) directed three *Five Fingers* episodes: "Dossier," "Man Who Got Away," and "Operation Ramrod." His career in show business was more unorthodox than most. He ran away from the family farm in his teens and became a patent medicine hawker with a traveling carnival. He attempted to break into acting in New York with limited success, so he moved to California in 1949. As he struggled to get into film or television, it occurred to Monty that perhaps he could get better parts by writing the screenplay himself. At this time, it was still possible, although unlikely, for a spec script to be submitted without an agent and actually be considered. In 1954, he sold his first script to *Four Star Playhouse*, the first of over fifty of his scripts to be filmed.

Almost immediately, Pittman took to a dislike to the way his scripts were being directed. With only five teleplays to his credit, he convinced the studios to let him direct an episode of *Luke and the Tenderfoot*. From that point, he would direct as many of his own screenplays as he could. Will Hutchins, the star of *Sugarfoot*, became a friend. Hutchins credited Pittman's five scripts and directorial efforts to revitalizing his show. Pittman was a frequent writer for *77 Sunset Strip*, also becoming a close friend of its star, Efrem Zimbalist Jr. Zimbalist, who delivered Pittman's eulogy, devotes a section of his memoirs, *My Dinner of Herbs* (2003), to his old friend, who died much too young of cancer.

Lamont Johnson directing. Copyright 20th Century Fox Studios. Photo courtesy of David Hedison.

Lamont Johnson (1922-2010) directed four episodes of *Five Fingers*: "Moment of Truth," "Unknown Town," "Assassin," and "Thin Ice." He also directed David Hedison's episode "Call Back Yesterday" of the *Bus Stop* series in 1961, starring Marilyn Maxwell. His career started as a radio actor at sixteen. He worked consistently enough as a voice actor, deejay and newscaster to underwrite his college education. Seeking a career on stage, Johnson ended up in New York, working as a voice actor in the soap operas and as a Broadway understudy.

While touring with the USO in Europe, he was befriended by Gertrude Stein, who gave him rights to her play *Yes is for a Very Young Man*. His first professional directing job was that show off-Broadway in 1948. He dabbled in television, appearing as a regular on *Prize Winner* in 1953-54, at which time he was also playing the lead role in the radio version of *Tarzan*. In 1955, he made his TV directorial debut on the live drama series *Matinee Theater* with Richard Boone starring in an adaptation of *Wuthering Heights*. The show was successful and Johnson went on to direct twenty-eight episodes of the series.

More important to Johnson's career, Boone was impressed, and would insist Johnson be allowed to direct six episodes of Boone's *Have Gun, Will Travel* series, allowing Johnson to enter the West Coast filmed TV series market. Over his career, he won two Emmys and four Directors Guild of America Awards. In addition to television, theater and film, Johnson also occasionally directed opera productions, including *The Man in the Moon* (1959), *Iphigénie en Tauride* (1962), and *Orfeo* (1990).

Allen Reisner (1924-2004) began his career in 1941 in New York as an actor. He worked on stage until he found himself more in demand for roles on live TV, appearing on such programs as *Philco Playhouse* and the *NBC Repertory Theater*. He switched from actor to assistant director at the suggestion of Yul Brynner, who was working as a television director in between his theater jobs. Assistant director quickly became director. Reisner remained under contract to CBS from 1950 to1956, which included directing six episodes of *Studio One* for Martin Manulis.

Reisner was popular and this translated to his directing multiple episodes of shows. Where a director might occasionally do several episodes of a program, with Reisner it was a regular occurrence. In addition to directing three *Five Fingers* episodes: "Emerald Curtain," "Final Dream," and "Search for Edvard Stoyan." He directed twenty-five episodes of *Climax*, thirteen episodes of *Hawaii Five-O*, eight episodes of *Lancer* and six episodes of *The Green Hornet*. He would direct David Hedison once again in an episode of the TV series *Shaft* called "The Capricorn Murders" in 1974.

Paul Wendkos (1925-2009) directed "Temple of the Swinging Doll." He had only been in Hollywood for two years when Harry Cohn, head of Columbia Pictures, saw his potential in *The Burglar* (1957), a film noir shot in the New York-Philadelphia area that was also the breakthrough role for Jayne Mansfield. This launched a career that was steeped in dichotomy. Even as Wendkos was making a name for himself in the industry with hard-hitting noir crime dramas, he was developing popular appeal as the director of three beloved teen surf movies: *Gidget* (1959), *Gidget Goes Hawaiian* (1961) and *Gidget Goes to Rome* (1963). Wendkos worked extensively in television, if not without the occasional hiccup. He directed eleven episodes of *I Spy*, only to be fired for making the spy show "too arty." Wendkos' response to that was to direct nine episodes of *The Invaders*. Starting in 1970, he began to concentrate on made-for-TV movies, a format that allowed him to use the fluid camera technique that was deemed too artistic for the *I Spy* producers, but had prompted Harry Cohn offer him a contract originally.

Gerald Mayer (1919-2001) directed "The Judas Goat." He began his career in the mid-1940s directing short films and shooting screen tests for MGM. Directing film at a major studio straight out of the military would be a remarkable feat, except Gerald was the son of MGM studio manager Jerry Mayer, which made Louis B. Mayer his uncle. Mayer broke into feature length films with *Dial 1119* (1950), a crime noir starring Andrea King and Virginia Field, both of whom Mayer was rumored to be involved with romantically in quick succession. From then on, Mayer found no shortage of offers to direct and leading ladies to woo. He directed *Bright Road* (1953); it became one of the most popular films of the year and marked the start of a romance with star Dorothy Dandridge.

By this point, Loews was exerting control of MGM and Mayer decided the increasingly popular medium of television was a better career choice for him. He was correct. Highlights of his busy career were nineteen episodes of *The Millionaire*, thirteen episodes of *Mannix* and four episodes of *Voyage to the Bottom of the Sea*.

David Greene (1921-2003) directed "A Shot in the Dark." He entered show business as the publicity man for the *Everyman Theatre* in London. Greene worked in British theater and films, then made the move to New York. He appeared on Broadway as part of a repertory cast that alternated between Shaw's *Caesar and Cleopatra* and Shakespeare's *Anthony and Cleopatra*. When the show closed on Broadway, it began a tour of Canada where Greene accepted an offer from the Canadian Broadcasting Company to join their television department. After three years of directing mostly Shakespearean adaptations, he returned to New York television. By the time Greene directed *Five Fingers*, he was becoming increasingly in demand both in Hollywood and in London, seamlessly switching from swashbuckling adventures like *Sir Francis Drake* (1961) to courtroom dramas such as *The Defenders* TV series (1961). Similarly, he was equally at home directing horror films like *The Shuttered Room* (1967) as he was directing a musical film such as *Godspell* (1973). In the mid-1970s, Greene cut back on travel and remained on the West Coast, specializing in made-for-TV films and miniseries. It was during this time he won three of his four Emmy Awards for Outstanding Directing of a Drama Series or Special.

Charles R. Rondeau (1917-1996) had directed a movie before directing *Five Fingers*, but since *The Littlest Hobo* (1958) was children's film starring only a dog, the episode "Counterfeit" should probably be considered his first directing credit, at least with a human cast. A theater actor and director with decades of stage experience, Rondeau came to Hollywood comparatively late. In the 1960s, he primarily directed TV dramas, including three episodes of *Voyage to the Bottom of the Sea* in 1968. As television evolved in the 1970s, so too did Rondeau.

Between 1969 and 1973, he directed forty-two episodes of *Love, American Style*, including David Hedison's first season appearance in "Love and the Other Love." Rondeau's forty-two episode credits from this series are all the more impressive, as a single episode could include several segments, all helmed by the same director. Rondeau retired from directing in 1980, ending a career that started with directing a dog by directing a monkey in four episodes of the television series *B.J. and the Bear*.

Series Writers (including writer, teleplay, story, and story editor credits):

L. C. Moyzisch (no dates) was the Nazi military attaché at the German Embassy in Ankara from 1943 to1945 and the handler for the mole in the British embassy that would lead to the book *Operation Cicero*. Moyzisch's book had absolutely nothing to do with the series. In the pilot episode he is wrongly credited as C. L. Moyzisch, but this had been corrected by the time the series aired in October 1959. The studio was using the *Five Fingers* name in hopes of cashing in on the 1952 James Mason film, for which they had the rights from the Moyzisch book, so each episode had to be credited as "based on 'Operation Cicero' by L. C. Moyzisch."

Author's note: See Chapter Eighteen.

Kenneth L. Evans (no dates) was Executive Story Editor for the entire sixteen episodes of *Five Fingers*, a job that juggled the demands of production with the shepherding of scripts through the creation and editing processes. The executive story editor position is one step below producer, making Evans responsible for most of the story editing and a number of producer-level tasks, such as rewrites, budget issues, and post-production. So, without a screen credit, Evans would have tweaked each script prior to putting it into the production timeline. It was a grueling job, as he was also simultaneously editing *The Many Loves of Dobie Gillis* (fifty-eight episodes, 1959-1961), *Adventures in Paradise* (twenty-eight episodes, 1959-1960), and *Hong Kong* (nine episodes, 1960). In 1967, Evans was named an executive at the new CBS theatrical film production and distribution division. By that point he had served as a Story Editor at Columbia, 20th Century Fox and Paramount. He tried his hand as an Executive Producer with the Lee Marvin/Gene Hackman film *Prime Cut* (1972) before semi-retiring to join the faculty at USC School of Cinematic Arts where he wrote a crime novel, *A Feast for Spiders* in 1979.

William E. Barrett (1900-1986) ["Assassin," "Operation Ramrod"] came to Hollywood in 1955 not to begin a career, but to observe the process of turning his best-selling novel *The Left Hand of God* into a film with Humphrey Bogart pretending to be a priest in order to hide from a Chinese warlord. Barrett had been a professional writer for over twenty years, with hundreds of short stories published. He was less impressed with the adaptation of one of his short stories into an episode of *DuPont Theater*, "Decision for a Hero," and decided to try teleplays himself. He wrote four scripts in three years that were produced, which does not sound prolific until also adding in the two novels and a history of warplanes he also published in the same time period. He returned to Colorado to concentrate on a new novel which was published in 1962. *Lilies of the Field* was immediately made into a film, earning five Academy Award nominations, including Sidney Poitier's Oscar for his role as a drifter who is coerced by German refugee nuns into helping them build a chapel.

Richard Berg ["Station Break"] See previous entry at beginning of this chapter.

Harry Brown (1917-1986) ["The Search for Edvard Stoyan"] was a Harvard-educated journalist whose work at *Time* and *New Yorker* was cut short by World War II. He was assigned to *Yank* magazine, published for servicemen, where he began writing war stories. Part of his output was the novel *A Walk in the Sun* (1944), a bestseller on the home front that was made into a 1946 film starring Dana Andrews. After his discharge, Brown headed to Hollywood to capitalize on this success, quickly becoming a sought-after screenwriter. He wrote back-to-back John Wayne scripts, *Wake of the Red Witch* (1948) and *Sands of Iwo Jima* (1949), the latter of which earned him his first Oscar nomination. He worked steadily, specializing in military films. Ironically, his only Academy Award win was for *A Place in the Sun* (1951), starring Montgomery Clift and Elizabeth Taylor, which had nothing to do with World War II. Although he would continue to work in war themed scripts, the Oscar allowed him to branch out. Even as his *Five Fingers* episode was being produced, he was hard at work on the script for *Ocean's Eleven* (1960) starring Frank Sinatra and rest of the Rat Pack. In the late 1960s, he moved to Guanajuato, Mexico, to concentrate on his writing, adding several novels and collections of poetry to his credits.

Whitfield Cook (1909-2003) ["Unknown Town"] was a long-time friend of Alfred Hitchcock, dating back to 1944 when Cook wrote and directed *Violet* on Broadway, based on his own popular "Violet" stories from *Redbook* about a teenage girl who complicates and then untangles her father's life. The show only ran for twenty-three performances, but it starred Alfred Hitchcock's daughter Patricia in her Broadway debut, and Cook was welcomed into the Hitchcock family's social circle accordingly. Cook moved to Hollywood in 1945 and signed with MGM, writing and scripting light film fare for June Allyson. Cook had been a regular companion of the Hitchcocks, and when his MGM contract was up, Hitch brought him to Warner Brothers where he was immediately put to work writing a script with Hitchcock's wife, Alma Reville. That film, *Stage Fright* (1950) changed Cook's career. While he was working on the next film for Hitchcock, *Strangers on a Train* (1951), he and Alma came perilously close to having an affair. After that, Cook began to distance himself from Reville. Whether it was his choice or Hitchcock had suspicions, Cook was far removed from the director's creative circle by 1952, working in television for the rest of his career, still writing teleplays that never entirely lost their vibe of mystery, no matter what the show's genre.

Robert C. Dennis (1915-1983) ["Dossier," "The Search for Edvard Stoyan"] was born in Courtright, Ontario, Canada, and was a mystery writer, first and foremost. For over a decade, his short stories repeatedly graced every major pulp mystery magazine. He parlayed that success into writing mysteries for radio. When he learned the struggling new ABC TV network needed scriptwriters, he sent them an episode of *Mysteries of Chinatown* (1950). As television and radio battled for dominance, Dennis worked in both camps. Dennis' credentials were such that he was able pitch series that played to his strength of mysteries in exotic locations. He created the series *China Smith* in 1952, the adventures of a private eye in Singapore, which was also brought back as 1954 as *The New Adventures of China Smith*. Dennis wrote thirty-two of the sixty episodes of the two shows. That series was barely off the air before he created another, *Passport to Danger*, starring Cesar Romero as a globe-trotting US diplomatic courier. Once again Dennis wrote half the scripts. A third series, to be set in Hong Kong, was not picked up, but Dennis was content to continue being a prolific script writer, which included penning thirty episodes of *Alfred Hitchcock Presents* and co-writing with Philip MacDonald the first of only three *Perry Mason* episodes where Mason lost a case. But to baby boomers, he and co-writer Earl Barrett will forever be remembered for creating the supervillain King Tut in the 1960's *Batman* series. Dennis wrote teleplays for the TV movies *Dan August: Once Is Never Enough* (1980), *Dan August: The Jealousy Factor*, *The Eddie Capra Mysteries* and *The Amazing Captain Nemo* (1978). Dennis worked prolifically for Quinn Martin, Jack Webb and Aaron Spelling.

Jerry Devine (no dates) ["Moment of Truth," "The Emerald Curtain," "Temple of the Swinging Doll," "Final Dream," "The Judas Goat"] was a child actor in the silent era who gave up his career onscreen for writing. Devine wrote for a number of radio shows from the 1930s through the1950s, including *Mr. District Attorney* and *The Shadow*. He produced, directed, and wrote for the Hoover sanctioned radio show *This is Your F.B.I.* (1944-1953). His first television credits were the five episodes of *Five Fingers*. Devine has nine other writing credits for the TV Shows *Naked City*, *Bewitched*, *Family Affair*, *Felony Squad*, *Voyage to the Bottom of the Sea* ("Man Beast"), *It Takes a Thief*, *The Doris Day Show*, and *The Six Million Dollar Man*. He was also a playwright, with his work reaching Broadway twice: *Amorous Flea* (1965) and *Children of the Wind* (1973).

David Karp (1922-1999) ["The Man Who Got Away"] had already published nine of his eleven novels when he was recruited to write for television. Like peers such as Rod Serling and Paddy Chayefsky, he parlayed his cachet as a novelist into teleplays tackling social issues of the day on the TV drama anthologies. Karp adapted his novel *One* (1953), a future dystopian tale of blind patriotism, into a script that aired on *Kraft Television Theater* in 1955 and the *Matinee Theater* in 1957. Karp wrote six novels and many episodes of television series, including *The Untouchables* and *The Defenders*. He wrote scripts for movies for over forty years, occasionally taking on the role of producer, most notably on *The Brothers Rico* (1960) with James Darren and *The Brotherhood of the Bell* (1970), which he adapted from his 1952 novel.

Andrew McCullough ["The Men with Triangle Heads"] d See previous entry.

Philip MacDonald (1901-1980) ["Thin Ice"] arrived in Hollywood after one of his books was adapted into the film *Lost Patrol* (1929). He became one of the most popular and prolific mystery writers of the 1930s, using five aliases to disguise how many books on the racks were written by him. This was appropriate for a writer whose work was constantly filled with plot twists involving disguises and make-up. Over the next thirty years, as mystery movies lost their popularity, he switched to radio and then television, including his *Five Fingers* episode, which not surprisingly, involved characters in disguise. Some of his better known film screenplays include *Rebecca* (1940), *Sahara* (1943), and *The List of Adrian Messenger* (1963), which may be the king of disguise movies.

William O'Farrell (1904-1962) ["Operation Ramrod"] was a crime novelist with a severe case of wanderlust, leaving a steady job as a reporter in Pittsburgh to wander across Europe from 1920 to 1922, before returning to attend college and then try his hand in theater in New York City. To avoid starving, the unsuccessful actor turned to writing short stories for the pulp magazines. The acting bug passed, but the writing continued until World War II. While serving in the Merchant Marines, his first novel, *Repeat Performance* (1942), was published. By the time he was discharged, it was already under contract for a film version that was released in 1947 (with Richard Basehart, in his first film role). By 1949, he had a second novel, immediately adapted for an episode of *Suspense*. His wanderlust remained unabated and he moved around constantly. His residences in New Orleans, New York, South Carolina and the Caribbean show up in his novels. A stay in California in 1959-1960 resulted in teleplays for *Five Fingers*, *Alfred Hitchcock Presents*, *Perry Mason*, and *Thriller*. By his early death in 1962, he had written over a dozen crime novels and countless short stories.

Michael Pertwee (1916-1991) ["Shot in the Dark," "Counterfeit"] was born into the Pertwee theater dynasty, the eldest son of noted screenwriter/actor Roland Pertwee and older brother of Jon Pertwee, the third actor to play the time lord Doctor Who. After twenty years as a successful scriptwriter in England, he wrote a script for *The Invisible Man*, a series produced in the UK which was also shown on CBS. He moved to Hollywood soon after it aired in 1959. His first credits upon arriving were his two *Five Fingers* episodes, followed by the screenplay of a Robert Bloch story for *Alfred Hitchcock Presents*. He returned to Europe in 1961 after scripting four episodes of *Adventures in Paradise*, and spent the next thirty years of his prolific writing career working in Europe on teleplays, British farces and theatrical productions. Among his credits were episodes of *The Saint* and *Danger Man*. The three fields combined in 1966, when he co-wrote the screenplay for the movie adaptation of *A Funny Thing Happened on the Way to the Forum*.

Philip Saltzman (1929-2009) was the story editor for the entire sixteen episode run of *Five Fingers*, the first step in a career that would lead to associate producer of *12 O'Clock High* in 1966, producer of *Felony Squad* in 1969, and executive producer of television movies in 1978. Additionally, he was also a producer for *The F.B.I.*, *Columbo*, and *Barnaby Jones*. Even more impressively, he made his climb up the studio ladder while also writing more than fifty episodes of various television shows.

Leslie Stevens (1924-1998) ["Counterfeit"] ran away from home at fifteen to join Orson Welles' Mercury Theatre after selling them his play *The Mechanical Rat*. Truant officers returned the fledgling playwright to his parents. He had a major Broadway hit in 1958 with his fourth attempt at Broadway, the comedy *The Marriage-Go-Round*. Stevens had been writing for New York television when he was hired to script *The Left-Handed Gun* (1958), based on Gore Vidal's teleplay. He arrived in Hollywood and wrote scripts for two years while also mounting his fifth play for Broadway. He founded Daystar Productions in 1960, one of the rare independent production houses that would successfully compete with the major studios. Stevens' first project was directing, writing and co-producing a low budget feature, *Private Property*, that briefly made him a cause célèbre in the American New wave cinema movement. He then adapted and produced his *The Marriage-Go-Round* play for film in 1961. Stevens, under the Daystar label, created the *Stoney Burke* and *The Outer Limits* television series. He also wrote and directed the 1966 movie *Incubus*, starring William Shatner in the only US film to feature dialogue spoken exclusively in Esperanto. It would be Daystar's final project. In 1968, he was bought out by Universal Studios. He began writing scripts and serving as executive producer for Universal television shows such as *McCloud* and *Buck Rogers in the 25th Century*.

William Templeton (1913-1973) ["The Men with Triangle Heads"] was a Glasgow playwright who, at the height of his popularity, began writing teleplays for *BBC Sunday-Night Theatre*. American television was in its Golden Age, and CBS took note of the Scotsman who could both write successful drama and adapt other writers' work for the small screen. CBS-TV producer Felix Jackson desperately wanted to adapt George Orwell's *1984* into an episode of *Studio One*, but Orwell's estate had been difficult. Templeton was hired to do the adaptation and the estate, well aware of Templeton's work on the BBC and on the West End, acquiesced. Templeton's 1953 adaptation of George Orwell's novel, which starred Eddie Albert as Winston Smith, proved so popular and acceptable to the estate, it was expanded into a 1956 feature film with Edmond O'Brien as Smith. Templeton's work on programs such as *Studio One, Goodyear Playhouse*, and *Matinee Theatre* raised the bar for live television drama. As television settled into crime dramas, westerns and comedies, Templeton's interest waned. He continued writing scripts until 1962, but he was producing more material for British markets than for the US. He returned to the UK to focus on theater.

David Raksin (1912-2004) [theme music composer] was a child prodigy on piano and woodwinds. Upon graduating from the University of Pennsylvania, he immediately got a gig tour with Benny Goodman. Goodman's pianist, Oscar Levant, was impressed enough to introduce and recommend Raksin to his lifelong friend George Gershwin, who in turn helped Raksin to get a job as an arranger with music publisher Harms/Chappell. Raksin had studied under Arnold Schoenberg and, initially, to the untrained producer's ear, his compositions were too avant-garde for anything but horror films. That changed when he was given the assignment for the theme of *Laura* (1944). Alfred Newman refused to score *Laura* (1944) because it had developed a reputation as an inevitable failure. To avoid the potential association with a bomb, he passed the project on to David Raksin. Newman was one of three brothers, composers and conductors who essentially controlled the music department at 20th Century Fox for over four decades. Raksin's score and the film both became hits. Johnny Mercer later added lyrics and the song "Laura" became a standard, still recorded to this day, and making Raksin a household name. No doubt there was some awkwardness when Raksin's boss on *Five Fingers* turned out to be Lionel Newman, the youngest brother of the man who passed *Laura* on to him. Raksin served eight terms as president of the Composers and Lyricists Guild of America (1962-1970) and taught film score composition at the University of Southern California. His concert works have been performed by the New York Philharmonic, the Boston Pops, and the London Symphony. Raksin also wrote the theme song for the television series *Ben Casey*.

Anne Klein of Junior Sophisticates [Luciana Paluzzi's fashions] was launched in 1948 by husband and wife Ben and Anne Klein. The company focused on petite women who had been limited to cutesy "little-girl" clothing. By 1959, the brand was one of the most popular sportswear design houses in the US, and was a perfect fit for Luciana's fashion requirements. Klein's fashions were stylish, polished and readily available for the 5'6" actress.

Lebow Clothes [David Hedison's wardrobe] was a Baltimore-based manufacturer of high-end men's suits and jackets, known for high quality and extensive hand tailoring. The firm was well aware of the advantages of product placement before the term was coined; their clothing can be seen on a variety of shows in the 1950s and 1960s, including *Bachelor Father*, *Gidget*, and *Peyton Place*.

George Robotham (1921-2007) was Hedison's stunt double at Fox for both *Five Fingers* and *Voyage to the Bottom of the Sea*. He started his career as a stuntman and character actor in the 1943 serial *Batman* and never stopped falling off buildings. Robotham appeared regularly as an uncredited extra in many of the same productions where he was already on set doing stunts. His better known credits include *Captain Video, Master of the Stratosphere*, *The Robe*, *The Egyptian* and *20,000 Leagues Under the Sea*. He was Dick Shawn's stand-in in *It's a Mad, Mad, Mad, Mad World*. Blake Edwards hired him for *The Great Race*, *S.O.B*, and *A Fine Mess*. He did stunts in *Charley Varrick* and *Magnum Force*, *Poseidon Adventure*, *Towering Inferno* and *Meteor*. George retired in 1988, but came back to do a few last stunts in *Monster* (1991) and *Mars Attacks!* (1996). His last recorded appearance was in *Bedazzled* in 2000. He was probably best known as the human sacrifice in *The Prodigal*. He also made appearances in *Spartacus* (1960), *The Ten Commandments* (1957), and *The Goonies* (1985), where he was also the stunt coordinator. Robotham was active in films and television for more than fifty years. In 1988, he married former Bond Girl Karin Dor, whom he met on the set of *Dark Echoes* (1977), his one foray into writing, directing and producing.

The Crew of *Five Fingers*

George Robotham (2nd from left) with David Hedison (in werewolf makeup) in an outtake from the 4th season episode "Man Beast." *Voyage to the Bottom of the Sea.* Copyright 20th Century Fox Studios.

Miscellaneous Credits:

Many of the following people were given credit on *Five Fingers* because they were Fox Studio department heads. That's how credit was assigned in 1959 under the studio system, but it's highly unlikely these multiple Oscar winners actually worked on the production. They ran the departments that gave out series assignments to their (uncredited) junior department members.

Associate Producer:

Teresa Calabrese (no dates) She worked as an assistant to producer Herbert Swope on all sixteen episodes. Calabrese may have started working for Swope as early as 1952. She was in New York with him in the mid-1950s, came to Hollywood as his assistant and most probably returned to New York with him when he left Fox. There is no record of her other television work besides *Five Fingers*. She may have also worked on some of Swope's Broadway productions.

Music Supervisor:

Lionel Newman (1916-1989) Lionel Newman was the youngest of a trio of Newman composers and conductors who dominated the music department at 20th Century Fox for more than four decades. A highly regarded pianist by the age of 15, Lionel went on the national vaudeville circuit as accompanist for Mae West. He completed his music studies under Mario Castelnuovo-Tedesco in Los Angeles and, by 1934, fronted his own musical ensemble, Newman's Society Orchestra, aboard the luxury cruise ship *SS Rotterdam*. Under the tutelage of older brother Alfred, who headed the music department at 20th Century Fox from 1939-1960, Lionel was first commissioned to write the title song for *The Cowboy and the Lady* (1938). For this, he shared an Oscar nomination for Best Song with lyricist Arthur Quenzer. In 1942, Lionel was hired by Fox as rehearsal pianist and songwriter. He scored his first major hit with the standard "Again" (written for the film *Road House* (1948).

From when they first worked together on *Don't Bother to Knock* (1952), he struck up a close working relationship (and subsequent friendship) with Marilyn Monroe. He became her favorite conductor on her films *Niagara (*1953) and *Gentlemen Prefer Blondes* (1953). He also wrote the title song for *River of No Return* (1954) (with lyrics by Ken Darby), plus another piece, "Down in the Meadow," both sung by Marilyn. Other notable films he worked on over the years include *North to Alaska* (1960), *Cleopatra* (1963), *The Sand Pebbles* (1966) and *Alien (*1979). Among his compositions are the theme for *The Proud Ones* (1956) and (as co-writer with brother Alfred) the stirring opening theme for *The Bravados* (1958), starring Gregory Peck.

Following Alfred's departure from Fox in 1959, Lionel was promoted to Music Director, then to Vice President in Charge of Feature and Television Music. During the following decade, he supervised the majority of musical segments at the studio in addition to composing some classic TV music, such as the theme from *The Many Loves of Dobie Gillis (*1959). Lionel won an Oscar (shared with Lennie Hayton) for Best Score of a Musical Picture for *Hello, Dolly!* (1969). The following year, Alfred died and Lionel took over the mantle of General Director of Music at Fox, a position he held until his own departure in 1985. He subsequently joined MGM/United Artists in a similar executive capacity for the remaining years of his life.

Known for his consummate perfectionism as well as his often raucous sense of humor, Lionel was greatly respected. His nephews Randy and Thomas Newman are equally well known for their more modern film scores. Randy finally won an Oscar after sixteen nominations in 2010.

Music Editors:

Leonard A. Engel (1930-1988). Engle edited the music on countless films including *Outland* (1981), *Breaking Away* (1979), *The Boys from Brazil* (1978), *Damnation Alley* (1977), *Breakheart Pass* (1975), *The Towering Inferno* (1974), *Cinderella Liberty* (1973), *Tora! Tora! Tora!* (1970), and *MASH* (1970). His TV movies include *Sherlock Holmes in New York* (1976), starring Roger Moore, *Outrage* (1973), *The Girl Most Likely to...* (1973), and *The Night Strangler* (1973).

He was supervising music editor on the following television series: *The New Perry Mason* for eleven episodes including the "The Case of the Frenzied Feminist" (1973) with David Hedison, 1973-1974; *Land of the Giants*, seventeen episodes, 1968-1969; *Daniel Boone,* 101 episodes, 1964-1968; *Voyage to the Bottom of the Sea,* 109 episodes, 1964-1968; *Judd for the Defense*, twenty-six episodes, 1967-1968; *Felony Squad,* fifty-six episodes, 1967-1968; *Batman,* 120 episodes, 1966-1968; *Lost in Space,* eighty-four episodes, 1965-1968; *The Time Tunnel,* thirty episodes, 1966-1967; *The Green Hornet,* twenty-six episodes 1966-1967; *The Monroes,* twenty-six episodes, 1966-1967; *Custer,* seventeen episodes, 1967; *Blue Light* sixteen episodes, 1966; *The Long, Hot Summer,* sixteen episodes, 1965-1966; *The Loner,* twenty-six episodes, 1965-1966; *12 O'Clock High,* thirty-two episodes, 1964-1965; *Follow the Sun,* thirty episodes, 1961-1962; and *Hong Kong,* fourteen episodes, 1960-1961.

Kenneth (Ken) Hall (no dates). *Five Fingers* was his first job. He went on to edit music on 347 episodes of the TV series *Peyton Place.* Hall is currently the Ken Wannberg Endowed chair and a professor of music and sound since 2005 at the University of Southern California's (USC) School of Cinematic Arts. His film score credits over the course of his six decade editing career are far too numerous to list here, but include two *Star Trek* movies: *First Contact* and *Nemesis.* Hall won awards for his music editing work on *E. T., the Extra-Terrestrial* and *Mulan.*

Directors of Photography:

Wilfred M. Cline A.S.C. (1903-1976) Films include: *Adventures of Tom Sawyer* (1938) and *Gone with the Wind* (1939). He was Director of Photography for seven episodes of *My World and Welcome to It* (1969-1970) and *The Big Valley* seventy-two episodes (1965-1969). He also worked on *Saints and Sinners* (1962), six episodes, and *Stagecoach West,* *Alcoa Theatre* and *Zane Grey Theater.*

Joseph Patrick MacDonald, A.S.C. (1906-1968) was an award-winning American cinematographer born to American parents in Mexico City. He moved to Hollywood and became an assistant cameraman in the early 1920s, advancing to cinematographer in the 1940s. MacDonald became known for his excellent photography with both black-and-white and color film. He was also equally at home filming indoors or out. Some of his later recognizable film credits at Fox include: *A Guide for the Married Man* (1967),filmed at Romanoff's Restaurant, *The Carpetbaggers* (1964), *Kings of the Sun* (1963) with Richard Basehart, *The List of Adrian Messenger* (1963), *Taras Bulba* (1962), *Walk on the Wild Side* (1962),*The Gallant Hours* (1960),*The Fiend Who Walked the West* (1958), *Ten North Frederick* (1958), *A Hatful of Rain* (1957),*Will Success Spoil Rock Hunter?* (1957).He was nominated for an Oscar three times: Best Cinematography, Black-and-White, for *The Young Lions*, 1959; Best Cinematography, for *Pepe;* 1961; and Best Cinematography for *The Sand Pebbles*, 1967. MacDonald was also the first Mexican-born cinematographer to be nominated for an Oscar.

Art Directors:

Duncan Cramer (1901-1980) He did series Art Direction for several other television series, including *My Three Sons* (forty-nine episodes) 1962-1971; *Family Affair* (138 episodes) 1966-1971; *Hong Kong* (seven episodes) 1960; *Adventures in Paradise* (twenty-two episodes) 1959-1960; *Yancy Derringer* (thirty-three episodes) 1958 1959; *Man with a Camera* (TV Series) 1958-1959; *Zane Grey Theater* (twenty-three episodes) 1956-1957; *Cavalcade of America* (fourteen episodes) 1954-1958; *Four Star Playhouse* (eighty-nine episodes) 1952 1956; and *Terry and the Pirates* (fifteen episodes) 1953. He is also credited with art direction for *The Lost World* (1960).

Walter M. Simonds (no dates) was active from 1955 to 1976. Some of his films include *The Gumball Rally* (1976), *McQ* (1974), *Cahill: United States Marshal* (1973), *Outrage* (1973), *Napoleon and Samantha* (1972), *The Omega Man* (1971), *The Green Berets* (1968), *Dead Heat on a Merry-Go-Round* (1966), *The Lively Set* (1964), *State Fair* (1962), *All Hands on Deck*

(1961), *Flaming Star* (1960), *The Lost World* (1960), *From Hell to Texas* (1958), *The Fiend Who Walked the West* (1958), *The Wayward Bus* (1957) and *Marty* (1955), for which he was nominated for an Academy Award in the category Best Black and White Art Direction/Set Direction.

Lyle R. Wheeler (1905-1990). Wheeler worked on more than 350 films, winning five Academy Awards for *Gone with the Wind* (1939), *Anna and the King of Siam* (1946), *The Robe* (1953), *The King and I* (1956) and *The Diary of Anne Frank* (1959). He was nominated for twenty-four other Oscars. He started at MGM in 1931 as a layout artist and soon worked his way up to assistant art director. In the mid-1930s, he began to work for David O. Selznick as a set designer. His first picture as associate art director was *The Garden of Allah* (1936). He applied the new Technicolor dye transfer process to its fullest advantage. In 1939, he created the sets for Tara and was responsible for the burning of Atlanta (they set ablaze the old *King Kong* (1933) and *King of Kings* (1927) sets) on the back lot.

Wheeler became supervising art director at 20th Century Fox in 1944 and head of the studio's art department in 1947. During his tenure, he worked on some of the most sumptuous-looking films of the period, including *Leave Her to Heaven* (1945), *Love Is a Many-Splendored Thing* (1955), *The Snows of Kilimanjaro* (1952) and, of course, *The King and I* (1956). His outstanding black-and-white films are equally well known: *Rebecca* (1940), *Laura* (1944) and *All About Eve* (1950). One of his Oscar winning masterpieces, *Anna and the King of Siam* (1946), had to be shot in black & white because of a painter's strike. Other TV series he is credited with include Perry Mason (fifty-nine episodes) 1957-1958; *How to Marry a Millionaire* (four episodes) 1956-1958; *Broken Arrow* (seventy-two episodes) 1955-1957; *20th Century Fox Hour* (ten episodes, including "Operation Cicero") 1955-1956; and *My Friend Flicka* for three episodes in 1961.

Jack Senter (no dates) John H. Senter was an art director and production designer, probably best known for his movie designs on *Far and Away* (1992) and *Oh, God!* (1977). He was nominated for two Emmys for his work on the miniseries *Centennial* and *Masada*. Other Fox television series he was part of include *Hong Kong, Follow the Sun, Dobie Gillis* (1963 season) and *Peyton Place* through 1965. Senter also worked for Walt Disney for two decades, both on the TV shows, beginning in 1959, and then on several movies in the 1970s, including *Freaky Friday*. He worked mostly in various television series until the mid-1970s (*M*A*S*H, Cade's County*), and then in movies until the early 1990s.

George Van Marter (1910-1963) began working in films in 1940 and then moved into television doing thirty-nine episodes of the *George Burns and Gracie Allen Show* in 1950 and later on twenty-two episodes of *Love that Bob* aka *The Bob Cummings Show in 1958-1959*. His credits end in 1961 with the films *Twist Around the Clock* and *Pirates of Tortuga*. Other films you may know that Van Marter edited are *Magnetic Monster* (1953) and *Champagne for Caesar* (1950). He wrote television series scripts with his wife, actress Margaret Hedin, from 1954 to 1956.

Ben Hayne (1897-1972) got his start in 1945. He is probably best known for the film *High Noon* (1952), after which he moved into Fox Television with the television series *Broken Arrow* (thirteen episodes), *20th Century Fox Hour* (four episodes, including "Operation Cicero"), and *Adventures in Paradise* (four episodes). His credits end in 1960 with his fourth *Adventures in Paradise* episode.

Set Decorators:

Ruby Levitt (1907-1992) was nominated four times for the Academy Award for Best Art Direction. The films were *Pillow Talk*

(1959), *The Sound of Music* (1965), *The Andromeda Strain* (1971), and *Chinatown* (1974). For over four decades, set designer Ruby Levitt was known for her versatility. Levitt also designed sets for television shows, most notably *The Addams Family*.

Walter M. Scott (1906-1989) He began his career in 1937 as an uncredited Set Decorator. He was hired to work on the *Mr. Moto* film series starring Peter Lorre. By 1939, he had worked his way to assistant art director, a position he held until 1959. During that time, he worked on several films, including *The Purple Heart*, *The Lodger*, *Heaven Can Wait* and *Forever Amber*. He became a department head at Fox in 1959, after working on most, if not all, of their TV series up to that point.

Costume Design:

Charles Le Maire (1897-1985) was known for his work on *All About Eve* (1950), *The Day the Earth Stood Still* (1951) and *Miracle on 34th Street* (1947). An Ex-vaudevillian, he became a noted costumer on Broadway in 1921, working on top shows like *The Ziegfeld Follies*, *George White's Scandals*, *Earl Carroll's Vanities*, among others.

He was under contract to 20th Century Fox (1943-1959) as supervising costume designer and wardrobe department head. He assembled a very strong team of designers for the studio, but kept designing for his favorite stars to himself. He left Fox in 1959 to open his own salon and retired from show business in 1962.

Assistant Directors:

Edward Haldeman (1913-1973) began as an Assistant Director on *The Adventures of Superman* television series, doing thirteen episodes in 1958. Haldeman then kicked around several series at Fox as a fill-in doing one or two episodes of several series through 1962. He had progressed to three and four episodes by 1964 until he finally got a semi-permanent gig on the *Flipper* series in 1964 doing thirty-eight episodes through 1966. He apparently did well enough on *Flipper* to retire to Hawaii. He died in Maui in 1973.

Stanley Hough (1918-1990) was hired on his first film in 1946. He worked as an Assistant Director in film and television until 1961. Some of the films he worked on were *The Day the Earth Stood Still* (1951), *Prince Valiant* (1954), *Carousel* (1956), *The Bravados* (1958), *North to Alaska* (1960), and *Misty* (1961). There is no record of where he went to work after he was let go from Fox, but Hough was rehired in 1974 to produce TV movies and the short-lived *Planet of the Apes* television series. He would go on to produce three TV movies based on the *Apes* television series and two *Gunsmoke* reunion movies, the last of these being *Gunsmoke: The Last Apache*.

Wilbur McGaugh (1895-1965) got his start in movie westerns in 1931. He worked steadily in film as an Assistant Director in all genres including *The Jolson Story* (1947), one Tarzan movie that did not star Johnny Weissmuller, *Tarzan's Revenge* (1938), as well as *Jungle Jim (1948)* which did, plus two Robin Hood features, *Bandit of Sherwood Forest* (1946) and *Rogues of Sherwood Forest* (1950). In 1953, when he branched out into television, he worked on multiple episodes of *Kit Carson*, *Ramar of the Jungle* and *My Little Margie*. He worked on *Sea Hunt* and *Perry Mason*. McGaugh did twenty-three episodes of *Adventures in Paradise* in 1963 before moving on to the *Peyton Place* television series, where he completed twenty-eight episodes before his death in 1965.

Ad Schaumer (1898-1977) was born in San Francisco as Adolph Schaumer. He was an Assistant Director in films starting in 1928. He worked in film for the next five decades, starting with the Shirley Temple films in the 1930s. His films include some classic Fox projects such as

The Ox-bow Incident (1943), *Hell and High Water* (1954) and *Sayonara* (1957). He worked on the films *Follow the Sun* (1951), *The Lost World* (1960) and the 1961 *Voyage to the Bottom of the Sea* movie. He was an Assistant Director on the pilot for the *Voyage to the Bottom of the Sea* series. His last credit is for the film *Fantastic Voyage* (1966).

Editorial supervisors:

Richard W. Farrell (1910-1980) first found steady work as a film editor in 1948. He moved into television editing with *My Friend Flicka* in 1953. He edited other television series: *Broken Arrow* (ten episodes) in 1957, *The Real McCoys* (five episodes) 1959-1960, and *The Twilight Zone* (ten episodes) in 1963-1964. His longest gig was on *Perry Mason*, thirty-three episodes from 1957 to 1966. He edited *Jumbo (1962)* and the Presley movie *Speedway (1968)*. He moved on to TV movies, most notably *The Scorpio Letters* in 1967. His last TV movie credit was *The Over the Hill Gang Rides Again* in 1970.

Art Seid (1914-2001) began editing Hal Roach shorts beginning in 1937 and this was his career until 1941, when he was promoted to editing movies. He was hired to do television editing very early on, editing the television series *Silver Theater* in 1950, *Crown Theater with Gloria Swanson* in 1954 and *20th Century Fox Hour* in 1957 as well as working on several other Fox series. Seid is probably best known for editing fifteen *I Spy* episodes, many of which are considered the best episodes of this series. He became a supervising editor in 1952 on the series *Rebound* and had parallel editing jobs for the rest of his career. He gave up supervising in 1976, but he continued to work editing TV movies and series until 1987. He worked on ten episodes of *The Paper Chase* through 1985.

Film Editors:

David Bretherton (1924-2000) was an American film editor with more than forty credits for films released from 1954 to 1996. The son of editor/director Howard Bretherton and actress Dorothea McEvoy, he was born in Los Angeles. He served with the United States Air Force during World War II. After World War II he joined the editing department at 20th Century Fox, helping other editors, including Barbara McLean, Robert L. Simpson, Louis R. Loeffler, James B. Clark, William H. Reynolds, and, in later years, Dorothy Spencer and Hugh S. Fowler. His first project as a film editor was *An Affair to Remember* in 1954. In 1995, Bretherton received the American Cinema Editors Career Achievement Award. His most noted work was the editing of the film *Cabaret* (1972), directed by Bob Fosse. Bretherton received the Academy Award for Film Editing, an ACE Eddie Award, and a nomination for the BAFTA Award for Best Editing for this film.

Fred R. Feithans, Jr. (1909-1987) got his start in film editing with *Kit Carson* (1940), doing mostly western and costume dramas for the next twenty years. He was promoted to supervising editor for the series *Adventures of Hiram Holliday* in 1955 and worked on all the early Fox series (*Hong Kong, Bus Stop, Adventures in Paradise*) that were *Five Fingers*' contemporaries. Then he worked on all the mid-1960s "beach party" movies. Some of his later films of note were *Dillinger* (1973), and *Frogs* (1972).

Hugh Fowler (1912-1975) was at Fox from 1952 to 1968. He won the Academy Award for Best Editing for the film *Patton* (1970). Other films of note include *Planet of the Apes* (1968), *7 Year Itch* (1955), and *Gentlemen Prefer Blondes* (1953). He edited the first Elvis film, *Love Me Tender*, in 1956. He also worked on *Will Success Spoil Rock Hunter?* (1957),

The Lost World (1960), *In Harm's Way* (1961) and *In Like Flint* (1967). His last editing credit is for *Life and Times of Judge Roy Bean* in 1972.

Lynn Harrison (no dates) Began editing shorts in 1932, and worked on the first *Dragnet* series (1951). His career high came in 1955 when he won an Emmy for "Operation Undersea," which was the documentary of the making of the film *20,000 Leagues Under the Sea*. It aired on the new *Disneyland* show that had premiered in 1954. He later was associated with several of Paul Henning's television series, most notably *Petticoat Junction, Green Acres* and *The Beverly Hillbillies*.

Daniel A. Nathan (1916-1971) His first major job at Fox was as a film editor on the *Amos and Andy* television series (1951). He was promoted to supervisor at the end of the series run in 1953, after doing fifty episodes. He worked on several Fox series, with his next longest employment on *Jane Wyman Presents the Fireside Theater* from 1955 to 1957 (sixteen episodes). He worked on *Bachelor Father* (thirty-three episodes), *Wagon Train, Follow the Sun,* and *Breaking Point*. His longest running gig was as Post Production Supervisor on the *Peyton Place* series for 416 episodes from 1965 to 1968. His last credited job was on *Bonanza* in 1970.

Aaron Stell (1911-1996) was a film editor known for *To Kill a Mockingbird* (1962), *Touch of Evil* (1958), and *Silent Running* (1972). Stell worked at Fox Studios from 1955 to 1961. He got his start at Columbia (1943-1954), mostly editing shorts. After he left Fox, he worked at Universal until 1962 and then for Alan J. Pakula/Mulligan Productions until 1965. He wrote and directed one independent film in 1964, *The Gallant One*. He remained an active editor, mostly doing TV movies, until 1986.

Eda Warren (1903-1980) was hired as an Assistant Editor in 1927 and worked on *Rough Riders*. Other films you may know include *I Married a Witch* (1942), *Strategic Air Command* (1955), *Taras Bulba* (1962), and *Son of Paleface* (1951). She was an apprentice cutter and was promoted to Editorial Supervision in 1947 with the film *California*. It is worth noting that she edited Bob Hope's first major film, *The Big Broadcast of 1938*, and her last credit is *The Private Army of Sgt. O'Farrell* in 1968. Warren didn't do much series editing; four episodes of *The Twilight Zone* was one of her longer gigs. The series she worked on the longest, twelve episodes of *Love on a Rooftop*, may be known to Judy Carne and Peter Duel fans, but it only lasted thirty episodes in 1966-1967. Both of these actors became better known for other projects. Warren had a very long career, considering the decades she worked in. There were other female editors who made it, as well, such as Verna Fields, but they were still a minority.

Chapter 17

Victor Sebastian: "The Proper Spy"
By Wesley Britton

To provide more historical background on the effect this series had on popular culture, Dr. Wesley Britton has written an overview of the Spy show genre and Victor Sebastian's place in it.

In an August 2007 radio interview, author Robert Sellers claimed that the first (1961) British season of Patrick McGoohan's *Danger Man* was the "first proper spy show." What he meant, as demonstrated in his 2006 book, *Cult TV: The Golden Age of ITC*, was that before the globe-trotting adventures of secret agent John Drake, UK television had offered very few series with the trappings most viewers associate with full-fledged spy adventures.

True, there had been the 1958-1959 *The Invisible Man*, a children's program featuring an unseen agent infiltrating anti-Western criminal cartels and Communist cells. From 1956 to 1957, the British-produced *Adventures of Aggie* starred Joan Shawlee as an American fashion buyer in London who was often drawn into the comic plots and plans of Commie spy nests. And there was *Four Just Men* (1959-1960) which offered alternating leads Dan Dailey, Jack Hawkins, Richard Conti, and Vittorio Di Sica in all manner of international adventures. Occasionally, this meant uncovering spies.

But Sellers can be forgiven for discounting these series as "proper spy shows" as none were essentially focused on espionage. However, American producers had indeed been creating "proper" spy shows a full decade before *Danger Man*. In fact, the 1950s had as many offerings on the small screen as any season during the Bond boom. In a very real sense, *Five Fingers* was a series on the cusp of the transition between black-and-white Cold War dramas and the more romanticized, Bondian-influenced heyday of TV spies during the 1960s.

For example, *Doorway to Danger* (aka *Door with No Name*) debuted in 1951 and ran for three seasons on both NBC and ABC. Mel Ruick, Roland Winters, and Raymond Bramley all played the part of Intelligence Chief John Randolph who dispatched various agents on missions around the globe. In the same year, the syndicated *Foreign Intrigue* began with Jerome Thor and Sydna Scott and then James Daly and Anne Preville as wire correspondents uncovering spy networks in Europe. In 1954-1955, the series was revamped to feature Gerald Mohr as a government agent posing as a hotel owner.

1952 also saw the first season of *Hunter*, a CBS and then NBC series which first cast future TV James Bond, Barry Nelson, as a playboy and free-lance Communist hunter before actor Keith Larsen took over the role in 1954. Another early adventure series, *Biff Baker, U.S.A.* (CBS, 1952-1953), was not specifically a spy series, but series leads Alan Hale Jr. and Randy Stuart, who played his wife, were a traveling couple who encountered Communist agents as often as they did counterfeiters, smugglers, and blackmailing spouses.

These early series set the stage for several trends in later 1950s spy shows. There were the professional officers of various governments as seen in *Door with No Name;* amateurs stumbling into international intrigue as portrayed in *Hunter* and *Biff Baker;* and then there were adventure shows that only occasionally featured counter-espionage in the scripts. Perhaps the first in the mold of *Five Fingers* and, later *Danger Man* in tone and style, was *Dangerous Assignment*. In 1952, this syndicated adventure show cast Hollywood leading-man Brian Donlevy as globe-trotting government agent Steve Mitchell. Each week, in both radio and TV scripts, the suave Mitchell used his wits, stunts, and improvised gadgets to serve U.S. international interests.

Then came gravely-voiced Charles McGraw as an international government troubleshooter for various organizations in the NBC and then syndicated *Adventures of Falcon* which aired in 1954-1955. In 1955, Robert Alda was a European-based intelligence officer in *Secret Files U.S.A.*

While not a "proper" spy series, *Mackenzie's Raiders* (Syndicated, 1958-1959) had Richard Carlson leading a para-military troop in the Old West under the secret orders of President Grant. This series preceded *Mission: Impossible* with the premise that if any of the raiders were captured or killed, the government would disavow any knowledge of their actions. Like the later series, *The Wild Wild West*, this group reported directly to the president.

Another popular vogue in the 1950s were programs in which various characters, untrained in covert operations, found themselves dealing with all manner of Cold War operatives of the Soviet bloc. One show often seen as a precursor to the 1960s breed of spies with dash and humor was *Passport to Danger*. From 1954 to 1958, Cesar Romero was a diplomatic courier who arrived in different cities each week bearing official messages, which naturally attracted the interest of the opposition.

FIVE FINGERS: ELEGANCE IN ESPIONAGE

In *Soldiers of Fortune* (Syndicated, 1955-1957), John Russell and Chic Chandler were international mercenaries who'd bump into guerilla leaders and agent provocateurs on remote islands and in jungles. One series of special note was *Crusader* (CBS, 1955-1956). Future *Family Affair* father Brian Keith starred as a news reporter who also battled Communist agents. His mother had been killed in a concentration camp, which led Keith to actively look for opportunities to go behind the Iron Curtain to assist anyone trapped by "The Red Menace," whether they were refugees or defectors.

Perhaps the sub-genre most remembered from the era were the various shows ostensibly based on actual case files of various law enforcement agencies. In fact, on film, radio, and television, producers and script-writers were happy to work with the U.S. military, the Texas Rangers, and police departments to dramatize stories that sang the praises of those who protected our communities and country like *Trackdown* and *Dragnet*.

In the case of spy series, matters became somewhat more complicated. Many sponsors and studios felt supporting spy shows would boost their patriotic images and, in the case of Hollywood production companies, help keep the "McCarthy" black-listers at bay.

A case in point was the most influential series of the decade, the very popular *I Led Three Lives*. From 1953 to 1957, and in syndication for years afterward, Richard Carlson played actual FBI informant Herbert Philbrick. While not a "proper spy," as Philbrick was not a government agent, he informed on New York Communist cells. Scriptwriters added many elements and plots to this series that romanticized Philbrick's work, resulting in the actual Philbrick becoming a very public spokesman on the dangers of the creeping presence of Communism inside the U.S.

With a similar premise, but much wider scope, Addison Richards, Larry Fletcher, and Edward Binns starred in *Pentagon U.S.A* (CBS, 1953). This was an anthology series based on Army criminal investigation files.

Victor Sebastian: "The Proper Spy"

The Man Called X (Syndicated, 1956-1957) featured Barry Sullivan as a government agent in stories loosely based on actual files.

Looking back to World War II, *O.S.S.* (ABC, 1957-1958) had Ron Randell as a World War II agent of the Office of Strategic Services. Like *Five Fingers*, *O.S.S.* began each episode with an operative tapping out a message in Morse code. Merging scripts set in World War II and the Cold War, *Behind Closed Doors* (NBC, 1958-1959) featured host Bruce Gordon introducing both fictional stories and some ostensibly based on actual case files.

England, too, had programming in this vein. One of the most highly regarded series of the decade was producer Robert Barr's *Spycatcher*. On the BBC from 1959 to1961, Bernard Archard played an Army interrogator skilled in unmasking German spies during World War II. The show was noted for its taut scripts set in a simple interrogation room. From 1959 to 1960, competing network ITV broadcast *Interpol Calling* starring Charles Korvin and Edwin Richfield as agents investigating international criminals, including occasional ones from the Soviet bloc.

Certainly, few would consider any of the cartoons or live-action series designed for youngsters as "proper" spy shows, but a quick review of what was available should help demonstrate just how prevalent espionage was on 1950s American television. There was *Atom Squad*, a daily fifteen minute NBC serial with a team that battled Communist subversives and mad scientists from 1953 to 1954. There was *Captain Midnight* aka *Jet Jackson* aka *Flying Commando* (CBS, Syndicated, 1954-1956) with actor Richard Webb as the leader of a "Secret Squadron" battling evil-doers.

There was the original *I Spy* (Syndicated, 1956), an anthology about spies from many historical periods. Spy stories from the American Revolution, the Civil War, and especially World War II were introduced by "Anton the Spymaster," played by veteran actor Raymond Massey. In the spirit of *The Invisible Man*, youngsters were also offered *World of Giants* (syndicated, 1959) in which Marshall Thompson played a six-inch tall FBI agent that lasted all of six episodes. Finally, from 1959 and for decades afterward, *The Rocky and Bullwinkle Show* gave viewers a moose and squirrel constantly at odds with Boris, Natasha, and Fearless Leader, all agents of Pottsylvania, a cartoon-surrogate for any East European satellite of the U.S.S.R.

The place of *Five Fingers* in this catalogue is both unique and, in many ways, trend-setting. One stylistic element it shared with many programs of the era was the use of first-person narrations, including a preamble at the beginning of each hour to establish the mission of the lead character. Set in Europe, it allowed for scripts that were not limited to Cold War fears of Russian agents, but also bouts with ex-Nazis, a trend that would continue into the 1960s in virtually every spy program. Perhaps the greatest distinction it had from previous dramas was that it was hour-long, allowing for more character development and script depth difficult to include in the prevalent half-hour format of the 1950s.

One fresh element in *Five Fingers* was Victor Sebastian's romance with Simone Genet (Luciana Paluzzi). While there had been married couples in previous shows (*Biff Baker, Secret Files, I Led Three Lives*), the ongoing relationship between the spy and the model added a touch of glamour and often very personal motivations for Sebastian to complete his mission as his partner became more and more involved in his assignments.

In addition, this relationship allowed *Five Fingers* to bring together the most prominent sub-genre in spy shows, featuring professional and amateur leads. In the tradition of *Dangerous Assignment*, Victor Sebastian was a well-trained operative able to think on his feet while maintaining his cover as a theatrical booking agent. Simone was the enthusiastic amateur who relied on her intuition, a characteristic that would become a popular thread in spy television from *The Avengers* to *Scarecrow and Mrs. King*.

Before *Five Fingers*, amateur spies had been portrayed from the beginning, as in *Adventures of Aggie* and *Biff Baker*, but "professionals" tended to work for the other side and were not recurring cast members.

Later, the principal architects of *The Man from U.N.C.L.E.*, Norman Felton and Sam Rolfe, reversed this trend by making it a staple of their show to always bring in an "innocent" as a contrast to the high-tech world of U.N.C.L.E. agents.

So *Five Fingers* was a series with one foot firmly planted in the trends of the 1950s while creating new templates that would become significant in television spies to follow. Had the show remained in syndication past 1967 or had it become available on video or DVD when similar shows gained second lives for new generations, the production values, scripts, and acting would no doubt have elevated the program's reputation and legacy for spy aficionados who missed the few syndicated reruns of the episodes. Perhaps Fox Home Video could rectify this oversight with a DVD release, if they have any additional episodes, in addition to the existing four that were donated to the UCLA Film Library from the Fox archive.

And now, for those of you interested in what actually happened during Operation Cicero, before Hollywood gave the spy incident their glamour treatment, here is author Dave Goudsward.

Chapter 18

The Real Operation Cicero
by David Goudsward

TURKEY WAS A DANGEROUS PLACE DURING THE WAR.

What was to become known as World War II broke out during 1938, the same year İsmet İnönü assumed the presidency of Turkey. İnönü was well aware that the fledgling republic was in no position to participate in yet another conflict after decades of war as the Ottoman Empire ended and Turkish independence began. As tensions in Europe heightened, İnönü was determined to maintain Turkey's neutrality and walked a tightrope between the Allies and Axis, both of whom wanted Turkey on their side of the conflict. By 1943, all of southeastern Europe was under Axis control with Italy and Germany occupying Greece, Albania, Yugoslavia and Bulgaria while Romania and Hungary had joined the

Axis. The Allies controlled the Middle East and had regained control of North Africa. The Soviet Union was advancing on the Nazi-controlled Balkans. And Turkey sat squarely in the middle of these three great forces.

İnönü's greatest concern was the Soviet Union. Stalin had made it obvious he wanted control of the Turkish Straits, so when the Nazis and Soviets signed a nonaggression pact in 1939, a nervous Turkey signed a treaty of mutual assistance with Britain and France. İnönü then signed a nonaggression treaty with Germany to counter any indication of favoritism. Soon after, Germany invaded the Soviet Union. This distracted Stalin from the Turkish Straits, but left Turkey still poised between the two powers. Each considered Turkey neutral but with sympathetic leanings.

Against this backdrop, the respective ambassadors played a dangerous game of diplomacy and espionage while maintaining the façade of civility expected in a neutral country. The importance that both warring factions placed on Turkey's potential ally role was reflected in their ambassadorial appointments. The Germans sent former German Chancellor Franz von Papen. England sent Sir Hughe Knatchbull-Hugessen. Both were experienced diplomats with extensive familiarity with the region. Sir Hughe felt Turkey could be swayed into allowing military operations within Turkish territory against the Axis, while Papen focused on keeping Turkey neutral. As long as Turkey remained neutral, Germany could continue to buy the Turkish chromite needed for bomb making, and the country's neutrality kept Allied forces out of Turkish territory and limited Allied overland routes to the oil fields of the Middle East.

Into this powder keg came a new player in the fall of 1943. A man who called himself Pierre, but who is still remembered by the code name assigned by his German handlers: Cicero. Cicero provided the German embassy with a constant stream of secret documents from the British embassy. Although his espionage career barely lasted six months (between October 1943 and April 1944), Papen's skillful use of the data was sufficient to counter the Allied influence and keep Turkey out of the war. Germany's use of Cicero's pilfered documents, however, was hampered by politics. Ambassador von Papen was a career politician, not a staunch Nazi. His moderate views had made powerful enemies in the party hierarchy and only his influential friends in Berlin served as a counterbalance. His greatest enemy was his immediate superior, Foreign Minister Joachim von Ribbentrop. This relationship was further complicated by Ribbentrop's sister being married to Albert Jenke, the next highest-ranking official at the German embassy in Turkey. Ribbentrop distrusted all information and opinions that came from Papen, which included the Cicero material. Were it not for the constant internal sparring between Ribbentrop and Papen, and a similar distrust among all the other espionage departments in Berlin, the potential of Cicero's thefts for damage to Allied war planning could have been staggering.

Cicero's espionage had nothing to do with ideology or politics. He was a spy because he wanted to become rich enough to be treated as a gentleman. Cicero's real name was Elyesa Bazna, a man who should never have been hired to be Ambassador Sir Hughe Knatchbull-Hugessen's valet in the first place. If a more careful background check of his employment record had been made, he would not have been.

Bazna had been recommended by First Secretary Douglas Busk of the British Embassy, and Sir Hughe incorrectly assumed Busk had vetted Bazna. Sir Hughe was from the old school where the recommendation of a British gentleman and peer was sufficient; a second background check would be a slight to Busk and was never considered.

Elyesa Bazna was born in Priština, then a city in the Ottoman Empire. Now the capitol of the disputed Kosovo region, it had been part of an area that was subsequently part of Albania, Serbia and Yugoslavia. As the borders of the Ottoman Empire contracted, Bazna's father and his Albanian Muslim family were expelled from Albania, ending up in Istanbul by way of Salonika in Greece.

In the aftermath of World War I, young Bazna had tangled with the Italian, British and French occupying forces, racking up an impressive list of criminal charges ranging from theft and destruction of military property to armed escape from arrest and illegal possession of a weapon. After stealing the weapon of a French soldier, he was finally shipped off to a labor penal camp in Marseilles for three years. Bazna's autobiography notes that he considered this arrest somewhat fortuitous; he learned French while in the camp and, when the occupying forces signed a treaty with the new Turkish government, the remainder of his sentence was commuted. Bazna stayed in Marseilles and learned a new trade as a locksmith.

Returning to Turkey, Bazna married and had children. Steady work was hard to find when one was as ambitious as Bazna was to improve his status in life. He drifted further and further from his family, going from job to job until he found himself in Ankara. Overstating his background as a brief stint as a taxi driver, he became the driver to the Yugoslav ambassador.

To his extreme distaste, Bazna now found himself a *kavass*, a Turkish term for anyone who serves a foreigner. After seven years as driver at the Yugoslav Embassy, he quickly went through a series of jobs as a kavass at the American Embassy, the German Embassy and finally the driver/valet of Douglas Busk. With a little opportunistic manipulation of Bazna's mistress, another kavass in the embassy, Elyesa obtained a recommendation from Busk to present to Sir Hughe Knatchbull-Hugessen for the now vacant position of Sir Hughe's valet.

Bazna learned Knatchbull-Hugessen often brought home documents from the embassy to read at his leisure. Bazna tracked Sir Hughe's unvarying daily routine and soon conceived a way to make the money he so desperately needed to elevate his rank in society. He knew when the document box would be unattended and when he would have time to slip in, find the keys, take the papers out and photograph them.

Bazna approached First Secretary Jenke at the German consulate. Bazna had previously worked for Jenke as a valet. Bazna's autobiography notes that he felt that he lost that position because he had been caught snooping through documents, an event that Jenke apparently did not remember. He approached Jenke with an offer to photograph the documents for cash, specifically English pounds. Jenke wanted nothing to do with a former valet he barely remembered, but dutifully passed the information on to Ambassador von Papen, who was equally suspicious of a Turkish national coming to the embassy unannounced with an offer to steal secret British documents.

Papen, who himself had been expelled by the United States during World War I under suspicion of espionage, had the embassy's "commercial attaché" investigate the offer, just in case. Ludwig Carl Moyzisch was nominally attached to the embassy but was actually the local representative of the German *Sicherheitsdienst* (SD) intelligence agency. Bazna demanded £20,000 for the first two rolls of film and £15,000 for each subsequent roll. The price was non-negotiable, and he was fully prepared to approach the Soviet embassy if his offer was rebuffed. Papen sent the proposal to Ribbentrop who passed it on to Schellenberg. To Moyzisch's surprise, the offer was accepted.

Suddenly the valet-turned-spy found himself in the midst of a power struggle in the crumbling Third Reich. It was fortunate for both Bazna and the Germans that Papen assigned Moyzisch to handle Bazna, or the deal never would have been worked out. The SD was the new foreign intelligence unit of the *Shutzstaffe* (SS) with tighter security and a seemingly unlimited supply of British currency to pay for the information. Thus Bazna's identity remained concealed for many weeks longer than if his photographed documents had been turned over to the more leak-riddled rival spy agencies, the *Abwehr* and *Reichssicherheitshauptamt* (RHSA).

Bazna's espionage came at a critical time in the war, with top-level conferences being held to decide future Allied plans. From Cicero's stolen documents, the Germans were able to read the minutes of the Moscow, Tehran and Casablanca conferences within days of the meetings, learn details of bomber offensives and discover that the Allies no longer believed the Axis had any chance of winning the war. The Reich also sought clues to Operation Overlord, which the Germans knew was the Allied code name for a second front in Europe, but Sir Hughe was not privy to the "where" or "when" intelligence on this action that the Germans needed.

Ironically, Moyzisch had been ordered by his superior, Schellenberg, not to share the documents with von Papen, primarily to prevent Ribbentrop and the Foreign Ministry from gaining access to the Cicero data for the RHSA, the Foreign Ministry espionage agency under Ribbentrop's direct control. Moyzisch disregarded that edict on numerous occasions, allowing the Ambassador to see some of the documents, and Papen would end up being the only one who actually used the data.

Unbeknownst to Berlin, Papen had abandoned efforts to get Turkey to join the Axis effort as an Axis co-belligerent. Instead, he returned to his original mission of dissuading the Turkish government from entering the war, hinting to Turkish Foreign Minister Menemencioğlu that the Germans were aware of the negotiations between the Allies and Turkish Government. It did not take Menemencioğlu long to recognize that Papen's information could only have been learned through espionage and that the details Papen provided suggested the source was the British Embassy.

The Americans already knew of the leak in the British Embassy by December of 1943. Neutral Sweden sent word that they had been given a summary of the Cairo conference from the Hungarian Embassy. Washington notified London but, because the origin of the data was unclear, the British chose to disregard the report. Part of that disregard was certainly due to the disdain the British held for American espionage efforts. The British felt that the OSS operatives were inexperienced and overenthusiastic, a combination that encouraged German sympathizers to feed the OSS false information whenever they could.

The OSS knew far more than they actually shared with MI6. In 1942, Fritz Kolbe of the German Foreign Ministry office in Bern,

Switzerland, contacted Allen Dulles, the chief operative of the OSS in Bern. He then approached the British Embassy in Bern with an offer to photograph secret documents. The British official refused to consider the offer and never passed it on to British Intelligence. So Kolbe went back to the Americans. Kolbe turned out to be the officer who screened communications for the proper distribution of the messages. Through the end of the war, Kolbe was able to provide a steady stream of information to the OSS about topics of interest including the mood in Berlin, German rocket program development and Japanese troop movements.

In 1943, Kolbe passed to Dulles a series of communications sent from Moyzisch to Berlin that included a photograph of a British document with Sir Hughe's handwritten notes in the border. The OSS had discovered unquestionable evidence that there was a spy in the British Embassy in Ankara. By January 1, 1944, OSS had notified MI6 they had a spy in their embassy without providing specifics. The British were still not convinced. Because of the strained relations with MI6, the OSS did not identify their source or specifics, such as Sir Hughe's handwritten notes. British Foreign Minister A. Eden downplayed the matter, suggesting to Churchill that the source was probably Menemencioğlu himself, sharing too much information with Papen.

Then, later in January, a concerned and confused Turkish Government advised Sir Hughe that Papen had filed a complaint about Allied plans to build radar stations in Turkey, a topic that Sir Hughe had not yet broached with the government. Papen had tipped his hand, and the British had no choice but to admit there was a leak.

Bazna was getting progressively more nervous. MI6 had sent investigators to the embassy. They soon focused on Sir Hughe's tendency to bring documents home to review at night, a serious lapse in security procedures that continued even after admonishments not to do so. MI6 interviewed the house staff, including the valet, but was unable to find an employee they considered bright enough to be a spy. With Knatchbull-Hugessen still insisting the leak was in the Turkish government and MI6 unsure where the leak was, security was heightened at the embassy as a precaution.

To eliminate Sir Hughe's security breach, a new vault with an electric alarm system was installed in the ambassador's quarters. It made it more difficult for Bazna to continue his clandestine photographing, but not impossible. Falling back on his locksmith training, he "borrowed" Sir Hughe's key to the safe, made a wax impression and had the Germans ship the impression to Berlin to have a copy of the key made. Bazna's increasing paranoia would not permit use of a local locksmith who might remember details if a British agent was investigating the matter. The newly-installed safe alarm was all but useless. The alarm was powered by electricity and had been retrofit into the fuse box. Bazna quickly learned which fuse to remove to kill the power to the safe, effectively disarming it.

The OSS was also dealing with the leak, albeit through sheer dumb luck. In December of 1943, Moyzisch's trusted secretary injured her hand and within a month it was obvious that she could no longer handle the stream of work single-handedly, literally and figuratively. A temporary replacement was sought. Moyzisch's press attaché happened to be in Sofia when he met Karl Kapp, a diplomat who had been recalled from his posting in the United States at the start of the war. Kapp was frantically seeking a way to get his daughter away from the bombs falling on Sofia. Cornelia Kapp was brought to neutral Turkey to work in the embassy.

Cornelia, however, had her own agenda. She loved the freedom of America and wanted to return to the boyfriend she had left behind. As such, it was easy for the OSS to convince her to help, since the beau she left behind was now an OSS agent. They would aid her in an attempt to get back to her life in America.

Before the Kapps even arrived in Sofia, Cornelia had been recruited to supply information to the OSS. Finding her suddenly working in the office of the German SD officer in Turkey was beyond the OSS' wildest expectations for their recruit. She was able to confirm that Cicero was attached to the British Embassy but was never able to identify Bazna as Cicero.

Kapp was crumbling under the stress of being a spy. Her increasingly erratic behavior convinced the Germans she was having a breakdown. Moyzisch felt it was time for her to go. Papen delicately approached her father suggesting she needed a long rest and made arrangements to have her sent back to Sofia. The night before her trip, the local OSS agent retrieved Kapp and she went into hiding.

The Germans believed Kapp had defected, and things began to unravel. Papen's enemies leapt at the opportunity to exploit the defection, and only his skills and contacts kept him in Ankara until Turkey severed ties with Germany. Ribbentrop tried to get Moyzisch to Berlin to have him shot immediately, which Moyzisch avoided by claiming illness and stalling long enough to allow cooler heads to prevail. An investigation was opened, but Berlin would fall before culpability was assigned.

Kapp was flown to Cairo where a decidedly smug OSS allowed her to be interrogated by British agents. She returned to Ankara with her blonde hair cut short and dyed black, wearing a British uniform while the OSS made arrangements to get her to America. Bazna claimed in his autobiography that he happened to see her on the street and immediately saw through her disguise. Bazna had no way of knowing if she could identify him, but it was obvious to him that she had defected to the British.

Bazna made arrangements to call on Moyzisch one last time. Moyzisch could not guarantee how much Kapp knew or had passed on to the Allies. Bazna shook Moyzisch's hand and said goodbye. On the last day of April 1944, Bazna packed his belongings and left the British Embassy. Cicero then disappeared, having received over £300,000 sterling from the Germans, worth about $1.2 million in US currency of the time.

By April 1944, the Turks were facing an old fear, the Soviets were gaining ground against the Nazis, and the territories Stalin controlled were getting closer to Turkish borders. Concerned at the prospect of facing the advancing Soviet forces alone, Turkey severed diplomatic relations with Germany in August 1944 and, in February 1945, declared war on Germany. Since Turkey and the Soviets were now allies, the threat of Soviet invasion was averted.

In their biographies, both Papen and Moyzisch noted Bazna's sudden departure amidst the growing chaos of the Third Reich collapse and Turkey's alignment with the Allies; both also assumed the valet had died soon after the events of Operation Cicero. In truth, Bazna was still in Ankara operating a used car business. He was among the anonymous crowd watching Sir Hughe's departure from the embassy for his new assignment in Brussels. When Douglas Busk advertised an embassy car for sale, Bazna bought it, testing Busk to see if he knew the identity of Cicero and relishing the option of buying the car he formerly drove as a kavass. Bazna paid for it with the English bank notes that Cicero earned.

Within a year, Bazna's fortune would change. Fishermen in Austria started pulling wads of British currency out of the River Traun. The Americas cordoned off the river and pulled over £20 million out of the water. It was quickly determined it was counterfeit, manufactured by the RSHA in the Sachsenhausen concentration camp in a plan to undermine the British economy. In his book on the Cicero Affair, Moyzisch had remarked that he was surprised how readily his superiors had agreed to Cicero's price for the photographed documents, apparently unaware that much of the currency he was passing on to Cicero was counterfeit currency that the SD obtained from the RSHA. Schellenberg estimated that about £150,000, or roughly half of Cicero's payments were made in counterfeit bills from the Sachsenhausen concentration camp.

The British determined which serial numbers the Germans had copied and began withdrawing those bills from circulation, making the identification of counterfeits easier. At this fateful moment, Bazna had become a partner in a construction contractor firm and was beginning to use his Cicero funds more extensively. He began work on what was supposed to be his great legacy, an opulent hotel and spa that would attach to and double the rooms of the iconic *Çelik Palas* hotel in Bursa. As the money made its way across Europe, it was soon identified as bogus and quickly traced back to the construction project in Bursa.

By the time Bazna reimbursed holders of the fake notes, he was where he had begun: no funds, no status and no future. He would live another thirty years, in anonymity and with limited income from again selling used cars. While Bazna struggled to survive, his alter ego, Cicero, would gain fame in books and films.

Recollections of the war were growing in popularity in Europe. The principals in the Cicero Affair also published biographical recollections and, while each author agreed on major points, each remembered the events in such a way as to make himself the hero of the book. Moyzisch published first with *Der Fall Cicero: die größte Spionage-Affäre des Zweiten Weltkrieges* in 1949 which was released in English as *Operation Cicero* the next year. Plans to convert the book to film were not far behind.

Franz von Papen's memoirs appeared a year after the film version. There is no question his recollections were colored by the film. His version of the events during the Cicero Affair, contained in a single chapter, read like a last-minute book addendum intended to ride on the film's coattails. Another clue to the chapter's motivation is that von Papen consistently calls Cicero by the name Diello, a revised name for the valet that was written for the movie.

Walter Schellenberg's posthumously published 1956 autobiography erroneously concluded that Cicero had heroically passed British documents to the Germans to prevent Turkey from joining the Allies, thus saving Turkey from the German decimation that would have resulted.

Even Allen Dulles, still smarting from his removal as head of the CIA by Kennedy in 1961, reinvented the story in his 1966 book, *Secret Surrender*, to claim his warnings to London via Washington, D.C. were the reason Cicero abandoned the espionage operation.

The one notable exception to the literary collection of Cicero participants was Hughe Knatchbull-Hugessen. His book *Diplomat in Peace and War* was published before Moyzisch published his book disclosing the espionage that took place on Sir Hughe's watch. The Foreign Office and Sir Hughe both initially maintained a stony silence but, as details were brought forth in Parliament, two things became apparent: the British were well aware the leak had occurred and that, as late as 1950, Sir Hughe was still in the dark about the details of the security breach.

Moyzisch's book proved popular. When the book appeared in English in 1950, there was an uproar in British Parliament over the public disclosure of their spy scandal. This merely served as an additional catalyst; the press coverage of the Parliament inquiry spawned editions of the book in over a dozen other languages from Chinese to Latvian.

As Cicero became a legend, Bazna still could not exploit the situation to achieve the financial security he so ardently desired. He unsuccessfully approached the studios to become a consultant on the film payroll. Adding insult to injury, his autobiographic retelling of the events did not sell well. When he died in 1970, the headstone in Munich's Perlacher Forest cemetery had the name Cicero emblazoned on it in letters larger than Bazna's name.

For further reading:

Bazna, Elyesa, in collaboration with Hans Nogly. *I was Cicero*. NY: Harper & Row, 1962.

Dulles, Allen. *The Secret Surrender*. NY: Harper & Row, 1966.

Langelaan, George. *The Masks of War*. Garden City, N.Y: Doubleday, 1959.

Moyzisch, L. C. *Operation Cicero*. NY: Coward-McCann, 1950.

Knatchbull-Hugessen, Hughe Montgomery. *Diplomat in Peace and War*. London: J. Murray, 1949.

Papen, Franz von. *Franz von Papen: Memoirs*. NY: E.P. Dutton & Co., 1953.

Schellenberg, Walter [Louis Hagen, trans.] *The Labyrinth Memoirs*. NY: Harper, 1956.

I Was Cicero by Hans Nogly.

INDEX

5 Fingers xiv, 1, *6*, 8, 9, *11, 15*

Abdullah, Joe 194, 293

Adams, Casey see Max Showalter

Adams, Neile (McQueen Toffel) 229, 308, 309

Adler, Buddy 10, 36, 68, 91, 239

Adler, Jay 230, 311

Adventures in Paradise 20, 34, 36, 49, 68, *69,* 88, 98, *257*, 258, 268, 319, 328, 333, 341, 343, 345, 347

Albertson, Jack 138, 261, 262

Anthony, Ray 203, 295, *296*

Askin, Leon 9

Atienza, Edward 130, 256

Ayer, Harold 230, 310, 311

Baccaloni, Salvatore 138, 261

Bailey, Mark 186, 290

Balsam, Martin 219, 304, 305

Banner, John 186, 289

Barrett, William E. 328

Bazna, Elyesa 2, 3, 5, 7, 8, 361, 362, 363, 365-370, *371*

Berg, Richard xiv, 1, 13, 43, 317, 328

Bergdorf, Herbert *6,* 94

Bergen, Edgar 92, 106, 121, 122, 127, 128, 250, 251

Brocco, Peter 194, 231, 292, 315

Brubaker, Robert 148, 266

Burke, Paul xi, 109, 110, *111,* 114, 121, 122, 137, 138, 148, 155, 163, 171, 173, 185, 194, 204, 211, 212, *218,* 231, *233*

Caillou, Alan 155, 270

Cook, Whitfield 329, 330

Couch, Bill 148, 268

Danova, Cesare 106, 185, *193,* 287, *288,* 289

David, Michael 172, *173,* 177, 278

DeKova, Frank 212, *217, 218,* 301

Dennis, Robert C. 330

Devine, Jerry 95, 331

Delevanti, Cyril 171, 279, 280

Dennis, Nick 164, 276

Donlon, Dolores 164, 273

Dunne, Dominick 88, 102

Emery, John *179*, 180, 181, 182, *183*, 285

Emhardt, Robert 138, 262

Enemy Below, The 75, 252, 308

Esmond, Carl 203, 297

Eustrel, Anthony 122, 252

Feld, Fritz 155, 270

Feldary, Eric 231, 313

Feldman, Charles 75, 91, 92

Fly, The 19, 26, 42, 47, 48, 54, 65, 75, 76, 84, 85, 91, 171

Fly at Fifty, The 84, 85

Frances, Arlene 163, 164, 170, 272

Franz, Eduard 9

Gabor, Eva 15, 25, 45, 46, 89, 92, 114, 249,

Gordon, Leo 163, 164, 272

Graham, John 212, 301, 302

Granger, Michael 231, 314

Greene, David 95, 326

Gulager, Clu 180, 182, *183*, 285

Haas, Hugo 219, 304

Halsey, Brett x, 23, 36, 56, 61, 63, 66-68, 70, *71,* 91, 93, *96*, 99, 100, 144, 146, 193, *196*, *199,* 200-203, 232, 254, 291, 292

Hoffman, David 148, 268

Holloway, Sterling 180, 285

Homolka, Oscar 203, 295

Howard, Ron 114, 250

Howard, Ronald 229, 308

Hoyos, Rodolfo 180, 286

Hoyt, John 185, 289

Hudgins, Earle 138, 264

Hunter, Arline *179*, 180, *184*, 287

Jenson, Roy 204, 298

Johnson, Lamont 95, *134*, 200, *323*, 324

Jolly, Pete 164, 275

Keller, Greta 15, 45, 46, 114, 248

Kendis, William 122, 254, 255

Kerrigan, J. M. 171, *278*, 279

Kjellin, Alf 229, 309

Klein, Anne 104, 335, 336

Krueger, Kurt 122, 252

Krugman, Lou 130, 258

Le Maire, Charles 62, 104, 334

Lawson, Linda 130, *257*, 258

Lewis, David 138, 261

Lindfors, Vivica 25, 92, 180, 181, *184*, 184, 283, *284*

Lindsey, Margaret 211, 212, 218, 299, 300

Lorre, Peter 9, 10, 92, 93, 193, 200, 201, *202*, 203, 236, *290*, 291

INDEX

Lost World, The 24, 25, 49, 78, 302, 307, 341, 342, 346, 378

MacLeod, Gavin 137, 138, 145, 262, 263

McCollough, Andrew 46, 88, 95, 114, 321, 331

McGiver, John 155, *157*, 269

McKay, Gardner 56, 57, 68, *69*, 88, 91, 99, 100, 107

McVey, Tyler 114, 249

Many Loves of Dobie Gillis, The 20, 36, 261, 319, 320, 328, 339, 343

Mankiewicz, Joseph 6, 7, 8, 192

Manulis, Martin 10, 20, 42, 43, 46, 76, 88, 102, 265, 306, 318, 319, 321, 324

Marcuse, Theodore 114, 248

Mason, James 1, *6*, 7, 8, 10, *11*, 15, 43

Mathews, Pamela 148, 267

Mattern, Kitty 212, *300*

Mayer, Gerald 95, 325, 326

Medwar, Maria 155, 271, 272

Montalban, Ricardo 9, 10

Minardos, Nicos 155, 269

Moore, Joanna 229, 230, *231*, 310

Morris, Richard 231, 314

Morton, Gregory 155, 269

Moyzisch, L. C. 1, 2, 4, 7, 14, 15, 327, 363-368, 370, 371

Napier, Alan 9, 10, 138, 193, 235, 236, *237*, 238

O'Brien, Erin 203, *209*, 297

Opatoshu, David 46, 114, 247

Otis, Ted 122, 254

Pertwee, Michael 332, 333

Persoff, Nehemiah 130, 136, 256

Phillips, Margaret 219, 305, 306

Phipps, William 164, 274

Pittman, Montgomery 95, 231, 254, 315, 322, 323

Platt, Marc 193, 293

Pollard, Michael J. 137, 138, 145, *260*, 261

Price, Vincent 85, 91, 291, 300

Raksin, David 335

Regis, Charlita 130, 259

Reisner, Alan 95, 324

Reichow, Werner 219, 307, 308

Rennie, Michael 7, *11*, 30

Robotham, George 93, 94, 336, *337*

Roerick, William 219, 306

Romero, Cesar 231, *233*, 311, 312, 353

Romanoff, Michael 15, 45, 46, 114, *121*, 130, 203, 238-245, *246*

Rondeau, Charles R. 95, 232, 326, 327

Ruskin, Joseph 231, 312

Ryder, Alfred 106, 148, 265

Schallert, William 138, 263

Seltzer, Milton 185, 289

Seven, Johnny 180, 287

Showalter, Max 180, 286

Skouros, Spyros 36, 37, 239

Sokoloff, Vladimir 211, 212, 301

Sterling, Robert 9

Stevens, Leslie 333, 334

Stevens, Robert 43, 88, 114, 321

Stewart, David J. 219, 305

Swope, Herbert B. 14, 20, 43, 44, 58, 59, 65, 88, 89, 93, 98, 102, 145, 200, 319, 320 ,321, 337, 338

Szabo, Albert 212, *300*, 301

Taylor, Don 155, 268

Vaughn, Robert *99*

Voyage to the Bottom of the Sea xi, 26, 78, 79, 80, 86, 95, 232, 248, 249, 251, 256, 265, 266, 269, 271, 280, 283, 289, 293, 305, 309, 312, 313, 326, 327, 331, 336, *337,* 339, 346

Warden, Jack 130, 136, *255*, 256

Waring, Joseph 231, 314, 315

Wendkos, Paul 95, 181, 325

Wexler, Yale 231, 313

Wingreen, Jason 148, 266, *267*

Winwood, Estelle 148, 265, 266

Williams, John 121, 122, 128, 251, *252*

Woolf, Frank 122, 253, 254

Woolley, Monty 25, 92, 148, 264, 265

Young, Alan 193, 201, 202, 292

Zanuck, Darryl 6, 7, 8, 10, 33, 36

www.ingramcontent.com/pod-product-compliance
Lightning Source LLC
Chambersburg PA
CBHW051624230426
43669CB00013B/2177